Rickey and Robinson

SELECTED BOOKS BY HARVEY FROMMER

A Yankee Century (2002)

It Happened in Manhattan [with Myrna Katz Frommer] (2001)

Growing Up Baseball [with Frederic J. Frommer] (2001)

It Happened on Broadway [with Myrna Katz Frommer] (1998)

The New York Yankee Encyclopedia (1997)

Growing Up Jewish in America [with Myrna Katz Frommer] (1995)

Big Apple Baseball (1995)

It Happened in Brooklyn [with Myrna Katz Frommer] (1993)

Shoeless Joe and Ragtime Baseball (1992)

It Happened in the Catskills [with Myrna Katz Frommer] (1991)

Holzman on Hoops [with Red Holzman] (1991)

Behind the Lines: The Autobiography of Don Strock (1991)

Running Tough: The Autobiography of Tony Dorsett (1989)

Growing Up at Bat: 50th Anniversary Book of Little League Baseball (1989)

Throwing Heat: The Autobiography of Nolan Ryan (1988)

Primitive Baseball (1988)

150th Anniversary Album of Baseball (1988)

Red on Red: The Autobiography of Red Holzman (1987)

Baseball's Greatest Managers (1985)

National Baseball Hall of Fame (1985)

Games of the XXIIIrd Olympiad (1984)

Jackie Robinson (1984)

Baseball's Greatest Records, Streaks and Feats (1982)

Baseball's Greatest Rivalry (1982)

Basketball My Way: Nancy Lieberman [with Myrna Katz Frommer] (1982)

New York City Baseball (1980)

The Great American Soccer Book (1980)

Rickey and Robinson

The Men Who Broke Baseball's Color Barrier

Harvey Frommer

Foreword by Monte Irvin

TAYLOR TRADE PUBLISHING
Lanham • Boulder • New York • London

Published by Taylor Trade Publishing
An imprint of The Rowman & Littlefield Publishing Group, Inc.
4501 Forbes Boulevard, Suite 200, Lanham, Maryland 20706
www.rowman.com

Unit A, Whitacre Mews, 26-34 Stannary Street, London SE11 4AB,
United Kingdom

Distributed by NATIONAL BOOK NETWORK

British Library Cataloguing in Publication Information Available

A previous edition of this work was cataloged by the Library of Congress as
follows:

Frommer, Harvey.
  Rickey and Robinson : the men who broke baseball's color barrier.
  Includes index.
  1. Robinson, Jackie, 1919–1972. 2. Rickey, Branch, 1881–1965. 3. Baseball
players—United States—Biography. 4. Baseball—United States—Team
owners—Biography. 5. Segregation in sports—Case studies. I. Title.
  GV865.R6F76   81-23646
  796.357'092'2   [B]

ISBN 978-1-63076-002-1 (pbk. : alk. paper)
ISBN 978-1-63076-003-8 (electronic)

∞™ The paper used in this publication meets the minimum requirements of
American National Standard for Information Sciences—Permanence of Paper
for Printed Library Materials, ANSI/NISO Z39.48-1992.

Printed in the United States of America

For Ian, my son,

who was born

on April 15, 1972,

a quarter century to the day

since Jackie Robinson

broke baseball's

color line

CONTENTS

FOREWORD

I was almost thirty-one years old when I joined the New York Giants on July 5, 1949. Three days later, against the Dodgers of Jackie Robinson at Ebbets Field, manager Leo Durocher called on me to pinch-hit against Joe Hatten.

Behind me was the history of more than a decade of Negro League baseball, of being a five-time All-Star. Nevertheless, as I got into the batter's box in Brooklyn, my knees started knocking, and they wouldn't stop. I called time, stepped out, and stepped back in. I worked the count to 3–2 and then walked. I was so excited, I ran all the way to first base. It was a great feeling just to get there. That was how it all started for me in the majors.

Whenever I came into contact with Jackie Robinson, we would talk. He had his stories, and I had mine. It was not a time without incident. You'd walk into a room and some people would walk out. You'd sit down on a train, and one person, maybe two, maybe more, would get up and walk away. This was 1949 in the United States of America.

I am grateful for my accomplishments in the eight seasons I did have with the New York Giants—helping them win two pennants, finishing among the league leaders in many offensive categories in 1951 and 1953, getting elected to the Baseball Hall of Fame in 1973.

But I regret that I did not get a chance to play major league baseball earlier. What happened to me should have happened ten years before. Still, had it not been for Jackie Robinson and Branch Rickey, who knows if I would have ever gotten the chance. I say look at Josh Gibson. Look at Buck Leonard—all those fellows. Those guys were as good as any players who ever lived. They never got a chance.

Rickey and Robinson tells the story of the man who did get the first chance and the man who helped it happen. Together they made it possible for so many others. It is an important story, and nowhere is it told better than in this moving account written by one of my favorite sports authors. That's why I am so glad *Rickey and Robinson* has now been reprinted. It should be required reading for all those who wish to know more about Jackie Robinson and Branch Rickey and the breaking of baseball's color line in that long ago year of 1947.

MONTE IRVIN

ACKNOWLEDGMENTS

To Myrna Frommer for a totally professional editing job, with much love.

To the team on the bench, who once again listened lovingly: Jennifer, Freddy, Ian, Caroline, "Granny."

And for the memories, the time, the access to information: Bill Bevens, Joe Bostic, Bob Broeg, Roy Campanella, Fred Clare, Dr. Dan Dodson, David Doyle, Mal Goode, Dr. George N. Gordon, Bill Griffin, Eleanor Heard, John Sidney Heard, Monte Irvin, Irv Kaze, Ralph Kiner, Jerry Lewis of the Jackie Robinson Foundation, Stan Lomax, Russ Meyer, Lou Napoli, Peter O'Malley, Pee Wee Reese, Mack Robinson, Rachel Robinson, Ed Roebuck, Irving Rudd, Red Schoendienst, Lee Scott, Bill Shea, Enos Slaughter, Duke Snider, Ben Wade, Rube Walker, and Willa Mae Walker. For dedicated attention to detail, thanks to Jeffrey Neuman. And special thanks to Maron Waxman, my editor at Macmillan, for her concise and careful editing.

For information and aid: Los Angeles Dodgers, New York Mets, Pittsburgh Pirates, St. Louis Cardinals, New York Yankees, Ohio Wesleyan University, Pasadena Junior College, UCLA, Office of the Baseball Commissioner, Jackie Robinson Foundation, *Journal of Educational Sociology*, 1954.

H. F.

It is not the critic who counts, nor the man who points

out where the strong man stumbles, nor where the doer of

deeds could have done better. On the contrary, the credit

belongs to the man who is actually in the arena—whose

vision is marred by the dust and sweat and blood; who strives

valiantly; who errs and comes up again and again; who knows

the great devotions; the great enthusiasms; who at best knows

in the end of the triumph of high achievement.

—THEODORE ROOSEVELT

THE MEETING

The signs and symbols of the end of a worldwide war were everywhere. Four catastrophic years of death, deprivation, and drama were drawing to a close. The last week of the eighth month of 1945 was more than just the end of another month, another summer. The death camps of the Nazis, the atomic mushroom clouds of Nagasaki and Hiroshima, the deaths of President Franklin Delano Roosevelt and the despots Hitler and Mussolini were reminders of what America and the world had endured.

Millions had awaited this time of their lives: the ending of horrors, the beginning of new ways, the picking up of old patterns.

A month before, the *Queen Mary* had sailed west. The lights of the great ship were ablaze for the first time since 1939. There were 15,278 excited troops on board, stuffed into space that usually accommodated 2,000. On August 15, Japan surrendered. On Monday, August 27, the French war hero Charles de Gaulle arrived in New York City for a twenty-five-hour stay. He drove sixty-two miles in an open car through three boroughs. More than two hundred thousand cheered the tall, impressive figure. He rode in an open car, his hands above his head, his fingers spread in a "V" for victory. It was a beautiful summer day, seemingly made especially for New Yorkers to greet a hero.

The morning after de Gaulle's visit, a well-built black man hesitated at the corner of Court and Montague streets in downtown Brooklyn. He stopped at the newsstand in front of Wallach's clothing store. A former United States Army lieutenant, he noted with interest the headline on the front page of the *New York Times*:

FIRST TROOPS LAND IN JAPAN FROM 48 PLANES
TO PREPARE WAY FOR VAST INVASION THURSDAY
FLEET UNITS BEGIN TO MOVE INTO TOKYO BAY

"It's the beginning of the end," he thought as he walked toward 215 Montague Street, an office building where the main headquarters of the Brooklyn Dodgers was located. Times were changing. The end of the war was bringing a new spirit of joy and unity to the nation. But for the young man on that Brooklyn street there were some things that never seemed to change.

While in the armed forces he had experienced firsthand the segregation that was so much a part of the military and so dominant a force in much of American life. An athlete, he had played baseball that summer in the Negro Leagues and was now prepared to meet one of baseball's most powerful executives to explore the possibility, he was told, of his playing for another all-Negro team.

Almost since its inception, organized baseball had been a segregated sport run by white men and played by white men. In the 1880s, Negroes had played major-league ball, but an unwritten law laid down by baseball executives— notably Cap Anson, the great hitter of the nineteenth century—had established a color bar by the 1890s. No Negro player had breached this unspoken agreement.

The young man hardly noticed the noise of people arriving for work on Montague Street and the sounds of traffic around Borough Hall as he walked into the building. He was greeted by a secretary and led into the private office of Branch Rickey, the sixty-four-year-old Dodger general manager.

Venetian blinds were drawn to shut out the morning sun. The large office was walnut-paneled. The visitor saw a blackboard that contained the names of all the players and other personnel in the Dodger organization, down to the lowest minor-league teams. He glanced at a wall decorated with four framed pictures. There was a snapshot of Leo Durocher, the Dodger manager; a portrait of Charlie Barrett, one of the all-time top baseball scouts; and a photo of Gen. Claire Chennault, leader of the volunteer Flying Tigers, who aided China in its war against Japan. The fourth and largest frame contained a portrait of Abraham Lincoln.

Rickey pushed aside his leather swivel chair and came out from behind his huge mahogany desk. His face nearly obscured by the smoke of his cigar, he extended his hand in greeting. "Jackie Robinson." He smiled. "It's very nice to meet you. I understand you're quite a ballplayer."

"It's my pleasure," the twenty-six-year-old Robinson responded. They shook hands. Years later, Robinson would recall his first impression at that handshake: "The hand holding mine was hard, gnarled with the often-broken fingers of an ex-baseball catcher. His hair was thick, deep brown. Heavy bushy eyebrows flapped like twin crows from side to side as he talked."

Jackie Robinson's meeting with Branch Rickey was the culmination of a three-year search that had cost thousands of dollars. Rickey had ordered his chief scouts to find the one player who would be best equipped to break baseball's color line. Rickey asked three questions about each prospect: (1) Can he run? (2) Can he throw? (3) Can he hit with power? Those who met these criteria would then be judged on personality, background, intelligence, and desire.

Josh Gibson, the veteran black star who had smashed gigantic home runs while playing in the ballpark of the Washington Senators, was scouted, but he was considered too old. "Piper" Davis, an infielder for the Birmingham Black Barons, had fine speed and was a defensive standout. He drew serious consideration but was ruled out because he lacked major-league hitting potential. A catcher named Roy Campanella and a pitcher named Don Newcombe were also high on the list, but the player all the scouts agreed on was standing before Branch Rickey that summer day in Brooklyn, New York.

George Sisler, the St. Louis Browns' Hall of Fame first baseman, had praised Robinson's running ability and limitless hitting potential. His only reservation concerned Robinson's arm, which he deemed just average. Sisler felt that Robinson's best position would be first base or second base —the side of the infield with the shortest throw.

Wid Matthews reported that Robinson could protect the strike zone better than any other rookie he had ever seen. While impressed with Robinson's hitting, Matthews shared Sisler's concern about his arm.

Rickey sent scout Clyde Sukeforth to Chicago, where Robinson's team, the Kansas City Monarchs, was playing. "Get to talk to Robinson before the game," Rickey advised his scout. "Ask him to throw the ball from the hole in practice. There is some doubt about his arm, but if you like his arm, bring him in. Get him away from his teammates, so nobody will know what you are doing. I need absolute secrecy here."

Robinson was unable to play in the game that Sukeforth watched, but the Dodger scout prevailed on him to make some pregame practice throws. "I asked him why he was discharged from the army," Sukeforth wrote in his report to Rickey. "It seemed an old football ankle injury had brought about his discharge, but as it proved it did not bother him. I reasoned that if he wasn't going to play for a week, this would be an ideal time to bring him to Brooklyn. I had him make a few stretches into the hole to the right and come up throwing. His moves looked good."

The Dodger scout and Robinson met after the game in a downtown Chicago hotel. Sukeforth explained that there was interest in making Jackie a member of the Brooklyn Brown Dodgers, a team Rickey was sponsoring in a new Negro league. "Robinson reacted favorably," recalled Sukeforth. The two men went to Union Station, where Sukeforth purchased tickets, and together they took the train to New York City.

And now Robinson was face to face with Rickey himself, the man who had built the St. Louis Cardinal dynasty. Rickey's first question startled Robinson. "Do you have a girl?" he asked. "Do you have a girl?" Rickey pressed.

Robinson was taken aback. It was a question posed by a white man. It was a question that seemed too personal, especially in the first moments of a new relationship.

Robinson avoided Rickey's eyes for an instant. "Mr. Rickey, I don't know," Robinson finally answered quietly.

"What do you mean, you don't know?"

"Well," Robinson responded, "the way I've been traveling about the country and not writing as I should, well . . . I don't know."

"Is she a fine girl? Does she come from a good family background? Is she an educated girl?" The questions came out in a gravel-toned rush.

"They don't come any finer, Mr. Rickey."

"Then you know doggone well that you have a girl. And you need one. You ought to marry her quick as you can. It will be the best thing in the world for you. When we get through here today, you may want to call her up, because there are times when a man needs a woman by his side."

There was a pause. The two men stood silently in the middle of the office.

Then Rickey smiled as he chewed on his cigar. "Sit

down, please," he said, gesturing to a leather chair facing the desk. "We have a lot of things to talk about, and we've got plenty of time to do it."

Robinson sat down on the overstuffed chair. He tried to relax. He was prepared to give simple and direct answers to all questions. But he was also on his guard, for he had been in other situations with other white men who had been positive and friendly and then suddenly changed.

Rickey struck a match and held it inches from the end of his cigar. "Do you have any idea, Jackie, why we are meeting here today?"

"I only know what Mr. Sukeforth told me. You are starting a new Negro league, and there will be a team called the Brooklyn Brown Dodgers that will play at Ebbets Field."

Rickey waved out the lit match and removed the cigar from his mouth. He leaned forward across the desk. "That is what he was supposed to tell you. The truth is that you are not a candidate for the Brooklyn Brown Dodgers. You were brought here to play for the Brooklyn organization, to start out, if you can make it, playing for our top farm team, the Montreal Royals."

The words staggered Robinson. He frowned as if he hadn't heard right and clasped his powerful hands together. "Play for Montreal . . ." he said softly. "Me, play for Montreal?"

Rickey nodded. "Yes," he said in his cavernous, oratorical voice. Someone once said if Rickey spoke to a fellow across a desk, he delivered a Gettysburg address. Now he intoned, "Yes, if you can make the grade, Jackie. Later on, also if you can make it, you'll have a chance with the Brooklyn Dodgers. I want to win pennants. We need ballplayers. We have scouted you for weeks. What you can do on the baseball field is a matter of record. But this is much more than just playing baseball, much more. What I mean when I say 'can you make it' is do you have the guts, do you have the guts and what it takes to make it?"

"Mr. Rickey," Robinson answered firmly, although he was somewhat unnerved by the older man's bombast, "I'll make it. I'll make it if I get the opportunity to make it."

"I know you're a good ballplayer." Rickey swung about in his swivel chair, continuing his booming rhetoric. "I know all about your ability. But there is much more here than just playing." Rickey paused for a moment, then continued in a low, confidential voice. "I wish it meant only hits, runs, and errors—those things you can easily see in the box score. You know, Jackie, a box score is one of the most democratic things in the world. What color you are, what your politics are, how much money you have, how big or small you are—a box score doesn't reveal any of these things. It just tells what kind of a ballplayer you were on any given day."

"Isn't that all that matters in baseball?" Robinson cut in. "Isn't that all that counts?"

"It's all that should count. Perhaps the day will come when it will be all that does count. That's one of the reasons you are here in my office today. Jackie, if you are a good enough ballplayer and a big enough man, we can start in the right direction. What it will take, what it must take, is a great deal of courage."

Rickey picked up a piece of paper from his desk. He looked it over for a couple of moments. "About the Kansas City Monarchs—do you have a written or oral agreement to play for the Monarchs for the rest of the season?"

"No, sir. We just play from one payday to the next."

"How about next year?"

"No. There is no agreement of any kind. All the players on the Monarchs go from payday to payday. They pay me a certain amount each payday, but either side could end the arrangement at the end of the month if they wanted to, Mr. Rickey. That's the way it works."

"That was my impression too, Jackie, but I wanted to see how much of the situation you understood."

The older man then proceeded to reveal to the astonished Robinson how extensively he had investigated Robinson's life. Rickey knew that Robinson was, like himself, a Methodist and a nondrinker. He had visited California, where Robinson had grown up and made a name for himself in high school and college sports. Rickey had spoken with a Californian who was close to Robinson during his days at UCLA and had criticized Jackie for being too competitive.

Rickey was also aware of Robinson's army career. Drafted in 1942 at the age of twenty-three, Robinson was designated for limited service as a result of bone chips in his ankle caused by an old football injury. At basic training in Fort Riley, Kansas, Jackie applied for Officer's Candidate School, only to be told off the record that Fort Riley did not accept members of his race for such training.

Robinson had had a chance meeting and a few rounds of golf with the most famous black athlete of the time, Joe Louis, the heavyweight champion of the world, who was stationed at Fort Riley for a brief time. Robinson got in touch with Louis, and Louis called Truman Gibson, a black civil rights leader and adviser to the Secretary of Defense. Gibson came to Fort Riley to investigate. OCS opened its doors for Robinson and a few of his black fellow soldiers.

Robinson's regard for the army was understandably not too high at this point, but just about the time of his birthday in 1943, he was awarded his second lieutenant's bars and was transferred to a Negro provisional truck battalion, where he was made morale officer for the troops.

Again Robinson found prejudice and segregation firmly entrenched in army life. At the PX, just a half dozen seats were assigned to black personnel. There were other empty seats, but they were reserved for the white soldiers. Blacks stood for long periods of time waiting to claim their six seats as they were vacated.

In his capacity as morale officer, Robinson phoned the provost marshal, Major Hafner, and complained. He was told that things were better the way they were and that nothing could be done. "Lieutenant Robinson," Hafner had concluded, "let me put it this way—how would you like your wife sitting next to a nigger?"

Robinson was enraged. Hafner, realizing now he was speaking to a black man, hung up. But the exchange had not gone unnoticed. The office of battalion commander Colonel Longley was near where Robinson had made the phone call. Longley had heard the screaming, and after interviewing Jackie sided with the highly agitated black man. He sent a scorching letter of reprimand to Hafner and a letter of commendation to Robinson for standing up for his men. The incident led to a change in the PX seating arrangements.

Lieutenant Robinson was getting into shape to play football for the Fort Riley team when he was suddenly granted a two-week leave. When he returned, he learned that the leave was given so that he would not be on the scene when Fort Riley played against the University of Missouri. That institution had served notice that it would not participate in a football game against a team with a black athlete. Robinson quit the Fort Riley team, saying that he would not play on a squad that yielded to racial prejudice. "You can order me to play," he told the colonel in charge, "but you can't control the quality of my performance." Shortly afterward, Robinson was transferred to a tank battalion at Camp Hood, Texas.

One blisteringly hot summer day in August 1944, the third and most potentially dangerous incident in Robinson's army career took place. A bus driver ordered him to move to the back of the bus in direct violation of a federal ruling against segregated buses on army posts. Robinson refused. There was a heated exchange between him and the bus driver, followed by another argument between Jackie and a captain in the military police. The incident led to a court-martial based on two charges: that 2d Lt. Jack R. Robinson behaved insolently and impertinently to Capt. Gerald Bear, the military police officer; and that 2d Lt. Jack R. Robinson had disobeyed Bear's order to remain seated on a chair on the far side of a receiving room. Robinson's acquittal on the charges was a victory, but also another one in a series of humiliating incidents. He had simply demanded his legal rights, but those rights so freely given to others were rights he had to fight for. Because he demanded his rights, he was subjected to the ignominy of a trial.

"I'll level with you, Jackie," Rickey now said to the young man he had met just that morning but knew so much about. "I heard about racial problems that you supposedly had. I made a thorough investigation. I know that if you were white, they would never call you a troublemaker. I'm satisfied on that count.

"I know all about your battles, Jackie. I know all about your fighting spirit. It's fine. We are going to use all those qualities."

For Robinson, the interview was becoming more and more astonishing—the plans being made for him, the questions being asked, the insights into his life, all from this legendary figure. A $400-a-month shortstop for the Kansas City Monarchs who thought what he was doing was "a pretty miserable way to make a buck," he was excited at the opportunity being offered. Whatever it was, whatever it took, he thought, it was better than the segregated hotels, the two-day bus rides from Kansas City to Philadelphia for the long doubleheaders and the long bus ride the next day. He was confident of his ability to succeed in organized baseball. And yet there was doubt. He knew firsthand about opportunity seeming so close and then being pulled away.

Rickey stood up. He took off the jacket of his dark three-piece suit. "Have you the guts to play the game? Have you the guts to play no matter what happens? That's an answer I want to get from you today."

"I can play the game," Robinson answered. Rickey moved next to him, his face very close to the black man's. Rickey's look was suddenly mean, antagonistic.

"Let's say I'm a hotel clerk, Jackie. I look up at you from behind the desk register. I snarl at you, 'We don't want any niggers sleeping here!' What do you do then?

"You're standing in the batter's box," Rickey continued, before Robinson could answer. "It's a very tense situation. I'm a beanball pitcher." Rickey used his smudgy cigar as a weapon, pointing it toward Jackie's chin. "I wing a fast ball at you. It just grazes your cap and sends you jumping back for cover. What do you do?"

"It would not be the first time a pitcher threw at me, Mr. Rickey. I'd just pick myself up and dig in."

"All right—another game situation now. I am playing against you in a crucial game. I smack the ball into the outfield. I'm rounding first, and I come in to second. It's close. It's a very close play. We untangle our bodies. I lunge toward you." Rickey lunged at Robinson, his big fist coming close to Jackie's face. " 'Get out of my way, you black son of a bitch, you black bastard!' What do you do now?"

Not giving Robinson a chance to answer, Rickey continued, shouting now: "You're positioned at shortstop. I am at first base. I come down at you on a steal. I slide. My spikes are high. I cut you in the leg. As the blood starts to show through your uniform, I grin. I laugh at you. 'Now, you black nigger, how do you like that?' What do you do now?"

Robinson was angered, but he also realized that Rickey was playacting. "Mr. Rickey, what do you want? Do you want a coward, a ballplayer who's afraid to fight back?"

"I want a ballplayer with guts enough not to fight back," Rickey said firmly. His hair matted and wet, his tie loosened, Rickey took a few paces to the right, away from Robinson. "It's kind of a coincidence, Jackie, and I think a happy coincidence, that you share the same birth date as my son. He was born on January 31, 1914, and my records show you were born five years later to the day. Branch Jr., you may know, came to Brooklyn before me to handle their minor-league clubs. A couple of years later he was my main reason for coming to Brooklyn. Branch Jr. is a wonderful human being, religious and fair-minded. Yet he has expressed to me on various occasions the fear that signing a Negro player will dry up sources of talent for the Dodgers in the South, sources that he, in particular, has worked on.

"Mrs. Rickey also has been quite upset about the ramifications of my course of action. 'Why you, Branch?' she asks me. 'Why not someone else for a change?' She is fearful of my health deteriorating as a result of the controversy signing a colored player is certain to generate."

Rickey walked over to the window and adjusted the venetian blind against the rising morning sun. "I want you to know, Jackie," he continued, "that there is no way for us to fight our way through this situation." He turned back, facing Robinson once again. "There is virtually no group on our side. No umpires, no club owners, maybe a few newspapermen. We will be in a very tough spot. I have a great fear that there will be some fans who will be highly hostile to what we are doing. Jackie, it will be a tough position to be in, an almost impossible position. But we can win if we can convince everyone that you are not only a great ballplayer but also a great gentleman."

"Mr. Rickey," Robinson said, leaning forward in his chair, his hands clasped tightly together, "the way you're talking it sounds like a battle."

"Yes, exactly, a battle!" Rickey's voice rose again. "But it's one we won't be able to fight our way through. We have no army, no soldiers. Our weapons will be base hits and stolen bases and swallowed pride. Those will do the job and get the victory—that's what will win . . . and Jackie, nothing, nothing else will do it."

Now Rickey was once again very close to Robinson. Waving his hand under the black man's chin, Rickey became the fan screaming obscenities, the rival manager cursing Robinson's parentage, the teammate refusing to acknowledge his presence, the reporter baiting him with rigged questions. Rickey spilled out the litany of prejudice, all the while probing for the strength of character that he knew would be needed.

"All right," Rickey continued, "you have an argument with another player and he makes a statement subjecting you to the lowest depths of scurrility—a sexual reference to you and your mother. What would you do?"

"I'd kill him!"

Robinson's answer showed Rickey that the strength of character was there, but the Dodger general manager was not pleased. He wondered how he could be assured that Robinson would keep that strength and, at the same time, control it in order to survive.

"That would not serve any purpose," Rickey lectured. "The taunts and the goads will be aimed at making you react, at infuriating you enough to set off a race riot in the ballpark. Then they'll say that is proof that Negroes shouldn't be allowed in the major leagues. They'll think that's a good way to frighten fans and make them afraid to attend games."

Robinson nodded as he listened. "I understand, Mr. Rickey. I know what you're getting at."

"All right. You have played for Montreal and you come up to the Brooklyn Dodgers." Rickey was moving about the room, gesticulating. "You get into the World Series. There they play for keeps. It's no holds barred." The older man's face wrinkled into an evil frown. "I hate niggers. I also want to win in the worst possible way. I come into second base and my spikes are sharp. I aim them right at you. You move out of my way and you jab me in my rib cage with the ball. I'm out. I have an aching side. I'm humiliated. I jump up. 'You tar baby son of a bitch,' I scream. 'You can't do this to me, you coon.' I punch you in the face." Rickey was close to Robinson as he said this, and he swung his clenched fist under Robinson's chin. Robinson didn't flinch. "What do you do now, Jackie? What do you do now?"

"I get it, Mr. Rickey. I've got another cheek. I turn the other cheek."

"Wonderful!" Rickey was finally satisfied. "Wonderful. You will hear much worse before you are through. I merely was testing you, and I apologize for it. But you are a pioneer, and this whole experiment depends on you. You can never forget that for a moment."

The role playing was concluded. Returning to the swivel chair behind his desk, Rickey smoothed his hair and wiped the sweat from his face with a large white handkerchief. He reached for a sheet of paper. "Jackie, I'd like you to read this and sign it."

Robinson took the paper and read the two-paragraph statement carefully. It was a contract with the Montreal Royals—an agreement for a $3,500 bonus and a salary of $600 a month for the 1946 season. The second paragraph held Rickey harmless against any oral or written claims that Robinson was under contract to any other person or organization.

Robinson looked up. "It seems fine, Mr. Rickey." Unscrewing the top of his fountain pen and twisting it into its bottom, Rickey handed it to Robinson. He thought of all the times he had handed a pen across his desk to a ballplayer. There were drinkers, dreamers, brave men, and cowards, some with limitless talent and limited desire, others with limited talent and limitless desire. The scene had been repeated many times before; yet the sense that this was a historic moment caused a slight flutter in his heart.

Robinson signed the agreement. "Mr. Rickey, this seems like a dream come true. But it seems like there will be trouble ahead for you, for me, for baseball, for my people."

"Trouble ahead." Rickey rolled the phrase about as he leaned back in his chair, his hands folded high across his chest. "Trouble ahead. Many years ago, the Rio Grande Railroad used to give tourists in Colorado a thrill. They

would put the tourists on a flatcar and haul them up a canyon. Mrs. Rickey and I took that ride years ago, and on the
ride the walls were so narrow and so limited our view that
all we were able to see was the blue sky up at the very end
of the canyon. It was a frightening ride. As we got near the
top, Mrs. Rickey remarked to me, 'Branch, there's trouble
ahead. I'm afraid we're going to run right over the top.'

Rickey sat forward now, struck a match and ignited his
half-smoked cigar. "Well, Jackie, the engineers had figured
it all out. Just before we reached the top, the road veered off
and went through a tunnel, so there was no trouble ahead at
all. And that is the way it is with much of the trouble ahead
in the world. We simply have to use the courage and common sense God gave us. The important thing is to study and
understand the hazards and build wisely."

The yellow pad on Rickey's desk bore a few words he
had jotted down, closing remarks he had prepared in advance. Rickey quickly glanced at them and looked up at
Robinson.

"I want to beg two things of you, Jackie. Give it all you
have as a ballplayer. As a man, give continuing loyalty to
your race and to the critical cause you are going to sym-
bolize. And above all, do not fight. No matter how vile the
abuse, you must ignore it. You are carrying the reputation of
a race on your shoulders. Bear it well, and the day will come
when every team in baseball will open its doors to Negroes."

Rickey thought to himself that punch for punch was by
experience, inheritance, and desire Jackie's natural reaction
to attack and insult. He wondered how such self-imposed
control would work on this strong-willed young man. There
would be a price, he had no doubt.

As the meeting ended, Rickey pulled open a desk drawer,
took out a book, and handed it to Robinson. It was *The Life
of Christ* by Giovanni Papini, an Italian priest. Rickey read
often from the book, claiming it instructed him along the

corridors of humility. "Jackie, I would like you to read silently from a few passages of Papini's philosophy just now. I think it will be valuable for you."

Settling back in the comfortable leather chair, Robinson turned to the place Rickey indicated and began to read:

Ye have heard that it hath been said. An eye for eye and a tooth for a tooth: But I say unto you, that ye resist not evil; but whosoever shall smite thee on the right cheek, turn to him the other also. . . . There are three answers which men can make to violence: revenge, flight, turning the other cheek. The first is the barbarous principle of retaliation. . . . Flight is no better than retaliation. . . . The man who takes flight invites pursuit. . . . His weakness becomes the accomplice of the ferocity of others. . . . Turning the other cheek means not receiving the second blow. It means cutting the chain of the inevitable wrongs at the first link. Your adversary is ready for anything but this. . . . Every man has an obscure respect for courage in others, especially if it is moral courage, the rarest and most difficult sort of bravery. . . . It makes the very brute understand that this man is more than a man. . . . To answer blows with blows, evil deeds with evil deeds, is to meet the attacker on his own ground, to proclaim oneself as low as he. . . . Only he who has conquered himself can conquer his enemies.

Robinson closed the book gently and handed it back to Rickey. "I understand," he said.

PASADENA: THE MAKING OF

AN ALL-AMERICAN

Jack Roosevelt Robinson was born in Cairo, Georgia, on January 31, 1919, the fifth and last child of Mallie and Jerry Robinson. Mallie's father had been a slave, and the feel of those times was always close by. Her mind often tarried in the vestibule of bondage. Jerry earned $12 a month for his labors on the Jim Sasser plantation near the Florida border. His wages were barely enough to feed the young family.

One December day, Jerry came home late after his hog-killing chores were completed. "Just liver, lights, and chitterlings," Mallie shouted at her husband. "Butchering all day and that's what they let you bring home. No tenderloin, not even a neckbone?"

Jerry reminded her that he was forbidden to take home anything but the organs of the hogs.

"We're no better off than slaves," Mallie said furiously. "Things have got to change around here."

Mallie and Jerry argued for days. Jerry felt strongly about keeping his place and accepting what the plantation owner allowed. But Mallie was a proud, deeply religious woman who was profoundly influenced by the stories of slavery her father had told her. She prevailed. Jerry would ask to become a half-cropper and split the profits of his labor with the white plantation owner. Sasser was unwilling to lose a strong and capable worker; angry and with reservations, he consented.

Ironically, the new arrangement doomed the marriage. With each passing month, flushed by the extra money he was making, Jerry spent more and more time away from Mallie and the children. He purchased dress-up clothes and made his way into Cairo, a town of three thousand, where he mingled with the crowd questing after the sporting life. Jerry and Mallie now bickered constantly.

On July 28, 1919, when Jack was six months old and Mallie was thirty, Jerry boarded train #230 with someone else's wife and ran away to Florida. The family never saw him again. "When our father passed away, I was in high school," says Mack Robinson, Jack's older brother. "We never saw him. We knew nothing of him. When my mother got a telegram from some relative telling us he had passed, it wasn't traumatic for us; we had no recognition of him."

With Jerry gone, Jim Sasser lost no time in getting Mallie and her children off his land. He had always disliked the spirited young woman and quickly found a new family to come in and do the work. And so Mallie and her children —Jack, Willa Mae, Edgar, Frank, and Mack—moved into the home of a family that Mallie had worked for as a domestic before her marriage.

The 1920s and 1930s were a time of the great Negro exodus west. "If you poor Georgia folks want to get a little closer to heaven," Mallie heard, "come on out to California." The Robinsons lived through another blazing Georgia summer, a rainy autumn, and a chilling winter. But with the coming of spring in 1920, they packed their belongings in baskets, boxes, frayed suitcases, and straw bags and filed onto a dirty Jim Crow coach with hundreds of other blacks heading west to California and a new beginning.

"When we first came out," recalls Willa Mae, Jackie's older sister, "we all lived together in an apartment with my mother's sister Mary Lou and Uncle Burton, their kids, and a cousin. With the six of us, there were about thirteen altogether. We were poor, but we made it. My mother worked as a domestic for a lady who had four girls. I dressed well. I would get four dresses at a time."

The apartment had no hot water. There was no sink in the kitchen. The family lived on a diet of day-old bread and sweetwater, a liquid substance made from sugar and milk. Mallie's wages from domestic work and some aid from the welfare department kept the Robinsons going.

Jack had many moments alone in the evenings with his mother. They would sit in the glow of the flickering light of the oil lantern, and he would look into her face, a young face but one carved and written on by the hard years. She would tell him the old stories about the slaves and their masters. He learned about the time the slaves were given their freedom and how they were afraid to take it, fearing both of freedom and their masters at the same time.

Mallie was not afraid. By 1923, her domestic wages, hand-me-down clothing from employers, welfare department aid, and some prudent budgeting made her realize that it might be possible to move the family out of their crowded apartment and into a house.

The house Mallie purchased was at 121 Pepper Street, a modest two-story home in the comfortable but spare northwest section of Pasadena, an all-white neighborhood. Mallie bought the house from a black man. He had acquired it through the efforts of his niece, who looked white.

Most of the Pepper Street residents reacted to their new neighbors with annoyance, hostility, and open prejudice. There was a plan to circulate a petition to force the blacks out. When the petitioners learned that what they were attempting was illegal, they switched tactics. They tried to raise money to buy the house from Mallie. This too was unsuccessful, for the potential buyers argued among themselves as to who should put up the money. Even if they'd raised the money, Mallie would not have sold. She considered herself lucky to have obtained the house for such a low price and was glad to have a piece of land on which to raise her children.

With the legal and financial schemes aborted, residents resorted to harassment. There were complaints about Frank. His roller skating on the sidewalks provoked one neighbor to call the police, complaining about the noise he made. Mallie cautioned Frank and the other Robinson children to watch their behavior but not to be ashamed of who they were.

Each morning, Mallie rose very early and left her sleeping children to go to work for her white employers. She made that family's breakfast while her own children fended for themselves, many mornings going without breakfast. Many evenings they waited with hope and hunger for the leftovers their mother might manage to bring home. To take care of the family, each child became a surrogate mother or father for the next-youngest child.

Mallie Robinson was not only a supportive mother for her own children, but "she was motherly to all of us kids in the neighborhood," recalls Sidney Heard, Jackie's childhood friend. "We'd come over to the house, and she'd be good to us, share with us what she had. She remembered certain parts of slavery times that had been told to her by her folks. She had no bitterness, though—maybe a little, but not enough to notice. She believed in doing to you like she wanted done to her."

"She was something else," says her son Mack. "She had a way of saying and doing things that brought out the best in all of us." Without a father and with a mother working most of the time, rambunctiousness characterized the Robinson children's behavior. At times Mallie became angry with the rebellious Mack. "I used to tease Mom a little bit," he says. "She used to tell me I was the worst child she had. Jack was the baby of the family. She was really proud of him."

When Willa Mae started kindergarten at the Grover Cleveland School, it posed a problem for the entire family. By this time there was no one left at home to care for Jack. Mallie reasoned that the best arrangement would be for Willa Mae to bring Jack to school with her each day. The school authorities did not approve of this plan at first. "If I stay home and take care of him, I'll have to go on relief," Mallie argued. "It'll be cheaper for the city if you just let him come and play." The authorities agreed, and every day for a year Willa Mae brought her younger brother with her and placed him in the schoolyard sandbox under the blue California sky. At the end of her school day, Willa Mae would come out and take him home.

At first Jack played in the sand and with small toys, but then he began to mingle with other children at recess. "I told my mother to save money by not fixing food for me," Jackie recalled later. "I was the best athlete there. The others brought me sandwiches and dimes for the movies so they could play on my team. You might say I turned pro at an early age."

Sidney Heard and Jackie became friends in the early years of elementary school. Their families had come to Pasadena from Georgia at about the same time. "I began to notice that Jack had something that the rest of us did not have," recalls Heard. "He was just an average student, but he loved games and sports. And he could do things in games and sports that the other kids could not do. We played dodgeball. One by one kids would be eliminated when they were hit by the ball. Every time we played, he was left. And the game had to stop because nobody could hit him. That's when I really began to notice him.

"As time went on we got into other sports and games,

and there was nothing he could not do. When marble time came, he played marbles. We would get up early in the morning and play marbles from eight o'clock to five o'clock. He didn't even take his lunch. We used to draw a big circle, which we used to call a 'Boston.' We would draw a little circle and put the marbles in it and put the agates in. Those were petrified wood almost crystallized and harder than rock. Those were precious marbles—almost like diamonds in those days. We used to put several diamonds, as we called them, in the middle of the circle surrounded by marbles until we cleaned them out and got to the agates. Boy, that dude Jackie, he cleaned us out. He could concentrate. He could concentrate better than any of us."

All through the year, there were outdoor games. The weather in California was almost always good. Pepper Street was about a mile from the Rose Bowl Stadium site, and Sid Heard's father and Jack's brother Edgar were construction workers at the football stadium. "When it was a half bowl," Sid remembers, "we would go down through the bowl site area and chase rabbits." But Jackie yearned to play one day in the football stadium that was just being built.

"We played games we invented ourselves on the vacant lot on Pepper Street," continues Heard. "We played 'Over the Line.' I do believe that's what made Jackie a pull hitter. We had six players in the game—three on each side. There were two left fielders and a shortstop that took care of second and third base. The batter on the other team had to hit the ball between second and third, and it had to go over the line—an imaginary line. It couldn't bounce over the line. It had to be hit over. You had to travel around first and get as many bases as you could before the fielder threw the ball back over the line. That ability of Jack to hit was no mystery to me. I know where he developed that swing. Sometimes we played the game using a rag ball. You had to hit it with tremendous power, with a tremendous amount of power to get it over the line.

"Playing jacks the regular way was too easy for him. He wouldn't even use a ball. He used the jacks. He threw them up and caught the jacks before they came down.

"He was the one who chose sides. I was the other one. He'd always pick the younger kids and play the older ones and then he'd figure out a way to beat us older boys with the younger boys. . . . He was some competitor, and he figured it out so that we all got to play.

"There were so few blacks in Pasadena at that time that we were just like a family. If you wanted to borrow something, you would borrow it and say later that you borrowed it. We knew where we could go—we knew where people were prejudiced. We knew how far we could go downtown. We used to go down to Brookside Park where the whites were and play their teams for ice cream and cake. We'd beat them. Jack loved that. We used to get an awful lot of ice cream and cake."

Pasadena, set in the shadows of blue mountains, with its sweet air and wide boulevards, was a lovely place to live. Yet Jack never felt completely comfortable. As a child he had been taunted with shouts of "nigger, nigger, nigger, nigger." He remembered a taunt—"Soda cracker's good to eat, nigger's only good to beat."

Pasadena had many of the same restrictions as the rural South the Robinsons had fled. Blacks were allowed to swim in the municipal pool only on Tuesdays—that was the day the water was changed. They were allowed in the YMCA only one day a week. They could view the Saturday matinees in the movie theaters only from the segregated balcony.

"If my mother and brother and sister weren't living in Pasadena," Jack would observe many years later, after his retirement from baseball, "I would never go back. I've always felt like an intruder there—even in school. People in Pasadena were less understanding in some ways than southerners, and they were more openly hostile."

It was sports that sustained him, that gave him succor,

that provided an outlet for his pent-up fury. The youngest in a family of gifted natural athletes, he was nourished by sports.

Mack remembers an incident from his youth: "We were raising some horses for a man, and I took a horse by the house one day. My mother came out. She got up there and rode the horse side-saddle. She rode the horse better than I did, and I was astride the horse. She went galloping up the street. I would assume she was about forty years old at the time. But she had native athletic ability.

"All of us grew up playing together, and each one improved the other. Edgar, the oldest, was a fantastic roller skater on street skates, and a fine softball player and bicycle rider. Frank, next to oldest, was like a father to Jack. He was a sprinter. He was faster than I was in the hundred-yard dash, and I was a tenth of a second off the world record in those days. Willa Mae made first-string on everything girls could play back then—basketball, track, soccer. She was also a top sprinter in her day.

"Jack got his start in long jumping from me. You think of his speed, but it was his deception on the base paths, his timing, his starting and stopping, his faking abilities—those were the things that made his speed great. He was a combination athlete. He was great in all four major sports. I saw this from the time he was in junior high school."

Jackie attended Washington Junior High School. Sidney Heard went to Cleveland Junior High School. The two schools used to meet every year for the championship. "We could never beat them," Heard recalls. "We were always second because of Jackie. He made their teams something else.

"We tried to get him mad, but we soon found out that the madder you made him, the better he played. We soon stopped getting him mad. . . . He never used any cuss words, he only used to say 'daggummit this' and 'daggummit that.'

. . . He was interested in the games, in winning, not in anything else. He never did start a fight. He could fight, but he would never take advantage of anyone . . . and he would never put himself in a position where he would be hurt."

Heard, Jackie, Warren Dorn—later mayor of Pasadena and Los Angeles County supervisor—and other youngsters banded together in a loose confederation known as "The Pepper Street Gang." They were a bunch of kids eager to compete in anything and ready to take risks.

"We all looked up to Jackie," recalls Dorn, "because he could hide in a storm drain, run out on a golf course, and grab a ball and get back faster than the rest of us. That's how we got our Coke money—and he could get oranges and a bunch of grapes so fast that he never got caught.

"During the Depression, things were tough for all of us," Heard remembers. "Things were especially tough for him. He didn't have a father. We kids all used to go down to chase after golf balls and make three or four dollars a day. He had tremendously good eyesight. We'd be down in the gullies, down among the big boulders. Sometimes he'd find six or seven golf balls. We couldn't find them. We used to get a quarter apiece for those golf balls. Jackie'd say, 'Okay, the next one is yours, Pete. The next one is yours, Sid.' He'd share with us.

"I remember one time we came across a couple of guys on the course finishing up the seventeenth hole. Jack had a couple of balls in his hand. Jack said, 'Would you like to buy a couple of balls?' And the two guys smiled. One of the guys said, 'Double or nothing.' Jack didn't know what that meant. 'What's double or nothing?' he asked. The guy said, 'We'll play from right here to the tee, and if you can't make it in less strokes than me, you give me the balls. And if you beat me, I'll give you a dollar and you keep the balls.'

"He handed Jack a putter. He took himself a seven iron. How Jack did it I'll never know, but he took that putter and hit the ball right onto the green just that far, almost right into the hole. Jack won the dollar. He was just about thirteen or fourteen, and the guy was an adult.

"When he'd come home in the evening," Heard continues, "he'd lay his money out on the table and save a little to go buy himself a pie or something. He loved sweets, big banana pie. He could have kept all the money for himself, but he gave most of it to his mother to help her out.

"The Pepper Street Gang was mostly a sport gang," Heard recalls. "We loved to compete. We weren't out to hurt anyone. We'd go miles to get into any type of sport. That gang was where Jackie and the rest of us learned that we all have to be brothers and sisters. We didn't have any racial restrictions. We played together—blacks, whites, Mexicans, Japanese. Anaheim and Long Beach were cities that were very prejudiced. Jack knew this, but he had no fear. He got us playing there because he knew we could play ball and win.

"Whenever we played, wherever we played, Jack was always the best. The grown-ups, the people from the city yard, used to come and watch us. They would come and watch every evening. They came mainly to see him. He was doing things that you just don't see young kids do. Jack just excelled in any kind of game, any sport, and he made an individual who played with him play much better."

The young Robinson followed the accomplishments of white sports stars, especially Lou Gehrig and Babe Ruth, and marveled at the way the New York Yankees kept winning. Although Sundays were family days, church days, he would rise at four in the morning and set out on his paper route delivering the *Los Angeles Times* and the *Los Angeles Examiner*. He read the sports sections, immersing himself in the statistics and the glories of the athletic world. Baseball's color barrier precluded any thought of playing major-league baseball, but he was sure of his talents and sure that his future lay in sports.

Growing up during the Depression, with no father at home, Jackie took any job that was available. He ran errands; he watered shrubs in the languid Pasadena evenings. He built a shoeshine box and went around polishing shoes. He went to many sporting events where, with one eye on the action and the other on hungry fans, he sold hot dogs. He ate meat sometimes on a Sunday when there was some extra money from his odd jobs and the supplemental employment his mother was able to obtain.

Growing into manhood, Jack felt new strength. Tall, lithe, and alert, he exuded the healthy handsomeness of a young man in full possession of his powers. He had the look of an earnest, clean-cut American kid, despite the hardships he had been through.

At John Muir Technical High School, he played with the same frenzy that he displayed on vacant lots with the Pepper Street Gang. He won letters in football, basketball, baseball, and track. Some mistook his will to win and his unwillingness to suffer incompetence gladly as cockiness and arrogance. Teams keyed on him. Rival coaches constructed game plans to cope with Muir Tech teams and ended their lecture with two words: "Stop Robinson."

He was the catcher on Muir's baseball team and played on the Pomona Tournament All-Star squad in 1937. His teammates included outfielder Ted Williams of San Diego Hoover and third baseman Bob Lemon of Long Beach Wilson.

Robinson's athletic career in college is the stuff of storybooks. He began inauspiciously as a freshman at Pasadena Junior College. In his first football practice, he broke an ankle. He missed the first four games. Pasadena lost every one of them. When he returned to action, the Bulldogs began a winning streak that did not end as long as Robinson was on the team.

He was the piston that powered Pasadena to eleven

straight triumphs in 1938 and the junior college football championship. Churning out over one thousand yards from scrimmage, he scored seventeen touchdowns and accounted for 131 of his team's 369 points. He paced Pasadena's 33–0 victory over San Francisco with a seventy-six-yard touchdown run on the second play from scrimmage; he scored three touchdowns in the game. Against San Bernardino, he ran for three touchdowns and passed for three more. He drew thirty-eight thousand fans to Pasadena's game against Los Angeles. In a 31–19 victory over Santa Ana, he racked up an eighty-three-yard run, a field goal, and four conversions. More than forty thousand watched him in action against Compton Junior College. He scored two touchdowns and passed for another. In the stands that day was a Compton student named Edwin "Duke" Snider.

"Jackie was the star," recalls Snider. "He wiped us out in football, basketball, baseball. He could have been a pro in all three. I still remember that game he played against Compton when he ran back that kick. He must have reversed his field three times. I think everybody on the field took shots at him, but they couldn't touch him."

At the Rose Bowl, where Robinson had chased rabbits as a kid, he brought thirty thousand fans to their feet in the season-ending game against Cal Tech as he dodged and scampered and powered his way for a 104-yard kickoff return.

On May 8, 1938, his multiple talents presented a problem, but in legendary fashion, he overcame this too. He competed in two different events in two different cities in the same day, and excelled in both. In the morning in Claremont, he was given permission to take three early broad jumps. His third jump measured 25′, 6½″, breaking his brother Mack's national junior college record. "I couldn't get over it," Jack said, "breaking Mack's record. My big brother had always been my idol, making the Olympics and all that . . . running second to Jesse Owens in the two hundred meters at Berlin in 1936."

Then racing to a waiting car, like Clark Kent transforming himself into Superman in a telephone booth, Jack Robinson, track-and-field star, changed into Jack Robinson, baseball player. The car took him to Glendale. He arrived in the third inning, took over at shortstop, and helped lead his Pasadena team to a 5–3 victory for the southern California baseball championship. Named the Most Valuable Player in Southern California Junior College baseball, he batted .417 and stole twenty-five bases in twenty-four games.

At Brookside Park, where Jack had once played baseball using a broomstick bat and a tennis ball, he played in an exhibition game against the Chicago White Sox. The date was March 14, 1938. The White Sox had agreed to the contest to help raise funds for Pasadena's baseball program. Robinson slapped out two hits and made three exceptional fielding plays—on one of them going deep in the hole at short to turn a sure run-scoring hit by Luke Appling, the American League batting champ, into a double play.

"Geez," exclaimed White Sox manager Jimmy Dykes. "No one in the American League can make plays like that. If that kid was only white, I'd sign him right now."

Dykes's statement did not surprise Robinson. "Growing up, I really gave no thought to becoming a baseball player," he recalled. "There was no future in it for colored players. I did love softball. I played it better and played it before anything else. I was really shooting at becoming a football, basketball, or track star. But I didn't think much of a chance existed for me in baseball."

California newspapers recounted his exploits. Robinson was referred to with hyperbolic nicknames—"Midnight Express," "The Dusky Flash," and "The Dark Demon." He was termed "the greatest all-around athlete in California sports."

As a forward on PJC's basketball team, he averaged nine-

teen points a game and was named to the all-state team. He
led Pasadena to the California Junior College championship.
He started alongside four white players: Clem Tomerlin, Al
Sauer, George E. McNutt, and Les O'Gara. During one
game, a white opponent continually fouled Robinson and
kept up a running stream of curses. "You've got no guts,
Robinson," the player shouted. "You're afraid to fight."

Robinson answered calmly: "If you want to fight, we'll
do it after the game. I'm not going to get thrown out and
hurt my team. We'll fight later, and we'll see who has more
guts."

The reply infuriated the player, who slammed into
Robinson, slugging away with both fists. Robinson did not
strike back, realizing that the racial overtones of a physical
confrontation might trigger a riot. Officials intervened, and
the opposing player was ejected from the game.

The athletic skills and winning ways he had displayed on
championship teams in elementary school, junior high, high
school, and junior college attracted scouts from many col-
leges. There were offers of athletic scholarships and part-
time employment. "I chose UCLA," he explained, "because I
planned to get a job in Los Angeles after I finished school,
and figured I'd have a better chance if I attended a local
university. . . . In school I majored in phys. ed. . . . My mother
wanted me to become a doctor or a lawyer, but I never
wanted to be anything but an athlete."

He became UCLA's first four-letter man, starring in basketball, football, baseball, and track. Sportswriters began to
refer to him as "the Jim Thorpe of his race." He became
college football's top ground gainer in 1939, averaging a
dozen yards each carry. He also returned punts for a twenty-
one-yard average.

Willa Mae recalls what it was like to have a brother
who was a big football star: "I went to a football game and
took along my oldest son, Ronnie, who was six. He started to
scream, 'C'mon, Uncle Jack! C'mon, Uncle Jack!' And soon

the whole stadium was calling out, 'C'mon, Uncle Jack! C'mon, Uncle Jack!' Jack didn't like that kind of publicity, and I knew I was in for it. After the game he came home and I hid. He was calling out, 'Willa Mae, who started that Uncle Jack?' I said, 'I couldn't help it. What was my Ronnie gonna call you?' And Jack laughed."

Jackie Robinson was not just Saturday's hero. It seemed that every day of the week he performed heroics in some athletic event or other. He won the Pacific Coast League conference championship in the broad jump, and a month later captured the national collegiate broad-jump title. He starred on the UCLA basketball team and twice paced the Pacific Coast League's southern division in scoring. Ironically, he only faltered in baseball, batting under .200.

Sidney Heard recalls Jackie, the 1941 football All-American: "Most people did not see him at his greatest like they saw Willie Mays, who came up when he was young. If Jack had gone up when he was twenty, there'd be records now they'd still be chasing. . . . I saw him run down to home plate and get within three feet and then go back to third base and be safe . . . that was his way. Whatever little flaws an individual or a team had, he took advantage of them."

Sidney's wife, Eleanor Heard, who was sixteen years old when she played with Jackie Robinson in the Pacific Coast Tennis Tournament, recalls how he capitalized on the weaknesses of opponents and maximized his own strengths: "Jack played to win, I can tell you that. He urged me to play in the singles. I knew I would be matched in the competition against this woman who was about twenty-two or twenty-three years old. He urged me to play her first in an intermission contest, just for fun. She beat me. Jack watched the contest carefully. Afterward he took me aside, and he knew all the things that she did that I could overcome. I played her again, and I beat her.

"Jack was a really fine tennis player. He would out-finesse you. If you had a strong serve and a strong volley, he'd pit-pat the ball and use his speed. He could move from one part of the court to another so fast you wouldn't even know he was moving. He had the ability to stop suddenly and get off a shot. He had a terrific cut that would make the ball hit the ground and just stay there. Nobody taught him these things. He just had to learn them himself. We won the Pacific Coast mixed doubles championship. But that was it. At that time, no matter how good blacks were, they were not allowed to compete in national tournaments."

Jack played tennis with Eleanor Heard, but the girl he fell in love with was Rachel Isum. An honor student majoring in nursing at UCLA, she was introduced to Jackie one afternoon in 1940. Rachel had no interest in sports. She agreed to the meeting only to be polite to the twenty-one-year-old athlete. She was refined, serious, intelligent, and outspoken. At this point in her life, she saw no reason to become involved with a cocky, highly publicized football hero.

"I could count on one hand the number of girls I went out with before Rachel," Jackie observed. With the feel of the poverty of his childhood still clinging to him, he was shy and uncomfortable in the affluent world of UCLA. Only in the arena, where his athletic talents cut off any feelings of inferiority, was he at ease.

He was defensive when he first met this pretty, obviously middle-class young woman who wore her long hair in the fashionable rolled-under style, and whose complexion was much lighter than his. But there was a certain melding of personalities, of opposites attracting, a mixture of the right moment with the appropriate person. "She never cared particularly about sports, but she took an interest in sports because of me. She became the most important and helpful and encouraging person I ever met in my whole life," Jack said. "When I became bitter or discouraged, she was always there with the help I needed."

But despite the sweetness of romance and the recognition for his athletic achievements, Jackie was still a poor black man in a white man's world. During his first year at UCLA, Robinson was in a car with a few friends. The car was bumped by a car driven by a white man. An argument ensued. When the police arrived, Robinson and his friends were taken to jail and booked on suspicion of robbery. A UCLA coach and some of Jack's friends came down to police headquarters and argued that Jack and his friends were innocent of any wrongdoing. The robbery charge was dropped, but UCLA's star athlete had to forfeit a $25 bond.

Twenty-one years after Mallie Robinson had carried little Jackie in her arms on the dirty Jim Crow coach to California, Robinson withdrew from UCLA. He had a job with the National Youth Administration and wanted to make money to help out his mother, for the other Robinson children had financial family pressures of their own.

Robinson's job with the National Youth Administration did not work out. The wages were meager, and the athlete in him was restless. A young black man without a college degree, lacking any specific job skill, faced with the responsibility of helping out his mother and supporting himself, he turned to the athletic skills that had thus far sustained him.

In the fall of 1941, he went to Hawaii to play professional football for the Honolulu Bears. There were many letters from him to Rachel, filled with thoughts of their life together in the future. Weekdays in Hawaii were spent working for a construction company near Pearl Harbor. On Sundays he played with the Honolulu Bears in an integrated league. The football season ended December 5.

Two days later, aboard the *Lurline*, Robinson was headed back to California. He was playing poker when the crew members began painting the ship's windows black. The captain informed the passengers that the United States was at war; the Japanese had attacked Pearl Harbor. Virtually all the passengers put on life jackets, but Robinson, obstinate and superstitious, refused. There was something about authority that brought out the iconoclast in him.

The war would unleash great demographic and social change for millions. Perceptions would alter. Momentous technological innovations would usher in a world vastly different from what had been. Jackie Robinson would be shaped by and would help shape much of what was to come in those turbulent years. Yet, what had been for him was past forgetting.

"When I saw him playing later for the Brooklyn Dodgers, it was part of the gang that had made it," says one link to the past, Sidney Heard. "I feel good because we all contributed to his becoming what he became. Not that we were as good as he was. We were good, but not like him. Still, I know when he got a touchdown playing out on the lots and then when he got a touchdown playing in school or college, and when he hit those home runs and stole those bases for the Brooklyn Dodgers, it was easier because we made him know how to hustle."

OHIO: PIONEER STOCK

A raft bearing a young family, a cart, and a yoke of oxen drifted down the Ohio River one spring day in 1819, and came to rest at Sciotoville, close by Portsmouth, Ohio. The powerful man unloaded the raft and placed all his earthly goods on the cart. He hitched up the wagon, lifted his wife and child onto it, and moved out toward the thickly wooded land. He headed deeper and deeper into the virgin land until he found a large tract of meadow. This, he decided, would be where he would settle. The man's name was David Brown. His wife, the former Hannah Hubbard, had been disowned by her family in Pennsylvania because her husband drank whiskey.

On the twelfth of March, 1874, Emily Brown, a granddaughter of David and Hannah, married Jacob Franklin Rickey. The young couple received a house, livestock, and two hundred acres as a wedding gift from the groom's father, Ephraim Wanser Rickey, a farmer and landowner. Ephraim was the son of a Baptist fundamentalist preacher who had broken the soil in Madison Township and later acquired extensive landholdings throughout the southern Ohio countryside.

Jacob inherited the religious fervor of his grandfather. Known as Uncle Frank, he was a pious, devout man. Emily, or Aunt Emma as she was called, was a Bible-reading, psalm-singing woman whose temperament melded perfectly with her husband's.

Emily and Frank had four children while they lived in Madison Township, but two died in infancy. With their two surviving children—Orla Edwin and Wesley Branch, born December 20, 1881—the Rickeys left Madison Township in 1883 and settled in Rush Township. A fifth child, Frank, was born in 1888.

Uncle Frank became Sciotto County commissioner. He took much pleasure in planting fruit trees on his land, aided by his son Orla. Wesley Branch, named for the founder of Methodism, spent much of his time with his mother. She read aloud to him from the Bible through the long evenings and told him hundreds of homespun folk tales.

During the 1890s, Branch, nicknamed "Weck," became caught up with baseball, like so many boys his age. An avid follower of the Cincinnati team, the strapping, broad-shouldered youth competed actively in sports. He and Orla formed a baseball battery: Orla was a fastballing southpaw, and Branch was one of the few around who dared to catch the hard stuff Orla threw. Always the manager or the catcher, Branch was already studying strategy, noting what made for good and bad players and what won games.

But Sundays were different. The Rickeys would eat a large breakfast and then hitch their horse, Old May, to a canopied surrey and ride off to church, filling the country air with the sounds of their hymns. It may have been on one of these Sunday rides that Emily extracted Branch Rickey's famous vow that he would never engage in any form of sport on Sunday.

When he had completed all the schooling available at the neighborhood school in Lucasville, a patchwork collection of courses that did not add up to a high school diploma, Weck got a teaching position at Turkey Creek. The salary was $35 a month. He made the eighteen-mile trip to the Turkey Creek schoolhouse by bicycle in all types of weather. The teaching was an exercise in discipline. Some of the boys he taught were as big and as old as he was, and he learned to dodge their tobacco juice sprays.

Rickey gave a portion of his monthly salary to his parents. Some he put away to save for a college education. With the rest, he bought books and taught himself Latin, higher mathematics, and rhetoric. Language fascinated him.

His routine of teaching and reading went on for two years. Then, encouraged by educator Ed Appel of Wheelersburg, Ohio, and Jim Finney, the superintendent of schools in Portsmouth, who tutored him and provided him with books, he prepared himself for the entrance examination for Ohio Wesleyan University.

"Two of my best friends had been at Ohio Wesleyan for a year," Rickey later recalled, "and they kept writing to me about it." He passed the exam for OWU and also for West Point. Rickey never intended to attend the military school, but took the examination for it, in his phrase, as a "brain test."

Admitted to Ohio Wesleyan even though he did not have a high school diploma, Rickey traveled on the Hocking Valley Railroad from Portsmouth to Delaware, Ohio, on a cool autumn day in 1900. A curious-looking figure dressed in an old suit, Rickey stepped off the train at West William Street. He carried his "other suit," his baseball suit, in his bag. The new freshman, dressed as he was and walking with a pigeon-toed gait, looked very different from the two well-dressed collegians who came to greet him. They were the two friends from Portsmouth who had written to him with so much enthusiasm about Ohio Wesleyan.

As they walked down the street, one of the boys whispered to the newly arrived eighteen-year-old, "Branch, turn your toes out when you walk. You look funny walking that way."

"Aw, turn your own damn toes out," was Rickey's response. The two friends were taken aback. "I answered that way," Rickey later admitted, "to show my independence right at the start in a new setting."

That was how Wesley Branch Rickey began at Ohio Wesleyan University—an institution that would remain special to him through all the days of his life.

"I never did go to high school, and never saw the inside of one until after I went to Delaware," he would write. "I was a preparatory student with two years of so-called prep work to do in order to become a freshman. I carried as many as twenty-one hours in one term and never did catch up with my class until the spring term of 1904. . . . I did the preparatory work and the four years of college work in three and a third years. . . .

"No boy could have had fewer clothes than I had in my first year in school. And no boy could have had less money than I had either. There was one month during which I did not have a single penny at any time. . . . Hormell [a professor] got a job for me waiting tables, and Walker [another professor] saw to it that I got the furnace job that gave me one-half interest in an attic room. Walker paid me eighteen dollars for copying some papers for him, which mystified me at the time because my penmanship was not too legible. During my first term at Delaware I had only one pair of pants, and nobody saw me wear anything else. I cleaned them myself and pressed them myself, and not infrequently. And they saw me through."

These penurious circumstances notwithstanding, Rickey threw himself wholeheartedly into campus life. "There was an old gymnasium that was too small for basketball. There were a couple of showers where the water was usually cold. One coach handled all athletics. There was not much game equipment. . . . One day we were playing baseball and a long foul landed near the railroad track, behind the catcher. A boy watching the game grabbed the ball. We chased him half a mile, even wading through the Olentangy River to get that ball back so we could continue the game.

"In the old days, we had padded sweaters, shin guards, and tight-fitting vests and pants for football. We usually bought our own shoes and had cleats nailed on by the shoemaker. Before the football season, we let our hair grow so our heads would have protection without head guards in the old center rushes. Five yards in three downs meant mass plays, and everyone piled up.

"Social life was pretty quiet. We went to the YMCA on Wednesday night and to church on Sunday. Monday, we signed slips in chapel to say that we had, or had not, been to church the day before. We might walk home to Monnett Hall with the girls after class and see them until nine o'clock on Friday or Saturday evenings. If we went walking, we confined our strolls to the halls and front porch of the dormitory. There were no dances, no picture shows, no college shows. We had a good lecture course, and it was a big event when a musical performance was given. The fellows wore dress suits, if they had them, and the girls wore formal dresses."

Poor, without a high school diploma, a product of country-schoolhouse education and largely self-taught, Rickey was ill prepared for some of the academic challenges of Ohio Wesleyan. He was at a particular disadvantage in classical studies. His knowledge of Latin, prior to his university days, had come from rote study of one Latin book. He knew the meanings of most words, but admitted that "what Cicero or someone had meant when he put those words together was a mystery to me."

Called to recite one day in Prof. Johnny Grove's class, Rickey stammered through a passage, embarrassed in front of the other students, most of whom were from big-city high schools and knew much more than he. When Rickey had completed his self-conscious recitation, the old professor peered at him over his glasses. "Whose Latin grammar did you study, Mr. Rickey?"

"*Grove's Latin Grammar,*" said Rickey, sheepishly.

The class erupted. Rickey immediately realized that the little black Latin book that he had studied so diligently back home had been written by the professor standing before him. One pudgy student was laughing so hard he nearly fell out of his seat. Rickey, crestfallen, stood in front of the room thinking, "When the next Hocking Valley train goes south, I'll be on it."

Professor Grove finally silenced the students and asked Rickey to remain after class. Alone in the classroom, Rickey and the professor sat at the desk in front of the room. "Mr. Rickey," the professor asked, "what's the difference between a gerundive and a verbal noun?" The question posed no problem for the eager student, and the answer satisfied Professor Grove.

"Mr. Rickey, you need some special work in translation. Come in to see me here tomorrow morning a half hour before class."

Rickey attended Professor Grove's special early-morning tutoring sessions until the professor said, "I think you are now prepared to recite. Get ready for tomorrow."

Rickey recalled the happy ending: "I don't think I went to bed at all that night. I knew that lesson from beginning to end. And then *horribile dictu!* He forgot to call on me. Next day, he did call on me. I was prepared. . . . And the class applauded. It was almost more embarrassing than the first day. 'Well,' Professor Grove said to the class, 'I think you will agree with me that Mr. Rickey has made considerable progress in his study of Latin.' "

Branch's spare time was taken up by athletic endeavors aimed at earning money to meet his educational expenses. At that time, collegians were allowed to engage in professional sports. Rickey played semipro baseball in the summer and football in the fall.

As a member of the backfield of the Shelby, Ohio, football team, he earned up to $150 a game. But in 1902, a double fracture of his leg ended his football career, and he decided to concentrate exclusively on baseball.

He became the catcher for the Laramie, Wyoming, baseball team in 1903, was moved up to Dallas in July, and a month later was promoted to the Cincinnati Reds. As backup catcher to Heinie Peitz, Rickey was placed in charge of the catcher's mask; Peitz looked after the chest protector. The Reds had just one of each for the team.

At the conclusion of a Saturday game, Rickey handed the catcher's mask to Peitz. "Look after it, Heinie," he said. "I won't be here tomorrow. It's a Sunday."

The manger of the Reds was Joe Kelley, a tough former member of the Baltimore Orioles. "What's that?" he shouted to Rickey. "What do you mean you won't be here tomorrow?"

"Didn't the Dallas team tell you when you bought me that I don't play ball on Sunday?"

"This is a Sunday town," snapped Kelley. "That's when the money comes in. How come you won't play Sunday ball?"

"It's just the way I was brought up," said Rickey. "It's against my principles to play ball on Sunday."

Kelley was livid. "You're not gonna go too far in baseball not playing on Sunday. What do you think you are? You think you're better than the other fellows?"

"That's not it at all, Mr. Kelley."

"Well, Rickey, whatever it is, we're not going to make an exception for you. You will catch when I tell you to catch or you can get the hell out of here. Pick up your money and get out if you won't play tomorrow."

Released and returned to Dallas, Rickey learned an important lesson. From that point on, for the rest of his career in baseball, Rickey always insisted on a clause in his contract—as both a player and an executive—stating that he was under no obligation to be at a ballpark on Sunday.

In 1904, Rickey was awarded a bachelor of literature degree from Ohio Wesleyan and enrolled at Allegheny College to study law and serve as athletic director and baseball coach.

Still a student, in 1905 Rickey became a member of the St. Louis Browns by way of Chicago. The White Sox had purchased his contract from Dallas and then traded him to the Browns for veteran catcher Frank Roth. He appeared in just one game for the Browns in 1905, but in 1906 batted a creditable .284 in sixty-four games. Perhaps his marriage to his childhood sweetheart Jane Moulton, a fellow student at Ohio Wesleyan, on June 1, 1906, had something to do with his playing performance. Rickey, who called his wife, a storekeeper's daughter, "the only pebble on the beach," claimed that he proposed to her more than a hundred times before she said yes.

It was an eventful year for Rickey. In addition to getting married and playing major-league baseball, he also served as athletic director and football coach at Ohio Wesleyan, earned a second bachelor's degree (this time in arts), and still found time to play checkers, a game he played avidly all his life.

In 1907, the Browns traded Rickey to the New York Highlanders. Years later he recalled the excitement of arriving as a country boy in the Big Apple that April, and riding uptown to 168th Street and Broadway, where the ballpark was located. Rickey may have been spreading himself too thin, though. He missed spring training because of OWU commitments, and that season he batted just .182—and was dead last in fielding percentage among all outfielders and catchers in the American League. In one eleven-game span, he committed nine errors. On June 28, 1907, he earned an ignominious niche in the record books. Catching against

Washington, he allowed thirteen bases to be stolen on him—
a record for a nine-inning game. The Highlanders released
him after the season ended, and he went back to Ohio and
his studies.

But it was not entirely a lost summer. Rickey had an
opportunity to prevail, if not in baseball, then in another
form of competition. In midtown Manhattan, there was a
storefront where customers could play checkers against a
large mechanical hand manipulated by someone behind a
curtain. The hand played four or five games at once, and
never lost.

Rickey was an old hand at checkers, having played many
games while sitting astride a cracker barrel in the country
store back home, and he couldn't resist the challenge. He
played the hand and beat it. The man behind the curtain
emerged to congratulate the victor. To the astonishment of
both men, it turned out that the "book" system Rickey employed was invented by his hidden opponent. Rickey had
mastered the technique, and the master had met his match.

Back in Ohio, Rickey took over the class of his onetime
mentor, Professor Grove, who had died. At the same time he
studied law at Ohio State University and coached football
and baseball at his alma mater. He was known to be especially sympathetic to homesick young players. Recalling his
own homesickness when he first attended Wesleyan, he told
them how he would go home for a day or two and return to
school feeling much better.

Herman M. Shipps, a member of the class of '13 and
later vice-president of Ohio Wesleyan, was a freshman when
Rickey was the college's football coach. He recalls another
aspect of Rickey's life:

"In those days there was a great deal of feeling in Ohio
about Prohibition. In fact, you were either 'wet' or 'dry.' One
evening Branch was walking up Sandusky Street after football practice with half the team gathered around him. At the

corner of William Street and Sandusky a man standing on a baggage truck was making a speech to a considerable crowd. Branch said, 'What's that fellow doing?' Someone said, 'He's making a "wet" speech.' Branch said, 'If you get a box over on this other corner, I'll make a "dry" speech.'

"He got on a box and started to talk, and pretty soon he had the whole crowd come across the street to listen to him. It must have been a pretty good speech, because the Anti-Saloon League heard about it and told him they would love him to make some 'dry' speeches in the small towns in Ohio, and they would pay him ten dollars and his expenses.

"The first place he went to was Chillicothe," recalls Shipps. Rickey was told by three hotel managers that there were no vacancies. The hotels were dependent on their bars for much of their income. "Branch wasn't quite sure what to do, so he started to walk down the street and met an old friend from Duck Run named Hunter. They stopped, shook hands, and Branch said, 'What are you doing here?'

" 'I'm tending bar. What are you doing?'

" 'I came to make a "dry" speech,' Branch said, 'and I can't find anyplace to stay. The hotels won't let me in.'

"Hunter said, 'That's all right, come on down and stay with me.'

"So Branch stayed with the bartender and made a good 'dry' speech. After that experience he made quite a few such speeches in Ohio and became widely known as a public speaker."

In the 1920s, Rickey was hired by the Reapath Lyceum Bureau in Columbus, Ohio, to speak in churches throughout the state. "Branch didn't like to drive a car, so he and I made a deal," Shipps recalled. "I would take him around to various small towns in Ohio where he was making speeches in the evening, and at dinnertime we would assemble the Ohio Wesleyan alumni who would come to have dinner together and to hear him talk about the university. Then we would all go to church and hear him talk about government. He was an ardent Republican, and at one time seriously considered running for senator in Missouri. I recall once we sat in front of my fire and talked for a couple of hours about whether he should stay in baseball or run. He finally decided, as it seemed he always did, in favor of baseball."

But even baseball had to wait back in the spring of 1909. Acute weight loss and a persistent cough were diagnosed as symptoms of tuberculosis. Rickey had to submit to a rest cure for six months at Saranac Lake, New York. The respite in the Adirondack Mountains worked. That fall, he enrolled in the University of Michigan Law School and served as baseball coach there. He completed the three-year course in two years, but the strain caused his health to break down again. Doctors suggested he go west, where the climate would be more beneficial. So the Rickeys headed out to Boise, Idaho, with two fraternity brothers and set up a law practice. It seemed as if he would spend his life as a western lawyer.

He had left with the understanding that if he wanted to return, he would be welcomed back. He wired the athletic director at the University of Michigan: "Am starving, will be back without delay." He told his partners he was making a leave and headed back to Ann Arbor to coach Michigan's baseball team. He doubled as baseball coach and part-time scout for the St. Louis Browns, sending in reports on players to the Browns owner, Col. Bob Hedges, who was so impressed with Rickey's reports that he hired him as an assistant presidential secretary. He was also allowed to continue coaching at the University of Michigan.

Nearing the end of the third decade of his life, Wesley Branch Rickey had been a country schoolteacher, earned three college degrees, played and coached collegiate baseball and football, played professional baseball and football, lectured extensively on behalf of Prohibition, and been a college instructor, an athletic director, and a lawyer. He had come through two bouts with tuberculosis. An abstemious, Sabbath-observing Methodist whose vilest expletive was "Judas Priest," he was primed to enter the rough-and-tumble world of major-league baseball. The sport would never be the same.

ST. LOUIS

In 1913, Ty Cobb of Detroit paced the American League in batting. Frank "Home Run" Baker of Philadelphia hit twelve homers to lead the league. Walter Johnson of Washington won thirty-six games and had an earned-run average of 1.09. The St. Louis Browns finished in last place, thirty-nine games behind Connie Mack's Athletics. Their three managers that season were George Stovall, Jimmy Austin, and Branch Rickey.

Col. Bob Hedges, the former Cincinnati carriage maker, prevailed upon his aide, Rickey, to take over the team for the final eleven games of the season. True to his old vow, Rickey would not enter the ballpark on Sunday; Burt Shotton, three years Rickey's junior, from Bronhelm, Ohio, became the designated Sunday manager.

Rickey piloted the 1914 Browns to a fifth-place finish. On August 25 of that year, the thirty-three-year-old manager was coaxed into a final major-league at-bat. His Browns were losing, 7–0, in the first game of a doubleheader against Connie Mack's Athletics in Shibe Park in Philadelphia. A nineteen-year-old southpaw named Ray Bressler was the Philadelphia pitcher. Veteran Ira Thomas, who had once been a teammate of Rickey's on the New York Highlanders, was catching.

"Get up and hit, Rick. Get up and hit," Thomas yelled. The other Athletics picked it up. Even the venerable Connie Mack joined in the chant. Rickey agreed to come to the plate if Bressler promised not to throw any curveballs.

"I was sure they'd curve me to death," Rickey recalled. "So I wasn't set for the first pitch, strike one, a fastball. Well, I thought, that was done to make me complacent. I just know they'd bend the next one over. The next pitch was a fastball and a strike. I was now ready for the curve and was utterly astonished to see a third fastball go by—strike three. My last turn at bat in the major leagues taught me that nothing is gained by distrusting your fellowman."

One of Rickey's early front-office coups was in signing George Sisler. He had starred as a member of Rickey's University of Michigan baseball team before signing a contract with the Pittsburgh Pirates. As an attorney, Rickey realized that the signing was illegal, since Sisler was underage and therefore not able to sign a legal contract. Rickey journeyed to Sisler's parents in Manchester, Ohio. After swapping some hunting and fishing stories, Sisler's father signed with his fellow Ohioan, binding the future Hall of Famer to the St. Louis Browns, where he starred for a dozen seasons. The signing caused an uproar, but Rickey was upheld by the National Baseball Commission.

Even with Sisler, the 1915 Browns were a hapless collection of athletes. They won only sixty-three games and finished in sixth place. Yankee third baseman Fritzie Maisel, who stole fifty-one bases that year—many against the Browns—recalled trying to ride Rickey, who was coaching at third base. "I told him to get behind the plate and try to stop me from stealing since I was having such a good time against his catcher.

" 'Judas Priest, Fritzie,' he shouted at me, 'will you kindly shut your mouth. I am suffering enough.' "

One contemporary claimed it was the players Rickey managed who suffered most. He droned on tirelessly about baseball theory, but his sermons on the game's intricacies befuddled and bewildered some of the semiliterate types, who could only scratch their heads when the man they called the "Ohio Weezeleyant," the exasperated professor of multiple college degrees, would declare: "I wonder why a man trained for the law devotes his life to something so cosmically unimportant as a game."

During the winter of 1915–16, the Federal League, which was formed to compete with the American and National leagues in 1914, folded. Hedges sold the Browns to Phil Ball, former owner of the St. Louis Federal League team. Ball, a fifty-six-year-old rough, growling Iowan, was the owner of an ice business. He encouraged the sale of liquor, which increased the sale of his ice. "So you're the goddamned Prohibitionist," was how the tough-talking Ball greeted the former Ohio schoolteacher. The two men never got along. Ball installed Fielder Jones, his former Federal League pilot, as manager of the Browns. Rickey was restricted solely to front-office duties.

Burdened with excess players as a result of the merger of Ball's two clubs, Rickey began to place surplus personnel with friendly owners of minor-league clubs. In return, he obtained the option to purchase players from their rosters for nominal sums, amounts much lower than the market value of these players. The seeds of the farm system, what would be Rickey's greatest baseball innovation, were thus planted.

Late in the summer of 1916, Helene Hathaway Robeson Britton, owner of the St. Louis Cardinals, hosted a meeting in her lavish home on Lindell Boulevard. "Lady Bee," plagued by domestic troubles and poor attendance at Cardinal games, ushered in manager Miller Huggins and her legal adviser James C. Jones. "Gentlemen," the striking brunette announced to the surprise of the two men, "I want

to get out of baseball. I guess I've had enough. I wanted you
two to be the first to know in case you're thinking of buying
the club yourself."

Huggins, in his fourth year as Cardinal manager, was
intrigued by the offer. "I'll take the club on verbal option,"
he told her. "I'll get a buyer." Jones remained silent.

The diminutive Huggins scrambled through St. Louis
and his native Cincinnati lining up financial backers. The
"Mighty Mite," as he was known, was prepared to present
Lady Bee with an offer when he read in the newspaper one
morning that the Cardinals had been sold. James C. Jones
had organized a stock company comprised of St. Louis fans
and supporters. The club, along with old League Park, was
acquired for $375,000. The money was raised by the sale of
stock ranging in price from $10 to $50 by the firm of Jones
and Hocker, which collected $25,000 for overseeing the
transaction.

The following year, further sales of stock kept the franchise going even though the club was $185,000 in the red.
Jones was feeling secure in his role as owner. He called
seven St. Louis writers and editors to his office. "Gentlemen,"
he announced, "our campaign has progressed nicely. We have
the club. We have a good manager. [Miller Huggins was in
his last year on the job, still piqued at the fact that Jones and
not he had wound up as club owner.] But I need a man to
run all of this as club president. You boys have been around;
you know baseball, and you know the St. Louis conditions. I
need, I want, your suggestions for this job. Would you be so
kind as to write the name of this person on a slip of paper
and drop it into my hat as I pass it around the room?"

The same name appeared on all the slips of paper—
Branch Rickey, business manager of the St. Louis Browns.

Across town, Rickey's efficiency had made him a valuable asset to ice tycoon Phil Ball despite their personal differences. But Rickey had not been happy working for the
Browns since Ball had taken over, and he was delighted

with the Cardinals' offer. Ball matched it, but Rickey chose to take the Cardinal job. Rickey claimed that his contract allowed him to switch jobs if a better position became available. Ball brought a suit against Rickey, and Rickey answered with a countersuit. When the shouting stopped, Rickey won and moved over to the presidency of the St. Louis Cardinals.

The Cards tied for last place in 1916. The 1917 club, led by a youngster named Rogers Hornsby who batted .327, second in the league, finished third. Most agreed that the climb in the standings was due to some key trades engineered by new club president Branch Rickey and the skillful managerial touch of Miller Huggins. Still miffed at losing his chance to own the Cardinals, Huggins went over to the New York Yankees in 1918. Rickey replaced him with Jack Hendricks. Rickey introduced several innovations, including sliding pits where players could practice their base running, and blackboard chalk-talks aimed at explaining baseball theory. Nonetheless, the 1918 Cardinals finished in last place under Hendricks in a season that ended on Labor Day. The War Department had introduced a "work or fight" order mandating the early end to the season.

Many baseball men became involved in the war effort. Those with good educational backgrounds and experience in strategic planning were placed in a special program supervised by the former president of Harvard University, Percy Houghton. Rickey was recruited by Houghton, and became part of the Chemical Warfare Service.

The Rickey home in St. Louis was closed for the duration of the war. Thirty-six-year-old Branch was sent east for training and then overseas. His wife, Jane, and their four little children returned to Ohio. Ambitious as ever, Rickey had attained the rank of major by the war's end.

When he returned to St. Louis, he found a team deep in debt. "We didn't even have the money to send the team south for spring training, so we trained at home," Rickey recalled. "We even wore the same uniforms at home and on the road. They were really ragged." Firemen patrolled the dilapidated Cardinal ballpark watching out for stray matches, fearful that the ramshackle wooden stands would burn down. Rickey had to pass up his own salary to meet the payroll. He borrowed a rug from his own home and placed it on the floor of his office to impress visitors. His ubiquitous bow tie, however, was not worn to make an impression. "It's cheaper than a regular tie," he explained, "and it takes less time to put on. It could also cover up a soiled shirt or a frayed collar," added the efficiency-minded baseball executive.

Rickey dismissed Hendricks and took over as manager himself. The look of the Redbirds began to change. His old Sunday manager, Burt Shotton, came over from the Browns, along with Charlie Barrett, one of the premier scouts in baseball. Players came and went as Rickey, carrying a black notebook in which he jotted down lengthy notes about each player's strengths and weaknesses, kept shuffling the Cards looking for the right combination. The 1919 team finished in seventh place.

Nineteen nineteen was also the year of the "Black Sox" scandal—the alleged attempt of several players on the Chicago White Sox to throw the World Series. The baseball world was too concerned with the scandal for anyone to notice Rickey's purchase of eighteen of the one hundred shares of stock in the Houston team of the Texas League.

The Houston stock purchase was the first primitive step toward the development of a farm system. "It was a case of necessity being the mother of invention," Rickey later explained. "We lived a precarious existence. We would trade one player for four and then sell one of them for some extra cash. We were always at a distinct disadvantage trying to get players from the minor leagues. Other clubs would outbid us; they had the money and the superior scouting machinery."

The rich New York Giants posed the biggest problem for the impoverished Cardinals. Owner Charles Stoneham and manager John McGraw formed a lavish spending combination. Every year they paid top dollar for players to give the Giants reinforcements for the second half of the season. There were times when Rickey or his top scout Charlie Barrett would spot a good prospect in the minor leagues and make an offer to the team. The team's owner would then approach the Giants or another wealthy major-league team and offer the player for a higher price. Rickey found himself in the frustrating position of scouting talent for his richer competitors. He concluded that since the Cardinals were too poor to buy players, they would have to develop their own.

The Houston affiliation was quickly followed by a purchase of stock in Fort Smith of the Class C Western Association. In 1920, Syracuse was added, a double-A club in the International League. Gradually, full control of the teams came into the hands of the Cardinals. "Experience had taught us," Rickey explained, "that a partial share of a minor-league team was unsatisfactory; the solution was to own the minor-league club outright."

More and more clubs were added. At one point, the Cardinals controlled the supply of players in both the Nebraska State League and the Arkansas-Missouri League.

New York Giant manager John McGraw called it "a pipe dream." But the farm system began to yield a rich harvest. A mythology emerged as fuzzy-cheeked recruits from tiny hamlets and backwoods villages across America poured into the St. Louis organization.

It was said that a Cardinal scout was once driving down a country lane when a rabbit shot out in front of his car, with a strapping youth in hot pursuit. The lad caught the hare just as it was about to enter the forest on the other side of the road. The astonished scout cried out, "What you doin' boy?"

"Huntin' rabbits," the youth replied.

"Is *that* how you hunt rabbits?"

"Is there any other way?"

The scout quickly whipped out a contract and said, "Boy, how'd you like to play for the Cardinals?"

Competing executives were outraged by Rickey's efforts to corner the market on young talent. Players in the farm system were called "Rickey's chain gang." Baseball Commissioner Judge Kenesaw Mountain Landis was a staunch supporter of independently owned minor-league teams and opposed Rickey's revolutionary farm system. He ruled that a major-league team could control only one team in each minor league.

In 1920 Rickey was joined by two men who would be key figures on the St. Louis scene for many years. One was a right-handed pitcher from Clayton, Ohio; the other was an Irishman from New York City's Greenwich Village.

Jesse Joseph Haines had kicked around in the minor leagues since 1914. Rickey saw Haines pitch just two innings for Kansas City in 1919, but his keen eye for talent told him that the twenty-six-year-old Ohioan could star for the Cardinals. Prevailing on a dozen stockholders to sign a bank note for $10,000, Rickey bought Haines's contract from Kansas City. Haines was the last player purchased outright during Rickey's years in St. Louis. He pitched for the Cardinals until 1937, winning a total of 210 games. In 1970, Haines, just one of the many players originally spotted and signed by Rickey, was admitted to the Hall of Fame.

The Irishman was Sam Breadon, a New Yorker who headed west in 1902 seeking riches. A year and a half younger than Rickey, he had made thousands selling automobiles in St. Louis during its World's Fair year of 1904. As Breadon bought more and more stock in the Cardinals, he became a major force in the organization. In 1920, with Jones's backing, Breadon was elected president of the Cardinals; Rickey became vice-president.

Breadon and Rickey were unlikely partners. Breadon,

known as "Singing Sam," was a boisterous, fun-loving man who loved to sing in barbershop quartets. The Bible-quoting, psalm-singing Rickey couldn't have been more different, yet they functioned very well together. They were both hard workers, both creative, inventive, and energetic enterpreneurs. Breadon introduced the Sunday doubleheader; Rickey introduced "The Knothole Gang," providing free tickets to Cardinal games for underprivileged youths, recognizing that today's youngsters were the paying customers of the future.

To save money, Breadon moved his club into Sportsman's Park as tenants of the Browns in 1920. The Cardinals finished in sixth place that year. It was a fairly nondescript team except for the glittering star at second base: Rogers Hornsby. The twenty-four-year-old Texan batted .370 and won the first of his seven batting titles. Charles Stoneham of the Giants offered the Cardinals $300,000 for Hornsby. It was a tempting offer, but Jones, Breadon, and Rickey turned it down.

The 1921 club had nine .300 hitters and finished the season in third place. Hornsby, grooving into his Hall of Fame batting form, finished the season with a .397 average. Stoneham, more anxious than ever to add the "Rajah" to his Giants, offered $250,000 plus four players for him. Breadon listened and then responded, "Hornsby is not for sale."

The next year, the first important product of Rickey's farm system reached the parent club. Sunny Jim Bottomley came to bat 151 times for the 1922 Cardinals and batted .325. The Cardinals, again led by Hornsby, who topped the magic .400 mark with a .401 average, wound up in a third-place tie with the Pirates, eight games behind the Giants, who had insured the pennant with the August purchase of pitcher Hugh McQuillan from the Braves for $100,000. McQuillan won six games down the stretch, and symbolized the history of late-season purchases that made the New Yorkers the powerhouse of the National League.

Rickey felt that the Cardinals' chances to beat out the Giants would have been better were it not for the late-season transaction. He complained to Commissioner Landis. The Judge ruled that no player purchases would be permitted after June 15 except for waiver deals. Rickey was pleased with the decision, which would limit some of the purchasing power of the rich teams like the Giants.

Breadon was delighted with the two straight third-place finishes, the developing farm system, Landis's ruling, and the Cardinals' home attendance of 536,343—then the highest in the club's history. He offered Rickey a ten-year contract. "Farmer Rickey," as he was then being called, refused and settled for a five-year pact, preferring not to tie himself down for quite so long a period.

The 1923 Cardinals dropped to fifth place, and the following year they finished sixth. Hornsby's fabulous batting skills kept improving; in 1924 he set a modern record with a .424 average. His relationship with Rickey, however, deteriorated. Hornsby disliked Rickey's cerebral approach. "This ain't football," the Rajah would moan. "We don't need the professor's blackboard in baseball." Hornsby spoke vulgarly about Rickey behind his back. They were men cut from different cloth. They came to blows in the clubhouse at the Polo Grounds in New York City late in the 1923 season. Burt Shotton stepped between the moody Texan and an angry Rickey. In September of 1923, Rickey fined Hornsby $500 for missing four Cardinal games without permission.

Rickey's family grew and prospered in St. Louis, and he became a well-known figure around town, with his neat bow tie and his omnipresent cigar. There were now five daughters and a son: Mary, Jane, Alice, Sue, Elizabeth, and Branch Jr. B. R., as Rickey was now being called, was earning a good salary, and also reaping a share of the team's profits. Each player sale added to his earnings, for he received 10 percent of every player deal as long as the Cardinal corporation made a profit. Because of his love for his large family, Rickey was a strong believer in life insurance and invested the first $14,000 of his annual income in premiums. Rickey was also active in community and church life, devoting time to YMCA board work and to Grace Methodist Church, where he was a lay preacher.

Convivial, gregarious, and outgoing, Rickey kept up old friendships from Ohio Wesleyan and Michigan while he was forming new ones in St. Louis. The Rickeys entertained often. Branch enjoyed company and liked nothing more than to spend an evening swapping tales with old or new friends. Herman Shipps, his old friend from Ohio Wesleyan, visited the Rickey home frequently. "I sat at the table with the five girls, the son, Branch, and Mrs. Rickey," Shipps recalls. "Branch would raise a question, take one side of it, and then say, 'Now, do you agree?' Some of the crowd surely wouldn't. Then he would conduct a debate until everyone had said what he wanted to. He would summarize, and they would go on to another subject. When he played bridge, his partner had a hard time. He would raise the bid that she made beyond what he thought she could accomplish and then seemed to enjoy seeing her struggle with the problem. It was an interested and an interesting family."

As more of "Farmer Rickey's produce" began to reach the majors, stories about the Cardinal general manager began to circulate around the league. It was reported that Rickey was sitting in the stands with his little black notebook watching several farmhands work out. "Who's that pitcher?" he asked scout Bennie Borgmann.

"His name is Hafey, Mr. Rickey. He's quite a pitching prospect."

"From now on he's an outfielder." Chick Hafey spent eight years in the Cardinals' outfield before being traded to Cincinnati. His career batting average was .317, and he was elected to the Hall of Fame in 1971.

Herman Shipps was in Cincinnati one winter attending an alumni meeting and talking to high school students.

"Branch had a large apartment in one of the hotels," Shipps recalls, "and took me in to stay with him and we had a good time visiting for three or four days. I remember distinctly coming back one afternoon from work. Going into the room I heard somebody speaking very loudly. There was Branch with his shirt off, with one foot up on a chair, and one of the baseball players—it could have been Tommy Thevenow [the Cardinal shortstop]—was sitting there listening. Branch was telling him why he ought to sign his contract. After hearing that conversation for a short time, I realized why it was that baseball players said, 'Never get into a hotel room with Branch Rickey if you don't want to sign a contract!' "

Rickey peppered his conversation with his pet expressions: "It's the history of this country that men are what they make themselves. Their education never stops." "Look for the best in everybody, but don't allow first impressions to sway you." "Nine times out of ten a man fashions his own destiny. You get out of life what you put into it." "Discipline should come from within and be self-imposed. It's more effective that way." "Evil is transient." "It is not the honor that you take with you but the heritage you leave behind." The moralistic expressions were not just words for Rickey; they were the bedrock of his philosophy of life; they were the windows through which he viewed the world.

In 1925, with the Cardinals in last place and attendance declining, Breadon discharged Rickey as manager over the Memorial Day weekend and replaced him with Hornsby. Rickey was angry over the loss of his job as manager to his bitter adversary, but Breadon told him, "What I'm doing for you is the greatest favor any man ever did for another. One day you'll see that I'm right."

The selection of Hornsby as manager may have been influenced by Breadon's desire to keep up with the times. There were several player-managers in the major leagues.

Rickey's Michigan State protégé, George Sisler, played first base and managed the Browns. Outfielder Ty Cobb was the Tiger pilot. Bucky Harris played second base and managed the Senators. Shortstop Dave Bancroft was the skipper of the Braves. In Cleveland, outfielder Tris Speaker was the manager, and Eddie Collins was the second baseman-manager of the White Sox.

The main reason for Rickey's demotion was that Breadon realized the Ohioan's skills were better suited to the off-the-field duties of a baseball executive. As a manager, Rickey had certain clear failings. His cerebral approach to the game confused players. His demands on them, as he later admitted, "made them too tense, too eager."

Hornsby took over. Rickey, hurt by the loss of the manager's job, sold off his Cardinal stock, which was quickly snapped up by Hornsby. Jesse "Pop" Haines, then the thirty-one-year-old leader of the Cardinal pitching staff, remembers what it was like with the new manager: "Rogers was all baseball during the game. And if you gave all you had, he was happy. But if you didn't, he'd give you hell. Rogers was a loner, though; even before he became manager he never palled around with the players."

Playing and managing agreed with Hornsby. In 1925 he batted .403, drove in 143 runs, and hit thirty-nine homers, and his bold managing tactics moved the Cardinals into a fourth-place finish, a game over .500 and eighteen games behind the league-leading Pirates. Breadon had found a winning combination: Rickey supplied the talent and Hornsby made it work.

The Breadon-Rickey-Hornsby combo lit up the city on the banks of the Mississippi in 1926. The "master trader" had added a few key players that season. Just before the trading deadline on June 14, Rickey shipped Heinie Mueller to the Giants in return for Billy Southworth. While Mueller went on to have a mediocre year for the New Yorkers and was relegated to part-time duty, Southworth batted .317 for the Redbirds and became a capable performer in right field. Grover Cleveland Alexander, picked up on waivers from the Cubs, was the other crucial addition. The grizzled veteran won nine games for the 1926 Cardinals, leading them to their first pennant. Rickey's years of building had finally paid off. St. Louis celebrated with a monstrous ticker-tape parade.

On October 10, a damp and dank Sunday, the Cards faced the Yankees, managed by Miller Huggins, in the seventh game of the World Series. Alexander had defeated the Yankees 10–2 the day before, scattering eight hits. He spent Saturday night celebrating. Hornsby, whose batting average had dropped to .317 that year, and who was so immersed in the business of baseball that he did not even go to his mother's funeral after she died on the eve of the Series, was intent on victory. In the seventh inning of that final game, with the bases loaded and two out, Hornsby called in Alexander to relieve. Hung over but clear-eyed, "old Pete" struck out Tony Lazzeri to end the inning, and then held the Yanks scoreless in the eighth and ninth to preserve the 3–2 lead and clinch the World Championship. "Pete was a silent drinker, and he'd probably had a little more than he should have," recalled Haines, "but I'll tell you, he was dead sober when he faced Lazzeri." It was a classic case of Rickey's recruiting a former star for one more round of glory. The championship was the first for the city of St. Louis since 1888.

After eleven full and productive seasons with the Cardinals, with six straight batting titles behind him and the distinction of having piloted the team to its first World Series victory, Hornsby could have run for mayor of St. Louis and won. Instead, incredibly, he was traded to the New York Giants for second baseman Frankie Frisch and pitcher Jimmy Ring.

The fans were outraged. Black crepe was hung around Breadon's home in mourning for the loss of Hornsby. It was the first of the many blockbuster trades that would become part of the Branch Rickey mystique. Fans in St. Louis that 1927 season had a lot of trouble forgetting the Rajah, but Frisch, nicknamed the "Fordham Flash," took much of the heat off Rickey and Breadon, batting .337 and stealing forty-eight bases. The Cardinals finished in second place behind the Pirates. Alexander won twenty-one games, and Rabbit Maranville, another great player now past his prime but still effective, was plucked from the Rochester roster to fill a weak spot at shortstop.

Pop Haines had perhaps his best year in baseball in 1927, winning twenty-four games and leading the league in complete games with twenty-five. He recalled what it was like dealing with the Breadon-Rickey tandem that winter:

"Oh, was Breadon mean with a dollar! We all tried to deal with Rickey, and he was no Santa Claus, but Sam was murder. The year was over and I went over to St. Louis to see Rickey. Well, Rickey was out, so Sam cornered me and said, 'I suppose you're here to talk contract.' I replied, 'I'm here to see Mr. Rickey, Mr. Breadon.'

" 'Oh, well,' said Sam, 'seeing as you're here, we might as well talk contract. You had a pretty good year, and I'm going to give you a five-hundred-dollar raise.'

"I like to fell through the floor. I said, 'Good day, Mr. Breadon,' and I went back to Phillipsburgh [Ohio]. A few days later I heard from Mr. Rickey, and I did get a bit more than a five-hundred-dollar raise."

Wheeling and dealing, patching and pruning, Rickey traded for catcher Jimmy Wilson, installed Maranville as the regular shortstop, and added Ernie Orsatti to the roster. The 1928 Cardinals, led by Bill McKechnie, who had replaced Hornsby's successor Bob O'Farrell as manager, won the pennant, but lost the World Series to New York. Babe Ruth and Lou Gehrig clubbed seven home runs to lead the Yankees to a four-game sweep.

The 1929 Cardinals finished in fourth place, as the pitching staff slumped badly. Alexander won just nine games; Haines posted a 5.71 ERA and only thirteen wins. Rickey decided that the top priority for the farm system, now valued at a million dollars, would be pitching help.

Some of the players that showed up at a Cardinal tryout camp at Shawnee, Oklahoma, in the spring of 1930 arrived without a penny in their pockets. Some had not had a meal for the past day or two. Most of them came from Oklahoma and Texas, determined to be signed by the Cardinal organization. Rickey sat in the stands observing, chewing on his cigar, and making occasional notes in his black book. With a network of cronies in small towns, coaches on college campuses, and franchises throughout the minor leagues, there wasn't a town in America where Rickey did not have some connection. Rickey had gotten used to traveling from big-city stadiums to his regularly scheduled rural tryout camps with just a small briefcase containing his papers, a towel, and a clean white shirt. When he reached a new location, the soiled shirt he had worn and the towel were sent out to the nearest laundry while, like a busy Broadway producer, he hurried about auditioning players for his cast.

"His judgment of players was unique, and the best I have ever seen," notes his former aide Bill DeWitt. "He would break a hitter down by observing his fundamental weaknesses, something he learned from John McGraw and Connie Mack." On this particular day at the Shawnee tryouts, Rickey was especially interested in observing pitchers. He had them hurl to a batter or two, or sometimes pitch a complete inning. "Pitchers were judged by the velocity and movement of their fastball," recalls DeWitt. "Mr. Rickey contended any pitcher could be taught other pitches such as the curve, change of pace, or knuckleball."

That day in Shawnee, a slope-shouldered right-hander came out to the mound and fired in a few fastballs to close out his warm-up pitches. Rickey edged forward in his seat. The right-hander threw with a fluid, cotton-picker's motion.

He threw just nine pitches to the first three batters he faced and struck them all out. The hitters couldn't get a bat on the ball for a foul tip. Rickey told an assistant to let the pitcher stay in for the next three batters. Again the pitcher threw nine pitches and again recorded three strikeouts. He left the mound like a satisfied cat who had just caught a delicious bird and flashed a big country-boy smile to Rickey up in the stands.

Relaxing in the lobby of the Aldridge Hotel that evening, puffing away on his cigar, full from his huge supper and pleased with the pitching prospects he had seen that day, Rickey was seated in a comfortable chair, leafing through a newspaper. A voice from above interrupted his reading.

"Hello, Branch. How ya doin'?"

Rickey put down his newspaper and looked up into a grinning face. It was the right-hander who had struck out six batters earlier in the day.

"I'm sorry," Rickey said sternly, "I don't know you."

"Sure you do, Branch," he was told. "I'm the pitcher that did so well today. You let me pitch more to strike out more batters.

"My name is Dean," the young man continued. "Say, when's you and me goin' to St. Louis? I can win the pennant for you, Branch. I can."

Rickey arose from his chair, a severe look on his face. He stared up into the eyes of the six-foot, two-inch loud young man who had disturbed him. "Mr. Dean," he said, "I have no idea where or when you're going. Those in charge will let you know. If you do not mind, I would like to continue to read my newspaper."

Dean backed away, a smile still across his big face. "Okay, okay, Mr. Rickey," he said. "Whatever you say is fine with me." It is reported that was the first and last time Dizzy Dean ever addressed Rickey as "Branch."

On September 28, 1930, Dizzy Dean arrived to pitch the final game of the season for the St. Louis Cardinals. "Just tell the boys to get me a couple of runs," he told manager "Gabby" Street. It was an impressive debut. Dean allowed the Pirates just four hits as the Cardinals won 3–1. "I just fogged it through," Dean told reporters after the game.

Dean's route through the minors had been swift and full of headaches for Rickey. After the hotel meeting, Dean was optioned to St. Joseph of the Western League. He won seventeen games and was promoted to Houston, where he won eight games, losing only two. He struck out ninety-five batters in eighty-five innings. When he arrived in St. Louis to pitch the last game of the 1930 season, he had already won twenty-five games that season. He had also accumulated a record of debts, fistfights with opponents and teammates, and an attitude that made him start every sentence with "I."

That winter Rickey arranged for Dean to live with the family of Oliver French, a Cardinal minor-league executive, in Charleston, Missouri. Dean lacked a home of his own and any way of supporting himself until the next season began. He kept himself busy in the French home by tossing coal into the furnace. It became a "coal-baseball game." Pieces of coal that were pitched into the furnace became strikes. Diz was setting new strikeout records in the cellar, and there were times that winter when the temperature in the French house made it seem as if they were living in the tropics.

Rickey had told the Frenches to advance Dean only small sums of money and to watch who his friends were. Dean soon wearied of the restrictions. After a couple of months he demanded a meeting with Rickey.

They met at Rickey's Country Life Acres in St. Louis. "What a swell place this is," Diz exclaimed, entering the huge, beautifully furnished living room. "What a pretty far piece to hit a ball!"

Spread over thirty-three acres in the suburbs of St. Louis, Country Life Acres was Rickey's retreat. It was a showplace that reflected his growing affluence. He lived there with his wife, six children, and all manner of fowl and livestock. There were ducks and geese that frolicked on a small lake, a peacock, ponies, a dozen dogs of various breeds, pigeons, pheasants, and turkeys. A goat named Goat roamed all over the huge Tudor house and the carefully landscaped property. There was an alfalfa field, and a concrete dam that created a pond where the Rickeys fished. The feel was baronial, bustling, and yet bucolic.

The Cardinal vice-president and the teen-aged pitcher met for three hours. Rickey did most of the talking. On the drive back to Charleston, Oliver French asked Dean how the meeting went. "A fine friend you are," complained Dizzy. "I was scratchin' aroun' for 'bout a hundred an' fifty dollars . . . an' all I wound up with was a sex lecture. When Mr. Rickey began to talk about the facts of life, I thought that meant money. That ain't what it means to him."

Around Christmas of 1930, Dean suddenly decided that he was in love. The object of his affection was a high school junior, and he was set on marrying her. When Rickey learned about Dean's plans, he telephoned him, attempting to talk him out of it.

"I'm very much in favor of ballplayers marrying," Rickey began, "but I am always deeply concerned that there should be the right kind of marriage. I will give you five hundred dollars to marry, boy, but I mean the right kind of marriage. I definitely do not believe in placing a premium on any old marriage and especially one that will have no chance of succeeding."

Whether it was the five hundred dollars or Rickey's persuasive sermon, Dean did not marry that high school girl.

Dizzy's eccentric behavior and immaturity convinced Rickey that one more year in the minors would give the young pitcher the best chance of succeeding in the majors. Dean returned to Houston for the 1931 season, where he matured as a pitcher, winning twenty-six games, posting a

1.3 earned-run average, and striking out 303 batters in 304 innings.

As Rickey had reckoned, the 1931 Cardinals had enough pitching that year without Dean. They romped to the National League pennant, finishing thirteen games ahead of the New York Giants. Former Cardinal farmhands Paul Derringer and Bill Hallahan combined with Burleigh Grimes, picked up by Rickey in a trade with the Braves, for fifty-four victories. Left fielder Chick Hafey batted .3489 to win the batting title. Jim Bottomley hit .3482 to finish third. (Bill Terry of the Giants finished second at .3486 in the closest batting race of all time.) Ripper Collins played in eighty-nine games and rapped the ball at a .301 pace. But the flash and fire of that Redbird club was Johnny Leonard Roosevelt Martin.

Born on February 29, 1904, in Temple, Oklahoma, Pepper Martin had come up through the Cardinal farm system, playing in Greenville, Fort Smith, Syracuse, and Houston. In 1930, Martin played for Rochester. In the spring of 1931, the twenty-seven-year-old Martin crashed into Rickey's office. "My lord," he screamed, "I am fed up. I wasn't born to sit on anybody's bench or spend my life in the minors, Mr. Rickey. You either play me or you trade me!" Regular center fielder Taylor Douthit was traded to the Reds; Martin took over and batted .300 in 1931.

Before the first game of the World Series against the Philadelphia Athletics, champions in 1929 and 1930, Rickey appealed to the Cardinal players in the accents of a former football coach. This was the moment for the achievement of all their boyhood dreams, he told them. He pounded away at the theme that all of them had gone hungry and struggled for the moment ahead of them. "This team has desire," he roared. "We will defeat the Athletics in this World Series!"

Pepper Martin recalled listening to Rickey's exhortations: "I personally got down on my knees in front of our dugout and kissed the ground. The theme of Mr. Rickey's speech was 'the greatest attribute to a winning ballplayer is a desire to win that dominates.' And I actually prayed to God to help me have the 'desire to win that dominates.' "

Martin almost single-handedly destroyed the vaunted Athletics, who were led by Lefty Grove, Mickey Cochrane, Jimmie Foxx, Al Simmons, and other stars. "The Wild Horse of the Osage" rapped out a dozen hits in five games and stole five bases. His .500 batting average and the verve with which he played made him a national hero—and a symbol of spirited St. Louis Cardinal baseball. Rickey had more like Martin down on the farm: Rochester and Houston had also won pennants in their minor leagues that year.

At the major-league meetings in 1931, Rickey purchased Hack Wilson from the Chicago Cubs. The powerful slugger had batted just .261 and managed only thirteen home runs that past season. The Rickey purchase was just for speculation. A month later, the Master Trader made a nice profit by selling Wilson to the Dodgers for $45,000 plus a minor league outfielder. The other clubs had such respect for Rickey's judgment that his interest in a ballplayer instantly upgraded that athlete's value.

Rickey was too smart a baseball man to let personal animosity interfere with his judgment. During the 1932 season, Rogers Hornsby was released as manager of the Cubs. Morale on the club was low, and Hornsby was spending too much time at the racetrack. Despite their shoving match a few years before, Rickey was prepared that winter to sign Hornsby as a pinch hitter. He was sure that the Rajah could help the Cardinals coming off the bench. Commissioner Landis objected. "The demoralizer Hornsby has been in baseball too long," said the commissioner. "He's a bad influence." The country lawyer in Rickey took over. He told Landis that he would draw up a contract that contained a clause banning Hornsby from gambling. "And when he signs it," Rickey asked Landis, "will you then be able to deny this man the right to earn a living as a baseball player?"

Hornsby batted .325 in forty-six games and then was released to allow him to take over as manager of the St. Louis Browns. It was a rare sentimental gesture for Rickey.

The 1932 Cardinals finished in a tie for sixth place, but that dismal season marked the arrival of Joe Medwick and Dizzy Dean. A twenty-year-old brought up from Houston, the New Jersey–born Medwick batted .349 in thirty-six games. He and the rest of the Cardinals that year were overshadowed by the irrepressible Dean, however, who once bragged, "If I had finished the second grade in school, I would have went a year longer than my old man." Dizzy won eighteen games while pitching more innings and striking out more batters than any other National League hurler.

Cardinal shortstop Charlie Gelbert, just twenty-six years old, suffered a shotgun wound while hunting near the end of 1932. The unfortunate accident created a weakness at shortstop. There was no adequate replacement in the St. Louis farm system, and Rickey spent much of the spring attempting to deal for a proven major-league shortstop. In May of 1933 he was finally able to pry one Leo Ernest Durocher, a twenty-seven-year-old dandy with slicked-back hair, loose from Sid Weil of the Cincinnati Reds.

While Rickey looked forward to adding Durocher to his colorful cast of characters, the feisty shortstop balked at the trade. "I won't go to that bushy-browed monster who runs a chain gang," Durocher protested to Weil. "I like it here in Cincinnati."

Weil prevailed upon Durocher to speak to Rickey. "Make your feelings known, and we'll see what happens."

Bursting into Rickey's hotel room the next day, Durocher found the Cardinal executive wrapped in a bathrobe, a cigar stuck in his mouth. He was nursing a bad cold. Durocher proceeded to deliver a monologue on his thoughts and feelings, and the rumors and gossip he had heard about Rickey and the Cardinal organization. He lit into Rickey for his push-button trades of ballplayers, for the frugality that he had heard was a way of life in St. Louis, for the low salaries dispensed to big stars. Slouched against a pillow, Rickey listened, chewing on the unlit cigar. Finally Rickey sat up. "I have heard many negative things about you, just as you have heard a lot about me," he said. "I could talk about your flashy clothes, your long string of debts, and the women in your life. But the trade has been made, and it will not be changed. We have a doubleheader this afternoon. I made this trade because I have a firm belief that with you at shortstop we can win a lot of pennants. You can do it for us. You can spark this team. You can help us win pennants. That's all I care about."

The combative Durocher was speechless. He had met his match. Rickey had his shortstop.

In 1934, his seventeenth year with the Cardinals, Branch Rickey was at the height of his power and the pride of the city on the banks of the Big Muddy. He lived on a lordly estate. He was constantly asked to run for political office, and he received daily requests to lend his name to social, religious, and civic causes. In the midst of the Great Depression he earned more money than the president of the United States, and was the highest-paid team executive in all of baseball. With the 10 percent commission he received for the sale of players, his annual income was over $75,000. He had total control of virtually everything in the St. Louis organization. He had signed practically all the players on the Cardinal roster; he hired and fired all personnel.

"Mr. Rickey used to have workouts at Sportsman's Park, and he would sit upstairs and watch those kids," remembers Stan Lomax, a former New York sportswriter. "Some of them were the darndest-looking people; some didn't even have spikes. He could see greatness. He could look inside of people. He looked inside a tall, skinny kid with a faded uniform and a pair of sneakers, and he saw Dizzy Dean. That fellow Medwick looked like a baggy-pants comedian on a stage, not like a ballplayer at all, but Mr. Rickey knew what was inside.

"He'd sit there in his paternal way using his cigar like a wand. 'We'll send this fellow to Cedar Rapids—we need a shortstop there. That fellow should go to Class D ball and be an outfielder.' Mr. Rickey had more players under his command than any other man in history."

The 1934 Cardinals, with Pepper Martin, Leo Durocher, Ripper Collins, Joe Medwick, Bill DeLancey, Ernie Orsatti, and Dizzy Dean and his brother Paul, were called the "Gashouse Gang"—a bunch of rubes who wore dirty uniforms and fought with each other and their opponents. But Rickey called them "a team of desire." Proud of these prime products of his farm system, he loved his collection of hungry ballplayers, even though some of them presented him with real problems.

Dizzy's younger brother, Paul, had cost Rickey more money than he was willing to spend. Rickey had a formula for signing young athletes: "Players of like age and like experience receive like compensation." Rickey had eleven players he wished to sign and was prepared to give each of them $450. But one of them was Paul Dean, and Dizzy insisted that his brother get $600 or there would be no signing. After offer and counteroffer, Rickey finally acceded to Dizzy's request. He signed Paul for $600, but then felt obliged to give each of the other ten players the same amount. Dizzy's demand cost Rickey $1,650.

The Gashouse Gang was a wild crew. Joe Medwick swung his big bat at pitched balls and sometimes at teammates. He was called the "Hungarian Rhapsody," a reference to his Hungarian background. Pepper Martin's play on the field was characterized by head-first slides. Off the field, he loved to ride fire engines. A midget-auto racer, he pushed the car that his partner raced and sometimes showed up for games too tired to perform with his usual drive.

Frankie Frisch played second base and presided over this colorful collection. He had replaced Gabby Street on

July 24, 1933, as Cardinal manager. "Gabby just kinda lost control of the team," recalled Pop Haines.

The Cardinals won the pennant and defeated the Detroit Tigers in the 1934 World Series. Through that tumultuous season, Rickey had to be a psychologist, lawyer, and marriage counselor to his troops. The Deans, who won forty-nine games between them that year, staged a two-man strike at one point, refusing to pitch in a midseason exhibition game scheduled by Breadon. Rickey suspended them. Frisch wanted the suspension lifted. Rickey argued that if the suspension were lifted, he would resign. Dizzy persuaded Commissioner Landis to hold a hearing, where Rickey prevailed. The Deans returned to action, and agreed they would pitch whenever Rickey told them to.

Durocher was smitten by the attractive dress designer Grace Dozier. Through most of the season, his mind was more on her than on baseball. Rickey telephoned her and suggested that for the good of all three of them she should marry Leo. The couple were wed on the morning of September 26, and Leo played inspired baseball down the stretch run of the 1934 season.

The Dean brothers, Ripper Collins, Pepper Martin, Joe Medwick, Frankie Frisch, Leo Durocher, and the other rambunctious Redbirds had no fear of the powerful Detroit Tigers in the Series. Diz trimmed the Tigers 8–3 in the first game. Paul Dean won the third game, 4–1. But Detroit proved tougher than the Cardinals had thought, and the Series moved to game six with the Tigers leading three games to two. Durocher's three hits and Paul Dean's pitching gave the Cardinals a 4–3 victory.

In the decisive seventh game in Detroit, the Cardinals poured it on. With Dizzy Dean on the mound, they led 9–0 after six innings. Joe Medwick's kicking, sliding triple in the sixth—his eleventh hit of the Series—added insult to injury. When he trotted out to left field in the bottom of the sixth, irate fans showered him with pop bottles, hard-boiled eggs, and anything else they could throw. Judge Landis ordered Medwick removed from the game to protect him from physical harm. The Cardinals won the game, 11–0, and with it the World Championship.

Stan Lomax remembers Rickey's amazing ability to judge young players and to tell when older ones were slipping. "Mr. Rickey was some character, some judge of human nature. He used to say, 'Never trust a guy with a bad ankle, knee, or arm. The day you need him, something will go wrong.' Mr. Rickey could look at a player and know in an instant if that player was a half-step slower, if he couldn't come in for a fly ball the way he used to, if he couldn't pull to his power the way he did a year before."

In May 1935, Rickey's mother died of a stroke. Rickey felt the loss deeply. He came from a tightly knit family whose members supported and sustained each other, and his mother had been a major influence on him. His own children were growing up, however, and a month after his mother's death his son, Branch Jr., and his oldest daughter, Mary, graduated from Ohio Wesleyan. The relationship between Branch and Branch Jr. was especially close. Branch Jr. was his father's confidant. Dubbed "The Twig," he was an extension of Branch Sr., attending the prep schools of his father's choosing, Ohio Wesleyan, and later the University of Michigan Law School.

Unlike the tender relationship between Rickey and his son, the relationship between Rickey and the eccentric Dizzy Dean was often tense. "Judas Priest," Rickey once declared, "if there were another player like Dizzy Dean in baseball, as God is my judge, I would most certainly get out of this game."

When Dean first signed with the Cardinals, he was paid by check. The trouble was, Dizzy kept writing checks even when he had no money to cover them. Through club secretary Clarence Lloyd, Dean was put on an allowance. He was given a dollar bill at the start of each day. It was generally spent by 11:00 A.M. "You could never say ol' Branch was free with a dollar," remarked Dean, "but he did get me to save some money."

In 1935, Dean posted a 28–12 record. He received a salary of $17,500 plus a $1,000 bonus. He also received $15,000 from General Foods for his comic-strip endorsement of a breakfast cereal. Rickey had arranged the deal through Clarence Eldridge, advertising director of General Foods and a classmate of Rickey's at Michigan Law School.

In the spring of 1936, pointing to his league-leading 28 victories and 324 innings pitched, Dean complained to the press that he was underpaid. "That man Rickey can talk longer and say less than any man in the game," Dean moaned. "But he's a skinflint when it comes to payin' up."

Upset by Dean's comments, Rickey sent him a long letter:

If you are agreed that my position is a correct one, then you should write me an unqualified letter of assurance that you will be found this coming season with your shoulder to the wheel . . . with the eagerness of a soldier in the ranks . . . and strive for the common cause . . . pitching your head off when called upon. . . .

For my part, I do not wish to discuss the terms of your contract until we have had a much better understanding about your intentions and purpose this coming year on the Cardinals. . . . If we do not come to an understanding . . . then I prefer not to handle the negotiations of your contract at all. Someone else can do it.

If we do come to an understanding, it is my opinion that you and I would not have any great difficulty in arriving at satisfactory terms for your contract.

With all good wishes to you and Mrs. Dean, I am

Very truly yours,
Branch Rickey
Vice-President

It took some time for Dean to get the letter translated, but when he finally understood its contents, he responded, "My shoulder is lopsided on one side. What does Mr. Rickey want me to do, play the outfield and lead the boys' band?"

Releasing Rickey's letter to the press, Dean circulated the letter he had written in reply:

If you really feel that way, why wouldn't it be best for you to sell or trade me? . . . You have been too good a friend to me, at least in the early days of my professional career, for me to want to get into any row with you. . . . As matters now stand, I ought to bring a fairly good price if you would offer me for sale or trade; and I could undoubtedly get hooked up with a club that would at least feel that I was not preventing it from winning the pennant.

A compromise finally settled the dispute. Dean signed a "loyalty pledge" that bound him to obey orders. In return, he received $27,500 for the 1936 season and, with Rickey's influence, the lucrative cereal-promotion contract was renewed.

Through all those years in St. Louis, Rickey was offered attractive contracts with other teams who wanted him to work his magic in their organizations. He tempered his refusals by recommending his protégés. Larry MacPhail had the distinction of being recommended twice. Rickey recommended MacPhail to the Cincinnati Reds in 1934. The redhead literally lit up Crosley Field. The first night game in major-league history was played in Cincinnati on May 24, 1935, with President Franklin D. Roosevelt pressing a remote-control switch to illuminate the field. Farsighted but short-fused, MacPhail had a few shoving matches with Cincinnati owner Powell Crosley, and on January 19, 1938— again on Rickey's recommendation—moved on to take over as general manager of the Brooklyn Dodgers. Warren Giles, another friend of Rickey's and president of the Rochester Red Wings, replaced MacPhail in Cincinnati.

Giles, who would go on to become National League president, was let out of a five-year contract to assume the position at Cincinnati. "You must think of your future," Rickey told him, "not mine."

On December 21, 1936, the future caught up with the boy they once called Weck. Rickey's daughter Mary was married a day after his fifty-fifth birthday. The proud father took the first of his five trips down the aisle with one of his daughters.

In 1938, Enos Slaughter moved up to the Cardinals. In 1937, at twenty-one, Slaughter had won the batting championship while on the Columbus farm team. Johnny Rizzo, twenty-five and a veteran of seven .300-plus minor-league seasons, was a teammate. He batted .358, third in the league. Pirate president William Benswanger was interested in acquiring some Cardinal farmhands. Rickey challenged him. "I'll name two players, and I'll bet you pick the wrong one for fifty thousand dollars." Benswanger selected Rizzo. Rickey knew he would be the pick, because the Pirates were already well staffed with left-handed hitters, and Rizzo batted right-handed. Rizzo spent five years in the majors, with a .270 batting average. Slaughter hit .300 in his nineteen-year career.

The outspoken Slaughter remembers that "Mr. Rickey had more knowledge of baseball than anyone else, but when you talked money to him you could get none of it. I played for a hundred dollars a month in Class B. In 1937, at Columbus, I was the Most Valuable Player and hit three eighty-two and made only one hundred fifty dollars. At the end of the season I asked Mr. Rickey for a little bonus and he snapped my head off, saying the old fellows had been talking to me. I didn't get any bonus. I came to the Cardinals in 1938 and they only gave me four hundred dollars a month. And in 1939 I hit three twenty and led the National League in doubles and made seven hundred and fifty dollars a month.

So Mr. Rickey knew his ballplayers, but when you wanted money he was in a different country."

Dizzy Dean was twenty-seven years old in 1938. In the All-Star game the season before, a line drive off the bat of Earl Averill had caromed off Dean's right foot. It was later discovered that Diz's toe was broken. He came back fast, returning during that 1937 season, but he was not the pitcher he had been. The pain in his foot caused him to adjust his delivery; his fluid cotton-picking pitching motion was gone. He finished the year with a 13–10 record.

Chicago Cubs owner Phil Wrigley was told by his aides that one more solid pitcher would give his team the 1938 pennant. Wrigley coveted Dean. Rickey told Wrigley that Dean's arm was "almost dead," but still he would not take less than $185,000 for him. The deal was made. The Cardinals received the money plus an outfielder and two pitchers. One of the pitchers was Curt Davis, also a sore-armed hurler in 1937. He won twenty-two games for the Cardinals in 1939.

In March 1938, Commissioner Landis issued a ruling that stunned Rickey and the Cardinal organization. Landis ruled that St. Louis had working agreements with one team and secret understandings or "wash sales" with others, in violation of the baseball law limiting each parent club to one team in each minor league. Teams cited by Landis included Springfield, Sacramento, and Cedar Rapids; specifically, Landis contended that Rickey had an unwritten agreement with the owner of the Cedar Rapids team to get first call for that team's players. Under the terms of Landis's decision some one hundred Cardinal farmhands were declared free agents.

The Landis decision—"the day they freed the slaves" in Stan Lomax's words—shocked the baseball world and stripped the Cardinals of many of their prize prospects. It also caused a rift between Breadon and Rickey that never fully healed. The frugal Breadon had been hurt financially and also suffered a loss of confidence in Rickey. In addition, it brought into clear focus the hostility between Rickey and Landis. "Landis had a real hatred of Mr. Rickey," notes Stan Lomax. "Mr. Rickey was too smart for him. He should have been baseball commissioner."

One of the players freed by Landis was Harold Pete Reiser. Rickey told intimates that Reiser had the potential to become one of the greatest players in baseball history, and he persuaded his former executive, Larry MacPhail, now the Dodger president, to sign him. The promising youngster was told to sign on whatever terms the Dodgers offered. Rickey wanted the Dodgers to hide Reiser in the low minors until 1940, at which time he would arrange a trade to bring the youth back to St. Louis.

There was no way MacPhail could hide Reiser. In spring training in 1939, the phenom slugged out eight straight hits, including four home runs. Durocher, whom Rickey had traded to Brooklyn in 1938 and who now managed the Dodgers, exclaimed, "That kid is the greatest prospect I've ever seen." Thus, the master trader lost Reiser twice: once to Landis and once to the Dodgers. Rickey settled for $132,000 and four no-name ballplayers and yielded Joe Medwick and Curt Davis to the Dodgers. It was poor balm to soothe the Reiser wound.

The Reds won the National League pennant in 1939 and 1940. Presided over by Rickey's protégé Warren Giles, Cincinnati's victories provided the Cardinal executive with a certain amount of backhanded pride.

In 1941, the Dodgers and the Cardinals fought for the National League pennant. The team from Brooklyn nipped the Redbirds by two and a half games to win the flag. Injuries to key St. Louis players hampered their pennant drive. First baseman Johnny Mize suffered a broken finger and a bruised shoulder. Center fielder Terry Moore was hospitalized after being hit in the head with a pitched ball. Right fielder Enos Slaughter broke his collarbone, and catcher

Walker Cooper broke a bone in his shoulder. Only shortstop Marty Marion of the St. Louis regulars played in every game of that 1941 season.

The end of the season brought Branch Rickey to another crossroad. Sam Breadon informed Rickey that his contract would not be renewed at the close of 1942.

Perhaps it was that the war years loomed ahead and Breadon was unwilling or unable to afford Rickey's huge salary. Perhaps it was the Cedar Rapids decision. Perhaps it was that the former Ohio schoolteacher attracted most of the publicity and the Cardinal owner felt he was not given enough credit for his team's success. Perhaps the huge stockpile of talent on the Cardinals and their farm teams made Breadon believe that the organization could virtually run itself in the years ahead. The 1942 Cardinals won 106 games—the most in their history—and there were those who felt the top St. Louis farm teams were better than some major-league clubs. Perhaps it was just all the years of turbulent differences of opinion adding up, leaving their mark.

Whatever the reason, in 1942, Rickey's quarter century with the Cardinals officially came to an end, just months after another St. Louis World Series victory. Rickey's family urged him to accept an offer to move over to the St. Louis Browns; they wanted to remain in the city on the banks of the Mississippi. He was invited to join the Phillies, a last-place team, and the challenge intrigued him. Also, Larry MacPhail had left an opening in Brooklyn by entering the armed forces. Finally, Rickey left the choice to "Rickey's Boys," nineteen of his most trusted scouts and business managers in the St. Louis organization. They opted for Brooklyn, arguing that the big-city population there would provide a strong financial base. Guaranteed a free hand to try out any and all new techniques with the Dodgers, Rickey said, "It was the kind of opportunity I just could not turn down."

The last superstar to rise from Rickey's St. Louis farm

system was Stan "The Man" Musial. Rickey's first glimpse of Musial was at Hollywood, Florida, in the spring of 1941. What he saw was a fair twenty-year-old pitcher who could swing the bat. Rickey pleaded with Springfield club officials to take a chance on the youth. The aspiring pitcher, who had damaged his shoulder, was converted into an outfielder. He played in eighty-seven games with Springfield and batted .379. Moved up to Rochester, Musial batted .326 in fifty-four games. Promoted to the Cardinals, the man from Donora, Pennsylvania, batted .426 in a dozen games at the tail end of the 1941 season. Musial fit into Rickey's historic pattern of the minor-league star brought up at the end of the season for grooming into big-league status and to help in a tight pennant race.

Moving on to Brooklyn, Rickey left behind in St. Louis a great team, including Musial, Red Schoendienst, Enos Slaughter, Terry Moore, Marty Marion, Whitey Kurowski, Mort and Walker Cooper, and Harry Brecheen. He had provided Cardinal fans with Jesse Haines, Dizzy and Paul Dean, Joe Medwick, Pepper Martin, Ripper Collins, Jim Bottomley, Chick Hafey. . . .

In two dozen years with the Cardinals, Rickey had earned more than a million dollars in salary and bonuses. Before Rickey arrived, the Cardinals had finished in the first division just three times in twenty years. With Rickey on the scene, there were nine pennants and six World Championships in twenty-one seasons.

Now in his sixties, at an age when most men are content to look back over times past and look forward to the serene years of retirement, Branch Rickey marched ahead to his boldest adventures.

BUILDING DAYS IN

BROOKLYN

President Franklin Delano Roosevelt had written to baseball commissioner Landis on January 15, 1942, in the second year of World War II, "I honestly think it would be best for the country to keep baseball going." Despite the number of major-leaguers in the service, the gas shortages that kept people at home, and the reduced attendance, baseball kept going with a patchwork of overaged veterans and deferred younger men. In 1942, 219 major-leaguers were in the armed forces. The number increased to 242 the next year. By 1945, 385 major-leaguers were in the service.

Retrenchment was the theme for virtually every major-league club. The dwindling supply of able-bodied ball-players convinced most executives that the war was something to be waited out. Most attempted just to get by with what they had and plan for the future when the war ended.

Installed as the new general manager of the Brooklyn Dodgers, a teetotaler in the freewheeling atmosphere of Ebbets Field where a cocktail lounge had been provided for the pleasure of visitors, Branch Rickey was not one to wait things out.

At a January 1943 meeting at the New York Athletic Club, the sixty-two-year-old Rickey outlined his plans for the future. The Dodgers had given him a five-year contract at $50,000 a year, an unlimited expense account, incentive bonuses if annual attendance topped 600,000, and a percentage of revenue from the sale of players. Rickey met with George McLaughlin and George Barnewall of the Brooklyn Trust Company, 50 percent owner of the team in trust for the Ebbets estate, Joe Gillauedeau of the Ebbets interest, and Jim Mulvey representing Ed and Steve McKeever, who owned the rest of the stock.

Rickey noted that while the Dodgers had won the 1941 pennant, they had been beaten out in 1942 by his old team, the St. Louis Cardinals. Rickey knew the talent that was in the Cardinal system, and he knew that they would be a formidable club for a long time to come. He maintained that the Brooklyn organization was faced with a bleak future unless radical innovations were put into effect.

He explained that he planned to hire "many more scouts, and to beat the bushes for talent, for new talent . . . to sign fifteen- and sixteen-year-olds so the Brooklyn club will be in possession of so large a complement of youth . . . boys of all skills and sizes . . . that our position for the future will be assured."

There were no objections, so Rickey added: "The mass scouting might possibly come up with a Negro player or two."

"I don't see why you can't come up with a Negro," McLaughlin interrupted. The two men had met secretly before the luncheon and had arranged this part of the talk. "You might really come up with something. If you find a man who is better than the others, use him."

"A Negro player or two," Rickey continued, "will not only help the Brooklyn organization—but putting colored players in the major leagues will also accomplish something that is long overdue. It is something I have thought about and believed in for a long time."

St. Louis sports editor J. Roy Stockton noted, "Rickey faces a new challenge this year; he cannot follow the old routine he originated—building a great farm system. The system depends on hungry young athletes, and baseball's fertile fields now are sending their young men into the armed forces. . . . For the duration, Rickey will be operating under a disadvantage. But those who know believe he'll find a way, and baseball will experience another revolutionary innovation of some kind."

There were those who looked upon the playing of wartime baseball as inappropriate. Rickey viewed baseball as a necessity in the war years. A month after the New York Athletic Club meeting, he issued the following statement:

"We need to hold on to such diversions as tend to relieve us from the ever-increasing sorrows of war. The good health of our people is not conserved by continuous and almost compulsory reflection upon their personal heartbreaking losses, which are bound to come and are coming even now. . . . We need to be cheerful fighters or as cheerful as we possibly can be. For the Japanese, to die is to be glorified. To live hopefully and joyfully is the American objective, and our fighting to live must match the religious frenzy of the Japs who fight to die."

Rickey was so caught up with "fighting to live" that he broke his personal ban on attendance at Sunday games. He appeared at the pregame ceremonies at a Dodgers-Phillies contest to make a speech to boost war bond sales. "For this occasion," he said, "and for this reason, because it's worthy, I will speak and then leave the ballpark."

By the summer of 1943, the scouting machinery of the man they called "The Brain" was in place. Approximately twenty thousand letters had been sent to high school coaches all over the United States asking them to recommend the best prospects available. The Dodger scouting staff was increased fourfold. As the high school coaches responded to the letters, Dodger scouts were dispatched to check out leads. More than four hundred players were signed to Dodger contracts. Most of them were too young and too inexperienced to be of immediate value, but as Rickey explained, "We are building for the future, and if the war is over in two years we expect wonderful results. We'll be fully developed, and after that I envision pennants, pennants, and more pennants!"

Hundreds of hopefuls showed up at an Olean, New York, tryout camp. Some were signed to minor-league contracts. One was selected for a personal evaluation by Branch Rickey at Ebbets Field. Just nineteen years old, he played one game with the Dodgers in 1943 at third base. He walked once and struck out twice. Rickey signed the Indiana-born youngster to a $1,250 bonus. Half was paid on signing, and the player received the other half two and a half years later when he returned from service in the United States Marines. Rickey made a note that the player would be best as a catcher or first baseman. In 1947, Gil Hodges re-joined the Dodgers and was positioned at first base, where he became one of the anchors of the powerful Dodger team. From 1949 to 1955, he recorded a hundred or more RBIs a season and averaged more than thirty-two home runs a year.

Edwin "Duke" Snider was another future Dodger star discovered by Rickey's extensive scouting system. As a seventeen-year-old, he had performed very well at one of the Dodger tryout camps and was invited to the 1944 training sessions at Bear Mountain. He pounded a three-run homer in an exhibition game against West Point. Assigned to Newport News, Virginia, the Brooklyn farm team in the Piedmont League, he showed the talent and the tempestuousness that one day would excite Dodger fans. His Newport News manager, Jake Pitler, once flashed the take sign to the young left-handed swinger. The sign so infuriated Snider that he kicked in rage at a water bucket and demanded that he be sent to play for another team in the Dodger organization. Nicknamed "The Duke of Flatbush," Snider starred in center field for the Dodgers and hit more home runs, drove in more runs, and recorded more extra-base hits than any other player in the team's history.

Newport News at one point had fifteen players under eighteen years of age. Manager Jake Pitler dubbed himself a "glorified babysitter" and kept a large supply of comic books and just a small supply of shaving cream on hand for the kiddie corps that included Tommy Brown, Preston Ward, Duke Snider, Clem Labine, Steve Lembo, and Bobby Morgan. The press referred to Rickey as "The Old Woman in the Shoe," developing players were called "Mother Rickey's Chickens." By 1946 the chickens were spread thick over the twenty-five farm teams of the Dodgers, from Montreal to Ponca City, from Abilene to Zanesville. The raw talents that were signed during the war years were now being developed into finished major-league products.

The heart of the Brooklyn Dodger team that would dominate the National League through the late 1940s and 1950s was recruited by Rickey's youth dragnet. Rickey began to implement his policy of moving out veteran players and replacing them with young players of unlimited potential. He traded away Brooklyn favorite Dolf Camilli, and angry Dodger fans hanged him in effigy. When he attempted to explain his moves, his Montague Street office was referred to as "The Cave of Winds." It was a pointed reference to Rickey's skill with double-talk. Once, when asked if he would have any influence in the selection of a coach by Dodger manager Leo Durocher, he responded: "Generally speaking, no. But I might. And could and should perhaps. In a given case, that is."

The man they called "The Deacon" was a collector of terms and phrases and expressions that he employed for effect over and over again. "Anesthetic" was his term for players like Camilli whose brilliant past obscured their limited current value. "There are anesthetic ballplayers," he observed. "You watch them all year, and you say they are not contributing much to the team. Then they show you a lot of impressive statistics. They put you to sleep with statistics that don't win games. It is time to trade a player as soon as he reaches the twilight zone of stardom."

A player who had poor reflexes and timing was a "dead body." A "pantywaist" was Rickey's way of referring to an athlete who was a nonwinner, a follower. He often used military language: a "captain" was a take-charge player, while those who did not have much of a future on his team he called "corporals." "Privates" were those who lacked any real future anywhere in baseball.

Among Rickey's tradable "corporals" were Gene Mauch, Rocky Bridges, Bob Ramizotti, Bobby Morgan, Stan Rojek, Eddie Miksis, and Danny O'Connell, all shortstops. In his turn each was touted as "the new Pee Wee Reese" by the old Ohio horse trader as he successfully dispensed them throughout the major leagues. The original Pee Wee Reese played shortstop for the Dodgers for sixteen seasons. While others on the team hit peaks and valleys, Reese was the steady man, the "captain" of the Brooks. He recorded more than two thousand hits in his career.

In Brooklyn, Rickey also continued his fabled trading. Baseball executive Bill Veeck once paid Rickey a backhanded compliment by refusing to make trades with Rickey face to face. "I would send and receive notes via a bellboy. I was afraid being in the same room with Mr. Rickey would mesmerize me." A holdout player advised to get together with Rickey to compromise on salary differences once declared, "Not me. I ain't going to see Mr. Rickey. Five minutes with him, I'll sign anything he hands me, and I won't be a holdout anymore."

One of Rickey's favorite expressions was "Luck is the residue of design." By covering every option, by planning five, ten, fifteen years into the future, by working while others slept, by maintaining careful and copious records, Rickey went about cultivating his own luck.

One of his favorite speeches was entitled "Paying the Price—Are You Willing to Do It to Achieve Success?" Two lines he always used were "I would prefer turbulent progress to quiet stagnation" and "I would rather have the errors of enthusiasm than the indifference of wisdom."

Bill Shea, for whom Shea Stadium is named, was an attorney for the Brooklyn Trust Company back then. He recalls some of The Deacon's choice declarations on youth, the subject he was much involved with at the time: "When you're eighteen years old and can't run fast, you'll never run fast. If you can't throw the ball hard at eighteen, you never will. If you haven't got a heart at eighteen, you'll never get one later on. If your morals are bad at eighteen, you'll never improve."

His oratorical skills, his fear of heights, his nonalcoholic, workaholic habits, his ten-room house in what was then suburban Forest Hills, his ten-acre saltwater farm in Chestertown, Maryland, and his Sabbath baseball ban—all fleshed out the image.

Back in Duck Run, the fundamentalists were not impressed with Rickey's boycotting of Sunday baseball. They argued that the cash that came in from Sunday games paid weekly salaries. "Drinking the devil's broth when you wouldn't eat the devil's meat" was their phrase. In New York City, reporters had choicer words for the man who refused to attend games on Sunday because of a promise he had made to his mother those long years back. When Rickey took refuge in the Bible and explained, "On the seventh day He rested," they didn't appreciate the comparison.

The bow-tied Ohioan became grist for newspaper copy and graphic material for cartoonists. Many stories echoed Enos Slaughter's comment, "Mr. Rickey was always going to the vault to give you a nickel's change." Cartoons depicted

Rickey in a stovepipe hat, offering shotguns and fishing poles to callow youths and then chaining them to a baseball diamond. He was shown struggling with chains and locks in front of armored vaults, depositing cobwebbed coins.

His bushy eyebrows, his ever-present cigar, and his pontificating manner helped make him an easy target. "There is a reasonable expectation of additional emolument," Rickey told a player during salary talks. "Ya mean more dough, doncha, boss?" the player asked.

Some of Rickey's critics referred to him as a "carpetbagger" because he had come from St. Louis to Brooklyn. Others used the phrase "the nonalcoholic Rickey," a slighting reference to his teetotaling ways. Sportswriter Tom Meany bestowed on him the title "Mahatma," inspired by John Gunther's description of Mohandas Gandhi as "a combination of God, your own father, and Tammany Hall."

John Carmichael, former sports editor of the *Chicago Daily News*, once suggested that Rickey be named as a replacement for secretary of state. "It is our firm belief," wrote Carmichael, "that if President Truman would sic Rickey on Russia, Joe Stalin would wake up one morning to discover that all he had left was Siberia plus a couple of southpaw pitchers who wouldn't report. By March 1, Rickey would have Stalin playing for Pepper Martin in Miami."

Jimmy Powers of the *New York Daily News* led the pack of Rickey detractors. He launched attack after attack in his "Powerhouse" columns. It was Powers who came up with the nickname "El Cheapo," claiming Rickey never dealt fairly with players in contract negotiations. In July 1946, Powers wrote, "This column will welcome suggestions from Brooklyn fans: what shall we do with El Cheapo? Shall we send him over Niagara Falls in a barrel? Shall we maroon him on Bikini Atoll? One reader suggests that all fans get together and each donate a $20 bill upon entrance to the ballpark. A grocery store chain has kindly consented to donate twenty empty barrels. If the fans will help fill these barrels perhaps Rickey's desire for milking money out of the franchise will be satisfied and he'll pack his carpet bags and go away to another town and run his coolie payroll there."

The comments enraged Rickey's family, friends, co-workers in the Dodger organization, and even other journalists. Rickey chose to ignore them, not wishing to dignify them with a public reaction. Privately, he seethed.

In what was apparently a public relations gesture aimed at defusing the El Cheapo image, Rickey gave each member of the 1946 Dodger team a brand-new Studebaker automobile. Even this did not satisfy Powers. He wrote that the gifts were a waste of money and that Rickey was simply attempting to "buy" the loyalty of the players with the new cars.

Arthur Daley of the New York Times came to Rickey's defense in a column he wrote on October 2, 1946, entitled "The Branch That Grows in Brooklyn."

"There's been a rather persistent campaign under way for most of this season to discredit Branch Rickey and, even though it has been waged by a writer whose credit rating in his profession is zero minus, it's been rather irritating," Daley began. Acknowledging that Rickey "is not an easy person to understand and to catalogue, and his intimates among those connected with sports are extremely few," Daley addressed himself to the question of Rickey's alleged frugality. The New York Times columnist pointed out that the Dodger players "bought the Mahatma a cabin cruiser as a token of their esteem . . . in a spontaneous, voluntary gesture . . . and players have never been known to be ultra-generous in handing out gifts to their own."

Daley concluded the column by praising the sound and productive program of Rickey for Brooklyn, "where he promises after winning one pennant to win it seven out of every ten years thereafter."

The world of high finance, speculation, calculated risk, investment—all of this intrigued Rickey. In 1944, the heirs of Ed McKeever offered to sell their share in the Dodgers. Rickey joined with John L. Smith, the head of a chemical company, and a forty-year-old-Brooklyn attorney named Walter O'Malley, representing the Brooklyn Trust Company, to purchase the stock. The trio was brought together by George McLaughlin. The following year, the trio purchased another 50 percent of the team's stock from the heirs of Charles Ebbets. By parlaying the sale of his Country Life Acres property that had been destroyed by fire in 1943, by cashing in some of his stock, by offering his life insurance as collateral, Rickey was able to become a 25 percent shareholder in the Brooklyn Dodgers.

The underage farm system and the thin supply of existing major-league talent during those war years forced Rickey to patch the Brooklyn roster with an interesting assortment of spare parts and innovations.

In August 1944, Rickey signed Ben Chapman. A former New York Yankee who had played in the same outfield with Babe Ruth in the 1930s, Chapman was thirty-five years old. He had learned how to pitch as a member of the Richmond Colts and won five of eight decisions for Brooklyn in 1944. His path would cross with Rickey's in the future.

Two other former prime-time ballplayers made their way onto the war-years roster of Dodger retreads. The Waner brothers were known as "Big Poison" and "Little Poison" when they starred for the Pittsburgh Pirates. Paul, age forty, batted .311 for the 1943 Brooklyn team, appearing in half its games. In 1944, he was on the roster most of the season but saw limited action. Lloyd joined his brother Paul for a part of the 1944 season. "Branch Rickey called me just before the season began," explained Lloyd. "He said he was going to lose two or three of his outfielders to the army and wanted me for insurance and wanted to know if I could get in shape." Lloyd batted .286 in fifteen games for Brooklyn before being released at the June 15 cut-down time to his former Pittsburgh team.

In July of 1945, the "Incredible Hoiman" was coaxed out of retirement in Glendale, California. Babe Herman, one of the madcap characters of the "Daffy Dodgers" of the 1930s, was forty-two years old, but he could still swing a bat and Rickey knew he was a crowd pleaser. Herman went nine for thirty-four as a pinch hitter finishing out the 1945 season with Brooklyn. He spent his last week out of uniform moving about gingerly on a bandaged knee with torn cartilage.

The same year, Rickey unveiled the original pitching machine. Invented by Byron Moser, a St. Louis banker and friend of Rickey's, the pitching machine was built on a principle similar to a crossbow.

"The thing can throw twenty-five hundred baseballs a day," Rickey bragged about the prolonged receptacle that had a baseball positioned against a rubber strip that was pulled back by electric power. "One pitcher averages one hundred twenty-five pitches in a nine-inning game," continued Rickey, the baseball efficiency expert in him excited. "This equals twenty pitchers working nine innings. And it takes only one man to operate it—and he does not have to be a pitcher . . . or even a baseball player."

In conjunction with the Brooklyn Eagle, Rickey launched a "Brooklyn Against the World" youth program. It was a move that capitalized on civic pride and created thousands of new Dodger fans. Sandlot teams of kids from Brooklyn and Long Island competed against teams from all over the United States who were sponsored by their local newspapers. The innovation proved to be a great source of favorable newspaper coverage, and an economical way of scouting new talent.

Late in 1945, when the Dodger organization had started to work out as Rickey had planned, Rickey was seized by a fit of dizziness and nausea while attending the major-league baseball meetings in Chicago. The symptoms were similar to those of a condition his brother Orla had died from, and that Rickey's mother had suffered through and survived. Rickey was examined in his hotel room by doctors who were unable to determine what was wrong with him but who agreed that he needed to rest and avoid stress.

The next day, Rickey traveled by train to New York City, where he suffered a more severe attack and was rushed to Brooklyn Jewish Hospital for tests. The malady mystified the doctors. They agreed, though, that rest and quiet were essential to Rickey's well-being. Finally, a top brain surgeon was brought in. He diagnosed the condition as Ménière's disease—a disorder related to deafness. It was determined that Rickey had a breakdown of the eighth cranial nerve, rendering him virtually deaf in his left ear. The crass joke that developed was that to be on his good side, "stand on Mr. Rickey's right side."

Like a caged tiger, Rickey impatiently spent two weeks in the hospital. When he was finally released, he was informed by doctors that stress and sudden moves of his body, especially his head, could provoke another attack. He was told to pace himself, to slow down.

Rickey promised to slow down, but he couldn't. He threw himself back into his varied projects, with a passion inspired by the time lost in the hospital. Early in 1946 he suffered a serious heart attack on the streets of Brooklyn not far from the Dodgers' office at 215 Montague Street, but he bounced back and kept on pushing. He told himself he had promises to keep; there was a color line to break and a dynasty to build. "I just can't slow down," he told a friend. "I'd rather die ten minutes sooner than be doing nothing all the time. But I do hope than on some distant day in the future my funeral cortège will move at a leisurely pace."

The war's end prompted him into more new beginnings. He activated the Montreal Royals franchise and designated it the top Dodger farm team. The Fort Worth club, acquired for $74,000 from the Texas League, became the Dodgers' first wholly owned minor-league affiliate. The purchase price gave the Dodgers control of the franchise, its ballpark, and twenty-two acres of park and parking space. Working agreements were arranged with St. Paul and Mobile. The Dodger scouting staff expanded; Rickey's brother Frank, a veteran of seventeen years of bird-dogging in the St. Louis organization, traveled all over the United States hunting for young talent.

In Indian River County, one hundred miles north of Miami, a former naval air base lay abandoned since the end of the war. Rickey had read Gen. Dwight D. Eisenhower's book *Crusade In Europe* and was impressed by its emphasis on efficiency and teamwork on the battlefield. Purchasing the Vero Beach, Florida, facility and borrowing Eisenhower's themes, Rickey created "Dodgertown," a complex for processing a huge number of ballplayers. There were multiple batting diamonds, sliding pits, pitching machines for batting practice, supervised calisthenics, pitching strings, charts that indicated each player's progress. All of this was part of the controlled frenzy that delighted Rickey, who sometimes shaved in taxi cabs, and who always abhorred any waste of time, money, or energy.

As many as four hundred and fifty players could be put through their training at one time at a cost of under $300,000. "Every morning," Duke Snider recalls, "Mr. Rickey used to give a forty-five-minute lecture. He covered every facet of the game and developed all types of drills. It was very intellectually and physically stimulating."

Rickey was as impressed with Snider as Snider was with him. "He's going to be a great hitter," said the man many thought was the greatest judge of talent in baseball history, "when he learns the strike zone is not high and outside."

To refine and discipline Snider's raw hitting talent, Rickey developed a special drill. Snider was positioned in the batter's box and was told not to swing but simply to stride at pitches. An umpire called out whether the pitch was a strike or a ball. "It was kind of tough," remembers

Snider, "but that's where I learned to smooth out my swing, how to judge the strike zone, how to become the hitter I became."

Lou Napoli worked at Ebbets Field as a private attendant to Branch Rickey, and when the Dodgers were on the road did maintenance work at the ballpark. When his wife gave birth to their second child, Napoli recalls, "I gave Mr. Rickey three Anthony and Cleopatra cigars. Those were the kind he smoked."

" 'What's this for, Lou?' Mr. Rickey asked. I told him that we had a new baby in the family. Mr. Rickey never stayed to the end of a game; win or lose, he always left at the bottom of the eighth. He came over in the bottom of the eighth and he wrote me out a personal check, not a Dodger check, a personal check for five hundred dollars. 'Here, Lou,' he said, 'give this to your wife for your baby daughter.'

"About a month later my older daughter came to the ballpark. She saw Mr. Rickey. 'I'd like to thank you for that wonderful gift you gave my baby sister,' she said. Mr. Rickey put his arm around my shoulder. 'Lou,' he said smiling, 'I always knew you were an honest man.' "

While Napoli and Snider remember Rickey with fond affection, others have less kind memories of the controversial executive. Rickey is recalled by Lee Scott, former traveling secretary for the Dodgers:

"I had a lot of respect for his baseball knowledge, but as a person, Rickey was full of crap. He laid it on with that Judas Priest. He said he didn't attend Sunday baseball, which he did; he said he didn't drink, which he did occasionally."

Scott, Brooklyn born and rooted, recalls one of his first meetings with Rickey. "I was a little friendly with Walter O'Malley," says Scott, who now lives in retirement in California not far from where Jackie Robinson grew up. "So I was able to get an appointment for a job interview with Rickey.

" 'Lee,' he said, 'all the jobs are taken except one . . . and that's in Decatur, Illinois. I know it's far from home, but would you like that?'

" 'Mr. Rickey,' Scott recalls responding, 'you're right. It is a little far. Incidentally, what would the salary be?'

" 'Thirty-six hundred dollars.'

"I was making more than that as a writer and with a few other things," Scott notes. "So I said, 'I don't think I'll take it. Decatur is entirely too far away for me.'

"And he said, 'Well, Lee, I don't think it was particularly appropriate for you anyway.'

"Rickey was not my kind of guy," Scott says with some emotion. "He thought anything he touched would turn to gold . . . he had that thing about money."

By the end of the 1946 season, Rickey had been with the Dodgers for five years. Sometimes he got lost on the subway or commuter trains or rode past his stop on the way home to Forest Hills. Occasionally, he found himself without pocket money, and he developed the dangerous habit of throwing lighted kitchen matches into the wastepaper basket in his Montague Street office. He still liked to play cards and passed much time at long games of hearts with his wife, Jane, and his cronies as he crisscrossed the country in his Beechcraft plane searching out new baseball talent. The old black notebook had been replaced by an index-card system containing the names of leading sandlot, high school, and college players in America. He had hired a statistician at a healthy $7,000 a year to travel with the Dodgers and chart pitches. Attendance at Ebbets Field in 1946 was almost two million. The Ebbets Field mortgage had finally been paid off. Sales of players that season brought in nearly a quarter of a million dollars. Television rights—a fairly new venture in baseball—earned the club an additional $6,000. Overall, the net profit of the Brooklyn Dodgers was nearly half a million dollars.

Things were looking up on the field as well. The Dodgers

and the St. Louis Cardinals tied for first place in 1946 with identical 96–58 records and met in the first playoff in National League history. It was Rickey versus Rickey, the team he had built pitted against the one he was building.

In the first game in St. Louis, Joe Garagiola and Terry Moore each collected three hits as the Cardinals, behind Howie Pollet, defeated the Dodgers and Ralph Branca, 4–2. In the second game, the Cardinals pounded out thirteen hits off six Dodger pitchers, defeating Brooklyn 8–4 to sweep the two-game playoff and win the National League pennant. It was the fourth pennant in five years for the Cards, and St. Louis manager Eddie Dyer acknowledged Rickey's role in the victory: "Mr. Rickey signed me as a pitcher in 1922 and when my arm went dead persuaded me to continue as an executive and taught me every bit of baseball I know. He got these players while he was still in St. Louis. If I'm a successful manager, it's because he made me one."

Some said Rickey was secretly happy his former team prevailed, but the Mahatma was looking ahead, not back. "The Cardinals deserved to win this one," he said, "but we will be the better team for a long time to come."

THE COLOR BAR DROPS

When Rickey mentioned the possibility that "mass scouting might possibly come up with a Negro player or two" at the New York Athletic Club meeting back in January 1943, the comment was not just idle banter. On the contrary, it was part of a carefully conceived six-step plan for breaking baseball's color barrier. He had accomplished step one at the meeting: gaining the support of the club's owners. Step two was the selection of a player with exceptional talent. Step three was making certain that the player selected would have the character to deal with the difficulties he would encounter on and off the field. Step four was laying the groundwork for favorable press reaction. Step five was enlisting the assistance of the Negro community. The final step was securing acceptance of the Negro player by his teammates.

Soon after the meeting, Rickey began his quest for "the one" who would break baseball's color line. He dispatched his chief scouts: George Sisler, Wid Matthews, and Tom Greenwade. He enlisted the aid of two university professors: Dr. Robert M. Haig of Columbia University and Dr. Jose Seda of the University of Puerto Rico. Dr. Haig, an old Ohio Wesleyan fraternity brother of Rickey's, visited Cuba and reported on the culture and capabilities of Cuban players, and Dr. Seda reported on players in Mexico and Puerto Rico. The search was under way.

This effort took place against the backdrop of World War II. All over the globe battles raged between the forces of tyranny and the defenders of freedom. In the United States, great social changes were launched loose in the land, triggered by the 1943 race riots in Harlem, Detroit, and Beaumont, Texas.

President Roosevelt issued Order 8802 creating the Fair Employment Practices Commission. Communist groups sought to capitalize on growing racial unrest and engaged in picketing, petitioning, and pamphleteering efforts in attempts to widen the schism between the races. Black activists and white liberals helped escalate the pressures. Political campaign rhetoric underscored the social upheaval.

The chafing pressures of racial tension in the United States in those years were symbolized by the Harlem riots in 1943. A white policeman had wounded a black soldier, precipitating the street violence. Most of Harlem was declared off limits to servicemen by Mayor La Guardia. The New York City mayor also formed a Committee on Unity aimed at keeping racial tension down to a minimum and preventing potential violence. Charles Evan Hughes, son of the chief justice of the United States Supreme Court, headed the committee that consisted of nineteen other prominent New Yorkers. Dr. Dan Dodson, a professor of sociology at New York University, was the organization's executive director.

Lily-white baseball became a prime target of the socially conscious. One brochure of the time depicted a dead black soldier and bore the caption "Good enough to die for his country . . . not good enough for organized baseball."

In December 1943 at the winter baseball meetings, the famous black singer-activist Paul Robeson led a delegation that met with Commissioner Landis and urged the admission of black players into the majors. Unofficially, Robeson was told that the American public was not ready to accept integrated baseball. Robeson, who was then appearing on the New York stage in the role of Othello, responded, "They said America never would stand for my playing Othello with a white cast, but it is the triumph of my life."

After the meeting, Landis issued a statement: "Each club is entirely free to employ Negro players to any and all extents it desires. The matter is solely for each club's decision, without restriction whatsoever." The statement was a public relations puff. "We knew it was mere rhetoric," says Mal Goode, who was to become the first black network news correspondent. "But back then, all we could do was ask; we couldn't demand."

Through his two decades as commissioner, Landis had strongly opposed breaking baseball's color line. In 1921, as a newly named commissioner, he forbade players to wear major-league uniforms in exhibition games against Negro teams. He hoped that this would hide the fact that many major-league teams lost to the Negro clubs. "In 1938," recalls Goode, "the two managing editors of the *Pittsburgh Courier*, the largest black newspaper in the world, met with Kenesaw Mountain. He said that the time wasn't right for blacks in baseball. 'You do whatever you want,' he told them. In those days, they would say to you, 'Boycott if you want, we don't care.' There weren't that many blacks going to major-league games." In the early years of World War II, Bill Veeck planned to purchase the Phillies and stock the roster with black players. "We could have run away with the pennant," recalls Veeck. Landis allegedly learned of the plan and squashed it. "I realize now that it was a mistake to tell him," notes Veeck.

Nonetheless, by May 1944 the last traces of segregation had been eliminated in the major-league stands, if not on the fields. The St. Louis Browns and St. Louis Cardinals did away with the segregated section in the right-field pavilion at Sportsman's Park. Equality among spectators had been achieved; the pressure kept building for equality on the playing field.

At the time, the only outlets for black baseball players were the existing Negro Leagues, the Negro National and American leagues. Each league had six teams that played approximately 110 games each season, which lasted from May through Labor Day. Many of them played in major-league stadiums when the home team was on the road. The Homestead Grays, for example, played at Forbes Field in Pittsburgh when the Pirates were on the road. This arrangement netted additional profits for white owners for use of their otherwise idle stadiums; after expenses the Negro clubs got just 40 percent of the gross. When major-league stadiums were not available, small-town ballparks were used instead. Black players were underpaid and suffered arduous bus trips and hard living conditions during the baseball season.

The Negro clubs asked for a committee from organized baseball to work with them for better scheduling and perhaps eventual recognition as part of the structure of organized baseball. At the major-league meetings in Cleveland in the spring of 1945, Larry MacPhail of the Yankees and Branch Rickey were designated by their respective leagues to select two prominent black figures and form a four-man committee to report on the Negro question in baseball. Tabbing Rickey for this role was purely coincidental; no one outside of Rickey's intimates knew of his search for a black player for the Brooklyn Dodgers.

Joe Bostic, a black sportswriter and the official announcer for the Negro National League and the Negro American League, felt that the time had come to act. Bostic, who could have had no inkling of Rickey's plan, staged a confrontation with Rickey and the white establishment at the Dodger training camp in Bear Mountain, New York.

"One of the things back then about being black or Negro

was keeping your place," recalls Bostic, "and I did not know my place. During World War II I had been in the forefront of trying to break the color line in major-league baseball. On two occasions I went down to Two fifteen Montague Street to plead my case, and I was bodily thrown out. Rickey was not there when these incidents took place. I was told that you can't accuse major-league baseball of being in favor of the color line—that no Negro had tried. We were Negroes; we hadn't become black as yet. One of my big arguments was the war. They had a one-armed man, Pete Gray, playing major-league ball, and yet they wouldn't let in a whole great pool of untapped American talent.

"I got the idea to demand a tryout and show up unannounced with a couple of players." One of the players was Terris McDuffie, age thirty-six, winner of five of eleven decisions for the Newark Eagles in 1944. The other was a thirty-nine-year-old first baseman, Dave "Showboat" Thomas of the New York Cubans. "At that point, those were the only two players I could get who were willing to face the wrath of the man," continues Bostic. "There was fear among black players that there might be people who could get to the Latin owners and deny opportunities to blacks to play in winter ball. There was also a feeling that what I was doing was senseless, that you couldn't break through the color barrier by stonewalling."

Bostic arrived with Williams and McDuffie, as well as several reporters. Workouts had already begun; there were about a dozen white players who also were being evaluated. "Rickey personally oversaw some pitching by Terris McDuffie. Durocher conducted infield practice and stationed Showboat Thomas at first base. He was called 'Twinkletoes' because of the way he handled his feet so slickly at first base. Rickey invited me to go with him into the Bear Mountain dining room. We sat at a table right in the very middle of the big room.

" 'You have not been as smart as you might have been,'

he told me. 'You should have informed me about what you planned to do. You should have written to me and told me that you wished to bring people for a tryout.'

" 'Mr. Rickey,' I said, 'I'm on the opposite side of the fence from you.' He was chewing on his cigar. He was infuriated with me. 'I can think of eight or ten reasons why you feel it is not possible to accommodate such an adventure as this,' I told him.

"He just listened and puffed on his cigar. 'You can probably think of thirty or forty reasons why I shouldn't be here,' I continued. 'This way neither of us has to do any thinking. The fellows are here and they're ready to play.'

" 'I don't appreciate what you have done, Mr. Bostic,' he said. He leaned closer to me. 'You've put me on a spot. If I didn't try these men out, you'd have the biggest sports story of the century. If I try them out and don't sign them, you have the biggest sports story of the century. Either way, it is an embarrassing situation for me and the Brooklyn Dodgers.'

"I told him not to worry about any of the complications, that the two guys I brought up could play ball. 'Let's not worry about the politics, Mr. Rickey. Let's get the Dodgers a good ball club.'

"At that point, he started talking about his concern for the black man. He actually put on a show for me. Rickey cried and talked about religion and so on. I was very cynical. I thought he was a phony. As it later turned out, I was right—at least as far as I was concerned. He didn't sign the two players, and from that day to the day he died, he never spoke to me again. Of course, my move might have been ill timed from Rickey's point of view. He might have already had his eye on Robinson."

Ironically, two years to the day after this Bear Mountain tryout, both Bostic and Rickey would be at Ebbets Field, witnesses to Jackie Robinson's first appearance as a Brooklyn Dodger.

The next day, April 16, 1945, three other black players

were given tryouts by the Boston Red Sox at Fenway Park. The players were Sam Jethroe from Erie, Pennsylvania, an outfielder for the Cleveland Buckeyes; Marvin Williams of the Philadelphia Stars; and Jackie Robinson, age twenty-six, from Pasadena, California. About a dozen white players were also trying out. They had already begun their workouts when the black athletes arrived with Wendell Smith, a black sportswriter. The *Pittsburgh Courier*, Smith's newspaper, had helped arrange the tryouts.

"Nobody put on an exhibition like we did," Robinson later recalled. "Everything we did, it seemed like the good Lord was guiding us. Everything the pitcher threw up became a line drive someplace. We tattooed the short left-field fence, that is Marv and I did . . . and Jethroe was doing extremely well from the left side, too. And he looked like a gazelle in the outfield."

The tryout ended and the three black players were given application blanks to fill out and were told they would be contacted sometime in the future. Boston manager Joe Cronin and his coach Hugh Duffy admitted they were impressed with the three black players, but they claimed it was too short a tryout to come up with any definitive plans as to what to do with the players.

"Tom Yawkey, the Boston owner, could have had all three of those players for nothing," said Wendell Smith. "They wouldn't take any of them." The Red Sox would become the last team in the major leagues to integrate; their first black player, Elijah "Pumpsie" Green, joined the club in 1959, one year before the Negro Leagues closed down.

During World War II, Sam Lacy had written in the black newspapers, "With us, the first man to break down the bars must be suited in every sense of the word. We can't afford any misfits pioneering for us, and for obvious reasons. Unwilling as they are to employ Negro players, they will be quick to draw the old cry: 'We gave them a chance and look what we got.' "

Now, Lacy and other black writers were openly hostile. Five black players had auditioned in two days and the bars were still up. Cum Posey in the *Pittsburgh Courier* wrote, "It's the most humiliating experience Negro baseball has yet suffered from white organized baseball."

Rickey still wished to conceal his plan to break baseball's color line, yet felt a statement was called for after the Bostic incident received so much attention. At a press conference, he argued that the Communists were using the tryouts as an issue to stir up racial conflict. Refusing to respond to questions about black players entering the major leagues, Rickey instead offered "a legitimate and valuable alternative for Negro players—the United States League."

The newly formed United States League consisted of six black baseball teams, one of which was the Brooklyn Brown Dodgers. Rickey announced that the Brown Dodgers would play at Ebbets Field when the Brooklyn Dodgers were on the road.

The existing Negro National and American leagues had exploited black players for years, Rickey claimed, but members of the black press could see no difference between the Negro Leagues and Rickey's alternative. The proposed United States League only fueled the deep-seated resentment the black community had for white baseball. "We want Negroes in the major leagues if they have to crawl to get there," wrote Frank A. Young in the *Defender*, "but we won't have any major-league owners running any segregated leagues for us."

An "End Jim Crow in Baseball" committee was formed to pressure major-league teams to sign black players. Committee members included the head of the Actor's Guild, Stella Adler; actors Louis Calhern, John Garfield, Sam Jaffe, and Paul Robeson; the lyricist Oscar Hammerstein II; black poet Langston Hughes; William O'Dwyer; and Adam Clayton Powell.

The New York Yankees' 1945 season opener at Yankee

Stadium was picketed. "If we can pay, why can't we play?" black demonstrators shouted.

"I have no hesitancy in saying that the Yankees have no intention of signing Negro players under contract or reservation to Negro clubs," Yankee president Larry MacPhail responded. "The solution of this problem in professional baseball must be compatible with long-established business and property rights. It is unfortunate that groups of professional political and social drumbeaters are conducting pressure campaigns in an attempt to force major-league clubs to sign Negro players."

The appointment of A. B. "Happy" Chandler as commissioner of baseball following the death of Judge Landis in 1945 cheered advocates of integration. Chandler publicly presented a different point of view from Landis's. His reaction to the picketing, the letter writing, and the articles in newspapers urging that blacks be allowed to play major-league baseball was candid. "I'm for the Four Freedoms," said Chandler. "If a black boy can make it in Okinawa and Guadalcanal, hell, he can make it in baseball. . . . I don't believe in barring Negroes from baseball just because they are Negroes."

At this point, Dr. Dan Dodson turned the Committee on Unity's attention to integrating major-league baseball. He began by getting in touch with Rickey and MacPhail to explore the possibilities. MacPhail responded immediately.

"We got together at the Squibb Building on Fifth Avenue," Dodson recalls. "MacPhail laid me out in lavender. 'You damn professional do-gooders know nothing about baseball. You're just trying to stir up trouble.' He said that Negroes weren't interested in baseball. 'They don't play on their sandlots. They don't play on their college campuses, and none of them would qualify to play in organized baseball. Satchel Paige would have made it, but he's over the hill now.' MacPhail argued that baseball was a business. 'I rented my ballparks to colored clubs this year, and the rental money is the profit I am able to pay my stockholders.' MacPhail said he didn't propose disturbing the Negro clubs by hiring one of their numbers; this would rob the black leagues and make it impossible for them to operate. He also said he wouldn't jeopardize his rental income or the Negro Leagues' investment until some way could be worked out that wouldn't hurt the Negro Leagues if the major leagues took an occasional player. But MacPhail had no suggestion as to how this could be done."

It was two or three weeks after Dodson sent his letter to Rickey that a meeting between them took place. Rickey apologized for the lag between his receiving the letter and their meeting at 215 Montague Street. He had made a considerable investigation of Dodson's background and of the Mayor's Committee on Unity. Rickey spent the first thirty minutes or so of the meeting quizzing the professor while chewing on his cigar.

"Now, Dan," Rickey said, "I have decided that I can trust you. I am satisfied that you are not going to cause any trouble. I am sure that we will be able to work together quite well on the cause. I am going to call you Dan because we are going to be working together for a long time. I am from the Midwest and you are from the Southwest. I understand people from out that way. We also share Methodism as a faith. We should be able to get along very well." Rickey went into a long story about his religious views and how he felt about baseball. "I once made a promise to my mother to never go to a Sunday baseball game. I have never broken that promise. Dan, I do not break any of my promises."

At this point, Dodson recalls, Rickey got up and opened a louvered arrangement on the side of the wall. Intricate charts detailed the entire Brooklyn Dodger organizational structure. All the farm clubs were identified—their location, their makeup, the names of all the personnel on them.

"This is the system we now have, Dan, but it will be changing. I will get to that, but first I want to tell you about an incident that has haunted me throughout my life, one that prompted a promise I made to myself.

"When I was a football coach at a midwestern college, I took my team to play in a nearby town. They would not allow a Negro player on my team to have a room at the hotel. I finally persuaded them to let him stay in my room on a cot.

"The player sat on the side of my bed and cried and pulled at one hand with the other and said, 'God, Mr. Rickey! If I could only change the color of my skin.'

"Dan," Rickey said, "this made such an impression on me that I decided that if I ever had the opportunity I was going to do something for the Negro race. I have never forgotten it. I thought of it often when I was in St. Louis and they made the Negroes sit in separate sections of the park. I couldn't do anything about that. I resolved when I came here that the time had arrived to do something.

"Now I am ready!" At this point, Dodson recalls, Rickey became excited, and his voice boomed. "I am ready. I have gone way out on a limb. I have taken a great deal of abuse. They have pilloried me in the press and in the Negro community. They do not know that I created the Brooklyn Brown Dodgers as a subterfuge, to mask my true intentions — to scout Negro players without tipping my hand.

"I have spent more than five thousand dollars scouting players. I feel now I have spotted the player who is most likely to succeed. I am not sure he is the best of the players, Dan, but he is the best hope for doing the whole job.

"The player I have in mind is named Jackie Robinson. He is college-educated. He is intelligent. He is playing in the Negro Leagues right now."

His evangelistic fervor nearly spent, Rickey sat down behind his desk and lit a fresh cigar. Dodson was stunned. He had come to the meeting hoping to reach first base. He found instead that Rickey was already rounding third and heading home. The first person outside of Rickey's inner circle to know of the secret plan to integrate baseball, Dodson vowed his support and any assistance he could offer.

"Mr. Rickey said there was a great deal of work to be done," Dodson remembers. "He asked for my help in getting material on Negroes in other sports. He wanted to know whom he could turn to for guidance in the Negro community and the community at large. He asked if we could get this Committee [the End Jim Crow in Baseball Committee, which Rickey was convinced was Communist-inspired] out of the way until he had a chance to do something. When, he wondered, should the signing of the contract be announced? What did we know about how integration is accomplished? What experience was there?"

There were to be many meetings between the professor and the baseball executive in the months ahead. They were to become allies and then friends.

"I was so sure of Mr. Rickey and his honesty that I was willing to do all he asked," Dr. Dodson said. The two Methodists meeting in downtown Brooklyn in the final months of World War II forged that day a union of trust and dedication.

7

THE SIGNING

Mrs. Effa Manley, owner of the Newark Eagles, organized a Negro All-Star team to play a five-game exhibition series against a club of white major-leaguers in October 1945. She recruited Roy Campanella to be the catcher for the Negro All-Stars. Four games were played in Brooklyn; one took place in Newark, New Jersey. After the game in Newark, Charlie Dressen, manager of the white team, approached Campanella. "To tell the truth," recalls Campanella, "I had no idea who Charlie was." Dressen asked Campanella if he would like to meet with Branch Rickey. "I remember I had to spend quite a time with Charlie to find out how to get to Mr. Rickey in Brooklyn," notes Campanella, but he eventually found his way through the New York City subway system to 215 Montague Street.

The meeting was different from the one Rickey had had in August with Jackie Robinson. "Mr. Rickey sat behind his desk and didn't do any talking for about four or five minutes," Campanella recalls. "He just looked me over from behind those horn-rimmed glasses."

Finally Rickey told Campanella that he had assigned Oscar Robertson, a former Negro Leagues first baseman, to look into the black catcher's life. "He had a black book," says Campanella, "and it was about four inches thick. It was in front of him on the desk. And he kept reading out of it. He knew everything about my family. He was interested in the fact that I had a black mother and a white father, that I went to an integrated school."

Rickey put down the black book and began a long speech; Campanella remembers thinking, "If I could catch like he could talk, I would have been a genius, for that Mr. Rickey knew how to catch from behind a desk."

"I've investigated dozens of players in the Negro Leagues," Rickey began. "I've tried to learn as much as I could about their personal habits, their family life, their social activities, their early childhood, their friends, their schooling. I have attempted to learn for myself all I could about them. I have rejected a number of possibilities who I am sure have the ability because they are lacking in other requisites. It's either character, habits, or what have you.

"You're different, Roy. Your record is good . . . no arrests, no trouble, a good family, a hard worker, a fellow who has the ability to get along with people." At this point, the Dodger executive paused. He lit a match and put the flame up against his half-smoked cigar, making the end glow a dull orange.

"What do you weigh, Campy?"

"Two fifteen to two twenty."

"Judas Priest!" Rickey shouted. "You can't weigh that much and play ball!"

"All I know is that I've been doing it every day for years and it's worked out fine."

Rickey knew how well it had worked out. A couple of months before he had sent Clyde Sukeforth to scout Newark Eagles pitcher Don Newcombe. Sukeforth was impressed by Newcombe but also impressed with the catcher on the opposing team, Roy Campanella of the Baltimore Elite Giants. A week after Sukeforth's scouting expedition, Rickey and his wife went to Jersey City. They watched Campanella catch both ends of a doubleheader. Rickey agreed with Suke-forth's high opinion of Campanella.

"Everything is fine," Rickey continued. "The one thing that puzzles me is your age. I have your age noted in this book," Rickey gestured down to the black book. "You sure this is your right age?"

"Sure, it's my right age. I'm twenty-three. I was born November nineteenth, 1921. I'll be twenty-four next month." Campanella was a bit annoyed.

"You look older."

"Mr. Rickey, I've been playing ball for a long time."

Rickey removed the cigar from between his fingers and placed it in a large ashtray on his desk. "I was a catcher, Campy, you know. You're a catcher. I think that's why we'll always be able to get along. I have had to ask you some of these questions. They were important. Now I am going to ask you the most important one: Would you like to play for me?"

Campanella knew about Rickey's sponsorship of the Brooklyn Brown Dodgers and thought that he was being offered a position with that team.

"I'm doing all right where I am, Mr. Rickey. I've been working for the same man for nine years. I like the man. I am one of the highest-paid players in the colored leagues. I make three thousand dollars a year and another two thousand from winter ball. I'm not interested, Mr. Rickey, in changing what I'm doing."

"All right," Rickey said calmly. "I understand, Roy. I want you to make me a promise. You promise me that you won't sign a contract with anyone else unless you talk to me."

Campanella had no trouble agreeing to the suggestion. "I don't sign contracts, Mr. Rickey. I just play ball."

Rickey stood up from behind the leather swivel chair and came out from behind the desk. He extended his hand.

Campanella could feel the gnarled fingers and Rickey felt Campanella's rough and bruised catcher's hand. "I'll be in touch with you," were Rickey's final words. Campanella was anxious to leave to get something to eat and to be out in the fresh air to clear his head of all the words.

Campanella returned to the Woodside Hotel in Harlem, where he was staying along with other Negro ballplayers who were enjoying a brief vacation in New York City before going to Venezuela for the winter baseball season. He settled down to a game of poker. One of the players was Jackie Robinson, the shortstop for the Kansas City Monarchs whom Campy had played against twice during the summer of 1945.

"We got to playing cards and talking," Campy remembers. "And Jackie told me, 'Roy, Mr. Rickey is signing up colored boys.' I had heard that kind of talk all the time from one player or another. They all had those kinds of pipe dreams. I told him, 'Jackie, I don't believe that kind of talk anymore.'

"Then Jackie told me that he had been signed up to play for Montreal and that the announcement was going to be made very soon. He told me not to tell anyone. 'They'll hear about it themselves,' he said, and he had a big smile, a real big smile on his face when he said those words."

On October 23, 1945, the announcement was made that Jackie Robinson had signed a contract to play for the Montreal Royals in the International League. The signing was the most dramatic and controversial sports story of the year.

When the news came over the radio at the Woodside Hotel in Harlem, there was loud cheering.

"I hope he makes it," said Sam Jethroe, who had been with Robinson at the Fenway Park tryout, "because if he does, I know I can."

"I'm afraid Jackie's in for a whole lot of trouble," warned fabled Buck Leonard, a longtime Negro Leagues star.

Roy Campanella was distressed. "I felt bad. Not that

Jackie had signed, it didn't matter to me who was number one. I felt bad that I had said no to Mr. Rickey. But he had said he would get in touch with me, so I decided to go to Venezuela and play ball and wait to hear from him."

Rickey heard from a lot of the owners. "When he finally decided to sign Jackie," Mal Goode reports, "men like Connie Mack in Philadelphia, Griffith in Washington, McKinney, who owned the Pirates, and Breadon in St. Louis were calling him. 'Branch, you're gonna kill baseball bringing that nigger into baseball now,' they said.

" 'You run your ball club, and I'll run mine,' Rickey told them."

The October signing was carefully planned. "A lesson of desegregation that I passed on to Mr. Rickey," explained Professor Dodson, "was that it succeeds best when management at the top takes a firm stand. I suggested that the contract with Robinson be signed before other players negotiated contracts for the spring, so that it would be clear that if they signed with the Dodgers for the coming year, they in all likelihood would be playing with black players in the future. I suggested to Mr. Rickey that he stand firm on this and not equivocate."

There had also been a question about where Robinson should play. Rickey personally decided on Montreal. "It is the best place," Rickey told Dodson, who recalls the twinkle in Rickey's eyes as he spoke of the city. "It has a heavy French influence, and their attitudes toward colored people are not what they are in the States. It also has the advantage that he would be playing in the eastern part of the United States most of the time, and the International League cities for the most part are urban places without the southern rural influence. Finally, the best press coverage would come out of Montreal."

Rickey told reporters, "My job is to build a baseball team. I have spent three years and twenty-five thousand dollars searching for Robinson. When I go after baseball players, sitting on the bench they all look as alike to me as doorbells. I never notice the color of their skins. I never meant to be a crusader, and I hope I won't be regarded as one. My purpose is to be fair to all people. My one selfish objective is to win ballgames."

A veteran player of many years in the Negro Leagues took a more cynical view: "That Branch Rickey was not just doing a little black boy a favor. He had more to offer to those sixteen prejudiced owners than just one black boy: He had those hundreds of thousands of Negro fans."

Minor-league baseball commissioner William Bramham also questioned the purity of Rickey's motives. "Father Divine [the flamboyant black evangelical minister] will have to look to his laurels," said Bramham, "for we can expect a Rickey Temple to be in the course of construction in Harlem soon. . . . Whenever I hear a white man, whether he be from the North, South, East, or West, protesting what a friend he is to the Negro race, right then I know the Negro needs a bodyguard. It is those of the carpetbagger stripe of the white race, under the guise of helping but in truth using the Negro for their own selfish interests, who retard the race."

Hall of Famer Monte Irvin was a star for the Newark Black Eagles then. His New Jersey scholastic sports feats had mirrored Robinson's accomplishments in California. "I was delighted," the soft-spoken Irvin notes, "but there was a certain amount of jealousy. I knew it would give us all a chance to possibly make it, but there was a certain amount of envy that he had been picked. There were real stars in the Negro Leagues—Josh Gibson, Satchel Paige, Roy Campanella. Those guys were proven stars. But they said Branch wanted a guy with talent and a college education, able to express himself with the press and in other situations. Jackie was perfect for all this. And we knew that if he made it there was a chance for the door to swing really open for all the black athletes not only in baseball, but for all the other professional sports. And it happened just that way. We were truly for him one hundred percent, but there was also a certain amount of jealousy."

Pee Wee Reese was aboard a ship returning to the United States from Guam. "I was told that a black had signed to play for Brooklyn," recalls Reese, "although I'd have to say that the word that was used was not 'black.' Like most Americans who were white, I didn't know what a black athlete was like. I just assumed they weren't good enough for the big leagues. I had heard the talk, you know, that if you threw at them, they backed down."

Reese then learned that the new man played shortstop. "Dammit, I thought," Reese recalled. "There are nine positions on the field and this guy has got to be a shortstop like me. I began to wonder what the people in Louisville would think about me playing with a colored boy. Then I thought, the hell with anyone who didn't like it—he deserved a chance just like anybody else."

Willa Mae Walker, three years and eight months older than her brother Jackie, remembers the reaction of the family. "We were all very happy," she says, "but we were frightened, too, because we knew there had never been any blacks in organized baseball."

Satchel Paige, the longtime pitching star who had toiled all those many years in the Negro Leagues for the Kansas City Monarchs, thought the Dodgers had signed the right man. "Jack's the number-one professional player. They couldn't have picked a better man," said the man who was now too old to be number one.

Paige was a prime example of how a black star made his living before the possibility of a major-league career. Estimated to have pitched thirty-three years, winning more than two thousand games, Paige traveled all over the world to play baseball. By car, by bus—some say even by horse— wherever there was a game, there was Satch. His nickname came from the fact that most of those years he lived out of a suitcase, or satchel. Breaking into the majors at an age when most players have since retired, Paige had a long career there. "Even though I got old, my arm stayed nineteen," claimed the Hall of Fame pitcher.

Many disagreed with Paige that Robinson was a good choice. Bob Feller, who had played against Robinson when a white All-Star team competed against the Monarchs, said, "He won't make it. That guy's got football shoulders. He's all tied up in the neck."

A week after Robinson's signing, *The Sporting News* attacked those who opposed him on racial grounds, calling them "un-American." Then the most powerful baseball newspaper in the United States proceeded to evaluate the black pioneer's chances: "Robinson, at twenty-six, is reported to possess baseball abilities, which, were he white, would make him eligible for a trial with, let us say, the Brooklyn Dodgers' Class B farm at Newport News, if he were six years younger. . . . The war is over. Hundreds of fine players are rushing out of the service and back into the roster of organized baseball. Robinson conceivably will discover that as a twenty-six-year-old shortstop just off the sandlots, the waters of competition in the International League will flow far over his head."

Walter O'Malley explained why Robinson's age was so important. "We wanted a fellow who was a little older than the average athlete, because we knew that what he would face would require maturity. It got down to two men, Jackie and Roy Campanella. Branch wanted Jackie because he knew Jackie had absolutely fierce pride and determination."

Rickey's motivations for signing Robinson have always been questioned. How much came from a moral conviction that the color bar must go, and how much came from a desire to make money and field a winning team? Monte Irvin suggests that what Rickey did is far more important than why he did it. "Regardless of the motives," Irvin observes, "Rickey had the conviction to pursue it and to follow through."

As Irvin points out, other owners had the chance to sign black players but didn't. "The Homestead Grays of the Negro Leagues used the ballpark of the Senators when Washington was on the road," Irvin recalls. "Josh Gibson and Buck Leonard were on the Grays. Today they are both in the Hall of Fame. They also had Roy Partlow, a fine left-hander, and Raymond Brown, a right-handed pitcher who hurled just like Red Ruffing. The Senators were at the bottom of the league, and those four players on the Homestead Grays were all at their peak. Josh was the equal of the Babe [Ruth]. Buck was just like Lou Gehrig. They used to draw big crowds—thirty-five thousand, forty-five thousand."

His scouts suggested to Clark Griffith, the owner of the Senators, that he sign those four players. "They would have played for nothing," says Irvin.

"But Griffith was a southerner. When faced with the idea of signing the four black players, all he could think was 'Where would they stay? How would they travel? Where would they eat? How would the other players feel about it?' That was the way of life back then and the way people thought," Irvin concludes. "It took Branch Rickey to come up with the answers, to do it."

Out of the limelight and away from the swirl of controversy from November 1945 to January 1946, Jackie Robinson and Roy Campanella played winter ball in Venezuela. Robinson was the shortstop; Campanella was the catcher-outfielder as their black All-Star team won eighteen of the twenty games it played. "Jackie and I roomed together," Campanella recalls. "We were able to get real close and have a lot of discussions about the situation. And Jackie would say, 'I just want a chance to play, and I think I can handle the worst of it.' "

Robinson told reporters that he was ready for what he knew would be a difficult ordeal. "I know I am heading for trouble in Florida next March when I must train with Montreal. I don't look for anything physical. I really believe we've gotten beyond that in this country. I know I'll take a tongue beating, though. But I think I can take it. I'm due for a terrible riding from the bench jockeys all around the International League circuit if I am good enough to play with Montreal all summer. I know about the riding white players give one another, and I'm sure it will be much worse for me because I am a Negro. They'll try to upset me and they'll have plenty of material, but we got that also in our league and I am prepared for it. These days keep reminding me of something my mother told me when I was a little kid. She told me that the words they say about you can't hurt you. And when they see that, they'll quit saying them. I've had plenty of nasty things said about me from the stands, especially in basketball, where you can hear everything they shout. I never let it get to me. I think it made me play better. I'll always remember what my mother taught me, and I think I'll come through.

"Joe Louis has done a great thing for our race. Without being conceited, I think I can say that I am going in with a much greater advantage than Joe had. . . . Therefore, I have a much greater responsibility.

"I think I am the right man to pick for this test. There is no possible chance that I will flunk it or quit before the end for any other reason than that I am not a good enough ballplayer. . . . That is the only thing I can be mistaken about now."

Robinson was the first black player signed to a contract to play in organized baseball. Rickey also signed the second, the third, the fourth, and the fifth, as America eagerly anticipated its first springtime peace in four years. John Wright, a twenty-seven-year-old pitcher, was signed in February 1946, following his discharge from the navy. On March 1, Campanella received a telegram advising him to report to the Brooklyn Dodger main office by March 10— "very important," the telegram said. It was signed "Branch Rickey."

"I got right back," Campanella recalls, even though the message came in the middle of the winter ball season. "I just got right out of there and lit out for New York. I signed up. The papers said I got a bonus. I got nothing except a salary of a hundred and eighty-five dollars a month to play with the Brooklyn Dodger farm team at Nashua, Class B."

Roy Partlow, pitcher, age thirty-seven, and Don Newcombe, pitcher, age nineteen, were also signed. The monthly salary for the five black pioneers was a grand total of $1,800. Robinson received the most, $600 a month. Campy was making the least.

The main man, though, was Jackie Robinson. Married to Rachel on February 10, 1946, the young man with his bride headed for spring training in Florida and the "trouble ahead" that Rickey had warned about. When they boarded the plane in California for Daytona Beach, Mallie Robinson presented them with a shoebox filled with fried chicken and hard-boiled eggs. At first they protested, explaining that they were just going to Florida, not to a wilderness. Then, not wanting to hurt Mallie's feelings, they took the shoebox with the home-cooked food along with them.

The American South, with its signs reading "For whites only" and "For colored women," its segregated drinking fountains, its layer upon layer of Jim Crow laws, was a shock to the Robinsons. When they arrived in New Orleans to get a connecting flight to Daytona Beach, they were bumped onto a later flight by the airlines. Informed that the law banned their eating at the New Orleans airport—they could only take food out—the man on the first steps of his mission to break baseball's color line became enraged. It accomplished nothing. The contents of the shoebox—succor provided by Mallie, who might have anticipated such a scene when she prevailed on them to take the food—eased their hunger if not their rage.

When they resumed their journey, they were bumped off

a plane at Pensacola, Florida, "for military priorities, so they said," Robinson noted. Determined not to waste any more time, the Robinsons boarded a bus to Daytona Beach. Although there were empty seats up front, they were forced to stay at the back of the bus—the Negro section. Jackie breathed the Florida air that mixed with the carbon monoxide fumes of the bus and thought about the adventure that loomed ahead and the price he knew he would have to pay.

On April 18, 1946, a new world quality enveloped the early spring day at Roosevelt Stadium in Jersey City, New Jersey. It was opening day of the International League season. It was opening day for Rickey and Robinson. After all the months of picketing and letter writing, of debate and dissent, Jack Roosevelt Robinson—a black man—would be playing second base for the Montreal Royals, the first of his race ever to play organized baseball.

Robinson had endured the hostility of that other country that was the American South. He had endured it and prevailed. As the Royals moved north, trouble ahead came daily. In Deland, Florida, a scheduled game between Montreal and Indianapolis was held up for almost an hour. It was claimed that electricians were at work repairing lights, even though the scheduled game was a day game. In Jacksonville, a city official padlocked the ballpark, canceling a game between the Jersey City Giants and the Montreal Royals. He claimed that public property could not be used for mixed racial competition. In Richmond and Savannah, too, games were canceled.

"I didn't realize it was going to be this bad," said Rickey. "Next year we'll have to train out of the country." Despite all the hardships, Robinson's play delighted the Mahatma. He admired the attitude, the aggressiveness, and the talent of this proud black man. To avoid confrontations over segregation, Rickey arranged lodging in private homes for Robinson and John Wright, also on the Montreal roster.

Jersey City was not Richmond or Savannah. The seating capacity for Roosevelt Stadium was twenty-five thousand, but on this dramatic day it was standing room only. Mayor Frank Hague, who was scheduled to throw out the first ball, declared the day a half-holiday. Many New Yorkers made their own holiday, taking the day off and traveling through the Hudson Tubes to witness Robinson's debut. Two bands, a tumbling acrobat, and hundreds of reporters and photographers added to the already electric atmosphere.

When Robinson made his first appearance on the field, the integrated crowd stood up and cheered. He played second base and batted second in the Royal lineup as Montreal blitzed Jersey City, 14–1. Robinson rapped out four hits in five trips to the plate, with three singles and a 335-foot homer. He scored four runs, and batted in four runs. He stole two bases. His dancing, taunting leads flustered Jersey City pitchers into committing two balks. When the game ended, it took the delighted rookie more than five minutes to reach the comparative safety of the dressing room. Squealing, adoring fans mobbed his path. Even Montreal manager Clay Hopper was delighted. Hopper, who hailed from Mississippi, had protested the assignment of Robinson to Montreal, and had once asked in all seriousness, "Mister Rickey, tell me—do you really think a nigra's a human being?"

In the Montreal clubhouse, a reporter asked Robinson to evaluate his situation. "Mr. Rickey has tried to foresee all the difficulties I would encounter." The voice was low but direct. "I have tried to follow his advice. I can thank Mr. Rickey that I am playing in the International League. I will give it all I have."

With Robinson on the scene, almost a million fans came out to see the Montreal Royals in 1946, setting a new minor-league record. Some Baltimore players objected to Jackie's presence and made it clear that they would not play against Montreal. International League president Frank Shaughnessy sent them a telegram: "If you don't take the field . . .

you will be suspended from baseball for the rest of your life." They took the field.

No minor-league ballplayer has ever attracted the kind of national attention that was focused on Jackie Robinson. Wendell Smith, sports editor of the *Pittsburgh Courier*, traveled along with Jackie. "Wendell's reports and stories," notes Mal Goode, "added one hundred thousand a week to the paper's circulation." Special charter trains came from Chicago to see Robinson perform with his Montreal teammates at Buffalo. After virtually every game, swarms of kids and their parents begged for autographs.

"We had rented a home in the French Canadian sector," recalls Rachel Robinson. "We were stared at on the street. We had very little privacy. Those kids were always trailing after us; they became an adoring retinue." John Wright, the black pitcher who was placed on the Montreal roster by Rickey, lasted only until May, when he was demoted to Three Rivers, Quebec, in Class C ball. Pitcher Roy Partlow replaced Wright on the Montreal roster in May, but he didn't last either and was also sent down to play at Three Rivers.

"John Wright," Robinson observed, "had all the talent in the world as far as physical abilities were concerned. But John couldn't stand the pressure of going up into this new league and being one of the first. The things that went on up there were too much for him, and John was not able to perform up to his capabilities.

"In a number of cities," Robinson later said of that first season with Montreal, "we had very little pressure. But there was always that little bit coming out. It wasn't so much based on race. But because John was the first pitcher, every time he stepped out there he seemed to lose that fineness, and he tried a little bit too hard. He tried to do more than he was actually able to do, and it caused him to be less of a pitcher than he really was. If he had come in two or three years later when the pressure was off, John could have made it in the major leagues." At the end of the 1946 season, Wright was released by the Dodger organization and went back to play with the Homestead Grays.

Robinson at one point nearly gave in to the pressures that ruined the chances of Partlow and Wright. Montreal won the International League pennant, but near the end of the season Robinson's reserve wore out. "My nerves were pretty ragged," he recalled. "I couldn't sleep, and often I couldn't eat. I guess I hadn't realized I wanted to make good so badly. I sort of went to pieces." At Rachel's urging, he went to see a doctor, who was concerned that Robinson might have a nervous breakdown. The doctor advised a brief rest. The rest was for one day. Robinson was concerned that if he won the batting title, people would claim he stayed out to protect his average.

He came back to lead Montreal against Louisville in the Little World Series. The Royals dropped two of the first three games to Louisville in Louisville. The Montreal fans were upset by the harsh treatment Robinson had received in Louisville, a border city, and Montreal sportswriters reported the abuse and racial epithets heaped on Robinson by Louisville players and fans. "Hey, nigger, go on back to Montreal where you belong," one fan had screamed. "Get out of here, nigger," another shouted, "and take your coon fans along."

The Royals swept three games in Montreal to win the Little World Series. The Royals' fans defended their beloved Jackie Robinson by booing and taunting every Louisville player. After the final out that clinched the Royal triumph, Montreal fans surged onto the playing field and mobbed Robinson. They lifted him onto their shoulders and paraded him around. When he finally was able to get to his feet, he made a frantic dash to the safety of the clubhouse. "It was probably the only day in history that a black man ran from a white mob with love instead of lynching on its mind," one reporter observed.

With the season over, Robinson could take pride in his

accomplishments as a Montreal Royal. His .349 batting average led the league, as did his .985 fielding average and his 113 runs scored. He added forty stolen bases. Montreal manager Clay Hopper, who had balked at having a black man on the Royals, told him, "You're a great ballplayer and a fine gentleman. You're the greatest competitor I ever saw. It's been wonderful having you on the team."

Back in New York, the pressure was intensifying for Rickey to bring Robinson up to the Dodgers. On the night of February 5, 1947, Rickey spoke to three dozen black leaders. The meeting was arranged by the executive secretary of the Carleton Branch of the YMCA, Herbert T. Miller. The only whites present were Rickey, his assistant Arthur Mann, Dr. Dan Dodson, and Judge Edward Lazansky, a close friend.

Rickey opened his after-dinner remarks with greetings, and then launched into the fifth step of his well-orchestrated plan: a speech aimed at insuring the complete understanding and backing by the black community of his program to break baseball's color line. "Someone close to me," he said, "remarked that I did not have the courage to tell you what I want to tell you; that I didn't have the guts to give this speech and that you people wouldn't be able to take it. I believe all of us here have the courage. I have a ballplayer named Jackie Robinson. He's on the Montreal team. He may stay there . . . he may be brought to Brooklyn. But if Jackie Robinson does come up to the Dodgers, the biggest threat to his success, the one enemy most likely to ruin that success, is the Negro people themselves." Rickey was aware of an uncomfortable stirring in the audience, but he pressed on with conviction.

"There is a weight of responsibility that rests upon the shoulders of you, the leading citizens of the community," he intoned. "For on the day Robinson enters the big leagues, if he does, we don't wany any Negro to add to the burden of Jackie Robinson. We don't want any Negroes to form gala welcoming committees, to form parades to the ballpark every night. We don't want Negroes to strut, to wear badges."

Rickey warned the audience of black leaders about white jealousy and sensitivity. "We don't want premature Jackie Robinson Days or Nights. We don't want Negroes in the stands gambling, drunk, fighting, being arrested. We don't want Jackie wined and dined until he is fat and futile. . . . We don't want what can be another great milestone in the progress of American race relations turned into a national comedy and an ugly tragedy." He paused and drew in his breath. "Let me tell you this!" The words came out fast and thunderously, in evangelistic tones. "If any individual, group, or segment of Negro society uses the advancement of Jackie Robinson in baseball as a triumph of race over race," he pounded the top of the table in front of him, "I will regret the day I ever signed him to a contract, and I will personally see that baseball is never so abused and misrepresented again!"

Rickey concluded his remarks, and he was applauded for several minutes by the black leaders. A lengthy discussion followed. The slogan "Don't Spoil Jackie's Chances" was adopted. "There was a real concern," Dodson notes, "that blacks would come to games drinking, being rowdy, making it unpleasant for whites to attend. The slogan would serve as a call for self-policing action. Cards bearing the slogan were placed in bars, restaurants, barbershops, and churches. Group meetings were held where Rickey's themes were disseminated." It was resolved that this program would be sustained throughout Robinson's first year in the major leagues. The sixty-six-year-old Rickey had achieved another important step in the plan that he had originally laid out at the New York Athletic Club in 1943—he had gained the support and cooperation of the black community.

While everyone agreed with Rickey's aims, not all members of the black community appreciated the tone of Rickey's remarks. "Rickey's speech was tremendously patronizing," recalls Joe Bostic. "He had the absolute effrontery to tell adults how to behave. I was not invited to that meeting, but I found out afterward what happened." Rickey apparently did not forget Bostic's bursting in on him at Bear Mountain, demanding tryouts, and so the journalist was excluded from the meeting. "I told those people that they should have shown their displeasure and indignation by walking out. 'You have been supporting major-league baseball for fifty years,' I told them. 'You don't need to be told how to act.' "

Bostic's objections notwithstanding, the self-policing activity moved ahead in the community. As spring training for the 1947 season loomed ahead, there were two problems that needed to be solved. One was where to train. The trouble in Florida had convinced Rickey that he should not expose Robinson to the rigid southern segregationist laws for a second straight year.

The other problem was what position Robinson should play. "The Dodgers had just about the best second baseman in the league in Eddie Stanky," notes Dodson, "and putting Robinson there, although it was agreed that this was his best position, would have led to the issue of a power struggle, the black man taking the white man's job. Robinson told Mr. Rickey that he thought he could do very well playing first base."

The Dodgers and Royals went to Havana, Cuba, for spring training. Three other blacks were assigned to the Montreal roster: Roy Campanella, Don Newcombe, and Roy Partlow. "The idea behind this," explains Dodson, "was to let the Dodger team have the experience of playing with, against, and among dark-skinned people, with people of different languages and colors around them. The idea was to bring both teams to Brooklyn playing exhibition games along the way and to introduce Robinson gradually."

"Down here in Havana," Rickey told Hopper, "you must stall and be vague. Tell the newspapermen that you're curious to see if Robinson can play first base, and that this is an experiment of no special significance. But when you bring Montreal to Panama, use him exclusively at first base. There won't be any writers there." Hopper was unhappy. He realized that Robinson was slotted for the Dodgers, and he wanted playing time for his own first-base prospects for the Royals. Robinson was also unhappy. Rickey had ordered that the blacks on the Montreal squad be quartered in segregated housing to avoid any possibility of racial problems. Robinson flared up. To him, it was like being in the American South all over again.

Rickey told Hopper and Robinson that there was too much involved to allow irritations of the moment to influence the great plan for the future. "This is the most important thing I ever did in my life and you ever did in your life," he told them. Hopper decided to be patient. Robinson, admitting that Rickey had been right in everything he had done to that point, relented and went along with the segregated housing.

But there were other problems as well. Pee Wee Reese asked to be traded. "My grandfather would turn over in his grave if he knew I was playing on a team with a colored boy," Reese said.

"Mr. Rickey did not want to lose Reese," recalls Mal Goode, "since Reese was the man he was building his ball club around. 'Pee Wee,' Mr. Rickey said, 'you're intelligent. I can talk to you. I'd like you to try it for a couple of weeks. If you still feel this way, then I'll trade you, because if Jackie makes this team, he's going to play.'

"Six days later Pee Wee came to see Mr. Rickey. 'You can still trade me if you want to,' said Pee Wee, 'but not for the same reason. Robinson is not only a great ballplayer but a gentleman in every sense of the word.' "

There were others on the team who did not want to see Jackie Robinson become a Brooklyn Dodger. Hugh Casey, Dixie Walker, Bobby Bragan, and Carl Furillo circulated a petition insisting that they could not and would not play on the same team with him. Duke Snider was amazed that anyone could engage in such overtly bigoted behavior. "That prejudice was not part of our life in southern California. When they passed that petition around, I told them, 'There's no way I can sign it. Jack's an idol of mine.' Nobody signed it except the guys who were passing it around."

The Dodger manager since 1939, Leo Durocher had ties with Rickey that went back to the days of the Gashouse Gang in St. Louis. "Mr. Rickey is just like a father to me," observed the forty-one-year-old Durocher. "Durocher is my pet reclamation project," observed Rickey. Their relationship was based on mutual respect for each other's talent and their desire to build better baseball teams. All of this contributed to Durocher's outrage when he heard about the petition. He called a midnight meeting of the entire Dodger team and unloaded his fury.

"I don't give a shit about the way you feel," he screamed. "It doesn't mean a thing to me whether the guy is blue or orange or black or if he is striped up like a fucking zebra. I manage this team. I say he plays. I say he can make us all rich. I say that if you can't use the dough I'll see to it that you get the hell out of here."

Rickey's reaction was calmer but just as forceful. The man who Jackie Robinson said "was like a piece of mobile armor who would throw himself and his advice in the way of anything likely to hurt me" called the mutineers into his office one by one. He was adamant that the Robinson experiment would continue. He informed each player that he was free, if he desired, to quit baseball.

"Bobby Bragan's argument was, 'I live in Fort Worth, Texas, and my friends there would never forgive me,'" notes Monte Irvin. "He was that blinded."

Rickey pointed out that Bragan was the third-string catcher on the Dodgers. "You're expendable," he said. Rickey sent Bragan down to the minors. "After a year or two," states

Irvin, "Bragan realized how wrong his attitude was. Later he went out of his way to help black ballplayers."

When Robinson signed with Montreal, Dixie Walker had shrugged off the news. "As long as he's not with the Dodgers, I'm not worried," he said. When the petition failed to gain momentum, the man Dodger fans called "The People's Cherce" hand-delivered a letter to Rickey in Havana.

"Recently the thought has occurred to me that a change of ball clubs would benefit both the Brooklyn baseball club and myself. Therefore I would like to be traded as soon as a deal can be arranged. My association with you, the people of Brooklyn, the press and radio has been very pleasant and one I can truthfully say I am sorry has to end. For reasons I don't care to go into, I feel my decision is the best for all concerned."

Business interests in Atlanta were among the reasons Walker didn't care to go into. Robinson, aware of Walker's objections, made a point of staying away from him as much as possible. "If he hit a home run," Robinson later recalled, "and I was on base, I never waited at the plate to shake his hand. I thought it would embarrass Dixie. He later changed his mind about me. He came to me in mid-June with advice about hitting behind the runner, something I didn't know much about."

Montreal and Brooklyn played seven exhibition games that spring. "Be a whirling demon against the Dodgers," Rickey told Robinson. "Go wild. Get on base. Make them know you are there." Robinson followed Rickey's advice. He batted .625 and stole seven bases in those showcase games. Robinson's dramatics were part of Rickey's overall plan. He reasoned that once the Dodger players saw the superb playing skills of the rookie, they would clamor for him to be placed on the Brooklyn roster. They did not. Only Montreal manager Clay Hopper spoke out. He noted that all five candidates for the Dodgers' first-base opening had not done well. "Why don't you take Robby to Brooklyn now?" he asked Rickey. "He's ready. He can't prove any more on my team. Besides, I got to break in my regular first baseman pretty quick."

Rickey decided the time had come. "Leo," he said to Durocher, "go to the press and tell them that if Robinson becomes the Dodger first baseman, Brooklyn will have an excellent chance at winning the pennant. I had thought the players, once they saw how good he was, would want him on the team. Since this has not transpired, I think we should do something to light a fire under them." Durocher agreed, but he was never able to carry out this plan.

On April 9, Commissioner Happy Chandler suspended Leo Durocher for one year for "conduct unbecoming to baseball." The Durocher suspension came as a result of a number of headlined incidents. The fiery manager had thrown a wet towel in an umpire's face, slugged a fan, lent his Manhattan apartment to actor George Raft, who was rumored to have connections to the underworld, and suffered embarrassment when a "crooked crap game" that was allegedly played in his living room made front-page news after a bust. His January 21, 1947, marriage to divorced actress Laraine Day resulted in still further adverse publicity and the withdrawal of support for the Dodger Knothole Gang by the Brooklyn Catholic Youth Organization.

The suspension left New York City's baseball community in shock. While the reason for the punitive action against the colorful "Leo the Lip" was never clearly specified, there were many who speculated that it was part of a move aimed at depriving Jackie Robinson of a bodyguard. Durocher, additionally, was silenced. He could not agitate the press, as planned, to urge that Jackie Robinson become a Brooklyn Dodger.

The suspension of Leo Durocher became the most sensational sports story of the year—for exactly one day. On April 10, as the sixth inning got underway at Ebbets Field, a Rickey assistant sauntered into the press box and began to distribute a news release. "Brooklyn announces the purchase of the contract of Jack Roosevelt Robinson from Montreal. . . . He will report immediately. Signed, Branch Rickey." The tens of thousands who had signed petitions urging the Dodgers to take this action were delighted. The thousands who wore "I'm for Jackie" buttons were delighted. And Robinson was delighted and ready. "Now I can relax," he told a reporter. "I have a few days before the season opens and I'll be ready then. The time element in making good won't be a factor anymore."

The final decision to sign major-league baseball's first black player was made at a secret meeting at Branch Rickey's Forest Hills, Queens, home just hours after Durocher was suspended. Rickey had received unanimous support for the decision from his coaches.

The next day, two signatures were affixed to a Uniform Player's Contract of the National League of Professional Ball Clubs dated April 11, 1947: Jack Roosevelt Robinson of 1588 W. 36th Pl., Los Angeles, California, and Branch Rickey of the Brooklyn National League Baseball Club, Inc. Four days later, it became official with the additional signature of Ford Frick, president of the National League.

NUMBER 42

With a blue number 42 on the back of his white Brooklyn Dodger home uniform, Jackie Robinson took his place at first base on April 15, 1947, at Ebbets Field. It was two years less a day since he had tried out at Fenway Park. It was thirty-two years to the day since Jack Johnson had become the first black heavyweight champion of the world.

Many of the 26,623 at that tiny ballpark on that chilly spring day were not even baseball fans but had come out to see "the one" who would break the sport's age-old color line. Rachel Robinson was there with the infant Jackie Jr.; Clyde Sukeforth, who had first seen Jackie Robinson in Comiskey Park in Chicago in 1945, was there as interim manager of the Dodgers. Many in the crowd wore "I'm for Jackie" buttons and badges and screamed each time the black pioneer came to bat or touched the ball.

He grounded out to short his first time up. It was a very close play and probably could have been called either way. Umpire Al Barlick called Robinson out. A scowl on his face, Robinson stepped toward the umpire, ready to protest. Then he backed off and returned to the Dodger dugout. Argument, Rickey had told him, might win a battle, but restraint would win the war. He was retired on a fly ball to left field in his second at-bat. He grounded into a rally-killing double play in his final appearance at the plate. "We had spoken on the phone a few days before," remembers Willa Mae Walker, "and he said he was doing it for his people. I listened to that game, and I was sitting down and shaking all the time." The Dodgers won the game, 5–3, nipping Johnny Sain and the Boston Braves. For Robinson, it was a muted performance, but the first of his 1,382 major-league games was now in the record books—and he had broken the color line forever. "I was nervous on my first day in my first game at Ebbets Field," Robinson told reporters later, "but nothing has bothered me since."

Duke Snider recalls that first game, too. "I never played with or against Jackie until spring training that year in Havana," Snider remembers. "While he was with Montreal, I wasn't even put on the Dodger roster until the latter part of spring training. All the attention that day was directed toward Jackie, and rightfully so, since he was the first black man in the major leagues. He played first base and did a fine job."

Lee Scott, then a reporter for the *Brooklyn Times*, remembers the scene at the start in the Dodger clubhouse at Ebbets Field. "Jackie had a spot on the right side, a little two-by-four. It was not as large as the other lockers of the regulars on the Dodgers. He was really almost all by himself on the other side of the clubhouse. I guess it was because we had a few guys from the Deep South and Rickey wanted to keep them apart."

Scott still remembers how reserved Robinson was at the start. "He never said a word. The only fellows who spoke to him in real conversations were Pee Wee Reese and Gil Hodges, and they became good friends. Jackie would go out and take practice and go into his little cubicle when the game was over and get dressed. He wouldn't say a word, and then he'd go about his business."

Robinson's behavior reflected a lesson in desegregation

Dodson had described to Rickey. "At registration time the dean of the law school at the University of Maryland called Walter White, head of the NAACP," Dodson explains. "The school was being ordered by the government to admit black students. The dean sought advice as to how this might be most smoothly accomplished.

"'How shall we admit this student to his class, Walter?' the dean asked. 'How shall we deal with it? Should we make an announcement that the law requires it?'

"'Do nothing,' responded White. 'Just have the student come early and sit in the middle of the room toward the front. Don't make it seem that the student has been forced on the white students. . . . Let him wait until they make their advances to him.'

"On the first day of classes, no one spoke to the black student. The next day one of the students greeted him. At the end of the semester the student had been elected president of the class. Mr. Rickey was very impressed with this story. And he decided to have Jackie keep a stance apart from the other players on the Dodgers and allow them to make their own adjustment to him."

Adjustment was a part of daily life for the tightly bound Robinson family—Jackie, Rachel, and Jackie Jr.

"It was postwar," Rachel Robinson remembers. "We couldn't get any housing. We were strangers in the city. We didn't have much money. We could afford only one room in the Hotel McAlpin in Manhattan." Diapers hung in the bathroom; the baby's things were pushed under the bed when reporters came clamoring for interviews.

"I was worried about Jackie Jr. He had caught a cold on opening day. We weren't even dressed for it. What I thought was a winter coat in California was nothing in New York. I just had a little spring topper. I was worried about Jack. I knew he still had to win a place on the team . . . and in baseball you have to beat someone else out to win a place on the team."

Jack and Rachel could not even go out and eat meals together. "In the back of the McAlpin," Rachel Robinson explains, "there was a cafeteria on a side street. One of us would mind the baby, and the other would go out and eat. I didn't use sitters. I didn't want to leave my baby with anyone. It was very much like going to work with your husband. I held on to Jack; he held on to me."

On April 18, 1947, at the Polo Grounds, in the shadow of the largest black community in the country, Jackie Robinson smashed his first major-league home run as the Dodgers defeated the Giants, 10–4. Writer James Baldwin had once noted, "Back in the thirties and forties, Joe Louis was the only hero that we ever had. When he won a fight, everybody in Harlem was up in heaven." On that April day the large contingent of blacks in the crowd of nearly forty thousand had another hero to be "up in heaven" about, another hero to stand beside Joe Louis.

"The one thing that concerned Jack," Rachel Robinson recalls, "was the possibility of an overenthusiastic black response. We saw it more in the South than we saw it in Brooklyn, but every time he came up to bat early on, even if he hit a pop-up, there would be a tremendous response. His concern was that this overresponse might lead to fights in the ballpark. But it didn't happen."

Part of the reason that it didn't happen was the work done in the community. Rickey had planned well. "In the churches," Goode remembers, "in the professional organizations, the word was passed along. If you hear the word 'nigger,' if you hear the word 'darkie,' ignore it. This message went from city to city wherever Jackie played. We all knew if Jackie made good, the door would be opened.

"Those of my generation and the one just behind us had witnessed the great black ballplayers. You sat at Forbes Field in Pittsburgh in the twenties and the thirties and watched the Homestead Grays play the Kansas City Monarchs or the Baltimore Black Sox when the Pittsburgh

Pirates were out of town. There were ten to twenty thousand in the stands. We saw 1–0, 2–1 games, skilled players. I saw Satchel Paige walk three men on purpose. He said to his first baseman, 'You sit there,' the guy at second base, 'You sit there,' the guy at third, 'You sit there.' I saw this. I didn't read it in a book. And then he struck out the next three guys.

"In 1938 I saw Josh Gibson hit a ball over the Barney Dreyfuss Memorial and over the center-field fence, which was marked at that point four hundred and ten feet; the ball went twenty feet above the wall into the trees in Schenley Park. It had to have been hit seven hundred feet if it was a foot.

"There weren't that many blacks going to major-league games. Who wanted to sit there and see eighteen white players when you knew when Saturday came along and the Pirates were out of town, you'd be able to sit there and see eighteen black players who were better than most of the white ones?"

Now with one of their own on the scene, blacks were coming out in large numbers to watch the Dodgers play ball. And those who didn't come out, or who couldn't come out, listened on the radio to the southern accents of Red Barber. One of those who listened was an elderly black woman. She was not a baseball fan, but she was a Jackie Robinson fan. Hearing that her idol had stolen a base annoyed her. "I knew they would accuse that boy of something wrong, of stealing, just 'cause he's colored," she told a friend. "But I know Jackie's a fine boy and wouldn't steal anything."

But he did steal—he stole the hearts of a generation who marveled at his burden and his bravado, who respected his dignity and his daring. For blacks and whites, Jackie Robinson represented a model for survival, of self-assurance in a crisis. "Anybody who says I can't make it doesn't know what I've gone through and what I'm prepared to go through to stay up in the major leagues," he once told a reporter.

In an early-season series between the Dodgers and Phillies at Ebbets Field, Robinson was put to a severe test. Before the series, Philadelphia owner Bob Carpenter allegedly phoned Branch Rickey and suggested that it might be best for all concerned if Robinson were kept on the bench. Carpenter said that with a black man in the lineup there was the real possibility that the Phillies would refuse to compete against the Dodgers.

After listening patiently to Carpenter, Rickey replied in measured tones: "It's all right with us whatever you do. You have to take the responsibility for your actions. We will not make a moral decision for you. If you do not choose to play, we will win all three games by forfeit."

The Phillies played, but some of them played dirty. "Hey, nigger, why don't you go pickin' cotton?" "Hey, snowflake, which one of the white boys' wives you shackin' up with tonight?" "Hey, coon, do you always smell so bad?" "Hey, darkie, you shouldn't be here in the big leagues—they need you back home to clean out the latrines." These were just a few of the racial slurs screamed out from the Phillies dugout, led by Alabama-born manager Ben Chapman. Inning after inning, the abuse, the vulgarity, and the invective kept building. Robinson was later to admit that that first game of the Philadelphia series brought him closer to the breaking point than any other day in his life.

The abuse continued in the second game of the series. "I didn't see too many bad things," Lee Scott remembers, "but I saw enough to make me sick and upset. They would lift up their arms and make believe they were smelling and that there was a stink. They yelled about black cats being Jackie's relatives."

When Robinson joined the Dodgers, Eddie Stanky said to him: "I don't like you, but we'll play together and get along because you're my teammate." After remaining silent for two games, Stanky came to Robinson's defense.

"You're all a bunch of cowards," Stanky shouted at the

Philadelphia bench. "What kind of men are you anyway? You're all yellow! Why the hell don't you pick on someone who can fight back! You know Robinson can't fight back— knock it off and just play ball!"

Stanky's challenge slightly reduced the racial vitriol, but one Philadelphia player yelled out, "If that black-lipped nigger was a white boy, he'd a been sent to Newport News a long time ago." Of all the taunts, Robinson was to admit the "Newport News" one affected him the most because of its aspersion on his playing ability.

Despite the venom, Rickey was elated when the series concluded. "The Chapman incident," he said, "did more than anything to make the other Dodgers speak up in Robinson's behalf. When Chapman and the others poured out that string of unconscionable abuse, he solidified and unified thirty men, not one of whom was willing to see someone kick around a man who had his hands tied behind his back. Chapman created in Robinson's behalf a thing called sympathy, the most unifying word in the world. That word has a Greek origin—it means 'to suffer.' To say 'I sympathize with you' means 'I suffer with you.' That is what Chapman did. He caused men like Stanky to suffer with Robinson, and he made this Negro a real member of the Dodgers."

The racist behavior was reported in various newspapers. The black press gave it extensive coverage, anxious to make its leaders aware of what had taken place. In a particularly critical column that appeared in the *New York Mirror*, sports editor Dan Parker said: "Ben Chapman, who during his career with the New York Yankees was frequently involved in unpleasant incidents with fans who charged him with shouting anti-Semitic remarks at them from the ball field, seems to be up to his old trick of stirring up racial trouble. During the recent series between the Phils and the Dodgers, Chapman . . . poured a stream of abuse at Jackie Robinson. Jackie, with admirable restraint, ignored the guttersnipe language coming from the Phils' dugout, thus stamping himself as the only gentleman among those involved in the incident."

Later on, to defuse the controversy that came as a result of the press coverage of the incident, Rickey prevailed upon Jackie to pose shaking hands with Chapman. "It will be good for the game of baseball," Rickey said. Robinson posed with Chapman but refused to shake hands. "It was one of my most painful moments ever," Robinson later admitted. "Deep in my heart, I couldn't forgive Chapman and the Phillies for what they did."

The first 1947 meeting between the St. Louis Cardinals and the Dodgers was scheduled for May 6. Stanley Woodward reported on May 9 in the *New York Herald Tribune* that a proposed strike by the Cardinals against Robinson's presence in the Brooklyn lineup had been scuttled. Woodward said that Ford Frick, National League president, had taken a strong stand. When Dr. Dodson had originally discussed bringing blacks into major-league baseball with Frick, the league president had not been enthusiastic, but now, less than two years later, he informed the Cardinals, "If you do this, you will be suspended from the league. You will find that the friends that you think you have in the press box will not support you, that you will be outcasts. I do not care if half the league strikes. Those who do it will encounter quick retribution. They will be suspended, and I do not care if it wrecks the National League for five years. This is the United States of America, and one citizen has as much right to play as another. The National League will go down the line with Robinson, whatever the consequence. You will find that if you go through with your intention that you have been guilty of complete madness."

Red Schoendienst, one of the last great players signed by Rickey to a St. Louis contract, denies to this day any knowledge of a strike threat. "I have been asked that question by a lot of people," he says. "I was there, but I don't know anything about it. Nobody said anything. We went out and we played. There was no reason for the Cardinals to go out on strike. The media just looked for a good story and picked the St. Louis Cardinals because we were the furthest south of any team at that time. The facts are that nothing was said with the Cardinals about going on strike."

The first physical threat came in a Brooklyn–St. Louis game. Harry "the Cat" Brecheen, a fine-fielding hurler, was on the mound for the Cardinals. With one out in the sixth inning, Robinson topped a bounding ball between the mound and first base. Brecheen pounced off the mound and fielded the ball in a direct line with first base. Instead of executing the routine play of flipping the ball to Stan Musial for the putout, Brecheen circled back and over to the baseline. With both fists extended, Brecheen positioned his body in a half-crouch, awaiting Robinson, who was speeding down the line. Robinson slowed and allowed himself to be tagged. "You'd better play your position as you should," Robinson snapped. "If you ever do that again, I'll send you right on the seat of your pants."

A second and potentially more dangerous incident took place a few days later against the Cubs, who were in the process of losing their fourth straight game. Robinson opened the ninth inning with a single and then stole second base. Cub pitcher Bill Lee kept throwing the ball to his shortstop Len Merullo in an attempt to pick off Robinson. The more he threw, the longer Robinson's lead became. Then, attempting to get back to second base to beat Lee's throw, Robinson slid between Merullo's legs. The bodies of the two players became entangled. Merullo was astride Robinson, who lay on the ground. Merullo lifted his right leg, and for a moment it looked as if he was going to kick Robinson. The Dodger first baseman jerked his left arm up, as if he was getting ready to throw a punch. Then the two players untangled. There was some glaring, and lots of tension, but no violence.

"It all seems inconceivable now," says Monte Irvin. "It's

like a bad dream." Physical challenges; crude epithets; crank phone calls that threatened to rape his wife, to kidnap his child, to assassinate him; aborted strikes; cold, demeaning stares; pitches aimed at his head; meals eaten alone in hotel rooms; a near nervous breakdown that few knew about at the end of the 1947 season, according to Don Newcombe— all of these pounded away at the "badge of martyrdom."

"Robby never spoke about the horror stories," recalls Joe Bostic. "And he didn't scare easily."

"I said to him, six or seven years later at my dining room table in my home in Pittsburgh, 'It must have been tough, Jackie,' " Mal Goode recalls.

" 'It wasn't that bad,' he said, shrugging his shoulders.

" 'Don't give me that b.s., Jackie, I sat in the stands.'

" 'Well, I guess I had to expect that, Mal.'

"He became philosophical about it. He never growled, never groaned. It was hard to get him to discuss what he went through. He was the right man at the right time. Willie Mays once said to me, 'I'm glad it wasn't me. I don't think I could have taken it.' Monte Irvin, Hank Thompson, I think they would have taken a bat and killed somebody. I think Jackie's coming on the scene was a divinely inspired thing. I think he was hand-picked by God Almighty."

Duke Snider maintains that he could never have taken the abuse that Robinson took in that first year and into the second. "Branch Rickey had to select someone who could take it, and Jackie could take it. He dished it out just by ignoring what was hollered at him and done to him. I don't think that Campy or Newk or Doby could have handled it, or anybody else. It takes a special type of person, a cocky type who can brush off the things done to him. I saw base runners go at him in that first year when he was playing first base. They'd try to step on him, try to cut his leg off."

Mack Robinson was never a witness to the abuse his brother had to endure, but he was a passionately involved listener to many of the details, later told to him by Jackie.

Never for an instant did Mack think his younger brother would not prevail.

"I had gone before Jack, and having gone through some of the trials and tribulations of the athletic world, I knew he could do the job," notes Mack. "It was made much easier because of Mr. Rickey. It was also made much easier because he was raised in California and went to school with a mixed group. Having played in interracial sports all his life, Jack had no fear of the white man. He was accustomed to just going out and playing. You have heard so many black players, like Satchel Paige and others, who have said they could not have done it. Most of those fellows were southerners. They were used to being bossed by the southern white man. Jack had not been bossed and could not be bossed."

Part sociological phenomenon, part entertainment spectacle, part revolution, part media event—day after day, the Jackie Robinson story played out its poignant scenes.

"Television was a major factor in helping him to succeed," says Dr. George N. Gordon, a noted communications theorist. "Jack Johnson was edited by photographs and Joe Louis was filtered by radio. But the unblinking eye of TV humanized Robinson. He was not a stereotype; he was an equal with the other players on the field. It was a lesson taught by example, like Ed Sullivan kissing Pearl Bailey. You couldn't deny his blackness. It was a visible, sustaining show day after day. Television magnified the social event and made it reflective and directed."

"I'm the grandson of slaves," observes Mal Goode. "Not just by history—I knew all four of my grandparents. I spent summers with them when I was a little boy in Virginia. . . . And then to see Jackie Robinson. . . . Maybe we overdo it, but you have to understand why."

Caravans came from Jackson, Mississippi, from Memphis, Tennessee, from Atlanta, Georgia. Charter buses carried thousands of blacks from all over the South to witness "the one." They would travel, whole families, to Crosley Field in Cincinnati, or Sportsman's Park in St. Louis. They would purchase the souvenir programs and scorecards and eat their home-packed food and marvel at the verve, the skill, the style of the man who broke baseball's color line. In the late innings of some games, buses would begin loading and an announcement would be made directing the fans to hurry back to their buses. Some would tarry a while longer hoping to see Jackie hit one more time, make one more fielding play, steal one more base.

Mal Goode recalls what it was like in Pittsburgh. "At a quarter to eleven on a Sunday morning people were piling off the buses and streetcars. They were coming to Forbes Field for a day game. At eleven A.M., an announcement was made on the loudspeaker. 'We are sold out. There are no more seats.' When Jackie came into Pittsburgh for a night game, traffic started to build at three in the afternoon. At four, it was crowded in the streets. People were parking their cars, getting off the bus. By six-thirty, you could not get into the ballpark. Pittsburgh at that time was a sorry team, but they came to see Jackie Robinson."

It was the same story all over the National League. When the Dodgers played the Cubs at Wrigley Field on the North Side of Chicago, thousands of blacks spilled off the northbound elevated trains and came out of automobiles, five, six, seven, eight in a car. Not many blacks in those days ever congregated in downtown Chicago: fewer still showed up for Cub games at the ballpark on the white side of town. But to see Jackie, they came. By noon, Wrigley Field was swarming with people. Hundreds clustered outside on the street haggling with scalpers for the few remaining tickets. The crowd was a curious collection of whites in casual clothes and blacks in suits—church suits, funeral suits, dress-up suits. They wore freshly starched white shirts and wide, multicolored ties. Many of the blacks had on straw hats, and their shoes glistened with newly applied polish.

They had come to celebrate the man who had broken through.

When the gates to that antique ballpark were closed, more than forty-seven thousand were jammed into a space meant to accommodate ten thousand fewer. They seemed uncomfortable in each other's presence; it was perhaps the first time many of the whites and blacks had been so close together. There was hardly any eye contact between the races. The whites carried themselves with a casual air. The blacks were dignified, proud, almost as if they were attending a huge church meeting.

Robinson came out of the on-deck circle in the first inning. Walking with mincing steps, he entered the batter's box. Long, loud, rhythmic applause filled Wrigley Field, like the kind that occasionally celebrates a great musical performance. Some of the blacks cried openly. Others pounded their hands together, clapping out their pride. Robinson took up his erect stance and Wrigley Field became silent. The Cubs, with Phil Cavaretta, Hank Nicholson, and Andy Pafko, were positioned on the field defending against the Dodger rookie.

Flailing with tremendous force at the first pitch, Robinson was able to get his bat or just a small piece of the ball. The white sphere jumped high in the air and then back into the seats—foul ball. For the thousands there, it might just as well have been a bases-loaded home run. Guttural basses mingled with soprano voices. The din could be heard blocks away. When Robinson struck out, the "ohhhhhhh" seemed to make him move more crisply back to his seat on the bench in the Dodger dugout.

"Why doncha go back and pick some cotton, you nigger," one of the rubes on the Cubs shouted at Robinson. "You're stinkin' up Chicaga." Robinson did not answer. He had heard worse. He was aware of all the blacks in the stands, and he was glad they had not heard the words.

What was said on the field could not be heard in the stands, but what transpired on the diamond was apparent to all. Positioned at first base, Robinson awaited a throw from Reese. The Cub base runner sped down the line. Robinson's foot took up just a small corner of the bag. As the runner approached the bag he made a stabbing move with his leg. The instant Reese's throw smacked into his glove, Robinson jumped aside. He had avoided the spiking, but the hostile act set off loud booing in the stands.

Mike Royko, now a journalist, was one of the many youngsters who attended a Cubs-Dodgers game on May 18. He caught a foul ball hit by Robinson, but he didn't keep it. While examining the major-league ball and looking at the scuff mark, Royko heard a voice behind him say, "Would you consider selling it?"

"I don't want to. I want to keep it," Royko told a middle-aged black man.

"I'll give you ten dollars for it," the man said.

Royko could not believe the amount of money he had been offered. There were men in his neighborhood who earned sixty dollars a week and considered it fine wages.

The amount convinced Royko to make the sale. The black man counted out ten one-dollar bills and handed them one at a time to Royko, who gave him the ball. "Thank you," the black man said, and he cradled the ball tenderly in his large hands.

"Since then," Royko says, "I've regretted a few times that I didn't keep the ball. Or that I hadn't given it to him free. I didn't know then how hard he probably had to work for that ten dollars. If that man is still around, and has the baseball, I'm sure he thinks it was worth every cent."

For those who watched Robinson in action, it was worth every cent they paid.

At times, the style with which he played appeared to be a case of trick photography. He was an illusionist in a baseball uniform, a magician on the base paths. The walking leads, the football-like slides, the change-of-pace runs—all were a part of Robinson's approach to the game.

In Chicago he twice startled even veteran sportswriters with his tactics during his rookie year of 1947. Once, he scored all the way from first base on a sacrifice by Gene Hermanski. Another time, he sent them running to their rule books after executing one of his unpredictable gambits. In the top of the ninth inning against the Cubs, with the score tied 1–1, he worked the count to three and two and then walked. While the Chicago catcher was disputing the base on balls with the umpire, Robinson loped down to first base, touched it, and then dashed to second and slid in safely. A lengthy argument followed, but there was nothing in the rule book against stealing second base on a walk. Robinson moved to third on a sacrifice, and then a sacrifice fly brought him home. His alert steal won the game for the Dodgers.

Even when Robinson was caught off base, he was dangerous. Opposing players used to say that trying to catch him was like trying to bottle mercury. The Philadelphia Phillies got a taste of what it was like in one of Robinson's most dramatic run-down plays at Ebbets Field. Hot-tempered Russ Meyer was the Philadelphia pitcher. He glared at Robinson, a darter, a darer, a dancer, at third base. Meyer threw, and Jackie was seemingly caught flat-footed, leaning toward third base but unable to get back.

It was a simple run-down play that the Phillies had practiced over and over again. Two of them covered third base; three of them protected the plate. Back and forth the white ball was thrown as the black man dodged and wheeled—down toward home plate, back to third. The ball was thrown slowly and deliberately, cutting off the amount of running space. The ball was thrown to the third baseman, Puddinhead Jones, who bobbled it for an instant. An instant was enough. Robinson wheeled and raced for the plate. Jones fired the ball to the catcher, but number 42 had already crossed the plate for another Dodger victory. Meyer swung at Robinson's face with his gloved hand. There was no racial malice in the gesture; he was just a frustrated pitcher who had had a well-pitched game turned into a loss in the most heartbreaking fashion.

"I said a few bad things to Jackie," remembers Meyer, "but I was really angry. The papers the next day showed he was definitely out at home. I was so angry I backed Frank Dascoli, the ump, all the way to the screen at Ebbets Field and got thrown out of the game, fined five hundred dollars, and suspended for a week.

"The next year I was traded from the Phillies to the Dodgers. Jackie was the first guy up in the clubhouse in Vero Beach. He held out his hand in front of everyone and said, 'Russ, we've been fighting one another—let's fight the other teams together now.' "

Robinson's competitive fury was especially spurred when he thought an opponent underestimated him or did not show the proper respect for his talent. At Forbes Field in Pittsburgh, there were about thirty thousand in the stands for a night game. Close to a third of them were black. The score was tied, 2–2, with Robinson on third base. Fritz Ostermueller was the pitcher. Dancing off the base, Robinson ran down the third-base line about ten yards toward home plate, and then ran back to third. "Then he went down about fifteen yards, and when he ran back he slid into the bag and dusted himself off," recalls Mal Goode. "Ostermueller probably said to himself, 'I know that nigger isn't gonna steal home now.' He turned his head and went into the full wind-up position. Jackie broke for home and stole it. The same fans who just a few moments before were screaming, 'Stick it in his ear and knock the black son of a bitch down,' were cheering. When the shouting died down, a guy who was screaming those negative things about Jackie just before turned to his friend and said: 'Goddamn, John, niggers shoulda been in baseball a long time ago.' " Robinson's steal gave the Dodgers a 3–2 victory.

The young Branch Rickey, coach of the Ohio Wesleyan baseball team in 1903.

A classic publicity photo from Jackie Robinson's college days, when he sparked the UCLA football team.

The 1934 Cardinals "The Gashouse Gang." The team that Rickey built included, from left to right, Dizzy Dean, Leo Durocher, Ernie Orsatti, Bill DeLancey, Ripper Collins, Joe Medwick, manager Frankie Frisch, Jack Rockroth, and Pepper Martin.

Jackie Robinson signs a major-league contract, breaking baseball's color bar forever.

Leroy "Satchel" Paige, left, one of the great stars of the Negro Leagues, played with the young Jackie Robinson on the Kansas City Monarchs in 1945.

Jackie Robinson was the center of attention both on and off the field. *Above*, the fans gather around their hero to grab an autograph. *Below*, Jackie Robinson crosses home plate in the classic manner.

A joyful group of Dodgers celebrate clinching a tie for the National League pennant on the last day of the 1951 season in a game won by Robinson's fourteenth-inning homer. In the front row are Rocky Bridges, Jackie Robinson, Pee Wee Reese, Roy Campanella, manager Chuck Dressen, and Carl Erskine.

Above, Branch Rickey in his role as a perpetual Ohio Wesleyan supporter. *Right*, Rickey back in St. Louis where it all began, with his ubiquitous cigar.

Jackie Robinson with his family—David, wife Rachel, Sharon, and Jackie, Jr.

Robinson with civil rights leader Martin Luther King, Jr., as they receive honorary degrees from Howard University.

Jackie Robinson Foundation

The Hall of Fame welcomes two baseball greats. *Above*, Robinson, at his induction with Rickey, Rachel, and Robinson's mother, Mallie. *Left*, Branch Rickey's plaque in Cooperstown, citing his baseball achievements.

"The supreme insult to him was if you were a pitcher and walked a batter to get at him," notes Joe Bostic. "I remember a game at Ebbets Field. Robinson came up after the pitcher had walked a batter intentionally to get at him. The count was two and one. He swung at a letter-high fastball. He swung at it with all the fury and all the venom the years had placed in him. That ball was a line drive that just screamed into the stands—it went in for a home run and it had all his pent-up emotion in it."

Toward the end of the 1947 season, a Jackie Robinson Day was staged at Ebbets Field. Rickey was no longer worried about such celebrations being premature. Robinson was now an assured drawing card, rivaling Bob Feller and Ted Williams in the American League. The black pioneer would push Brooklyn's attendance in 1947 to 1,807,526—the first of ten straight million-plus years for the Robinson-led Dodgers. With the first tumultuous season virtually in the books, Rickey felt secure enough to allow Robinson to receive the official adulation.

"I thank you all," Robinson said over the microphone in his high-pitched voice. He acknowledged the gifts: a brand-new car, a gold pen, a television and radio set, cutlery, silverware, an electric broiler. "I especially thank the members of the Dodgers who were so cooperative and helpful in helping me improve my game."

The great dancer, Bill "Bojangles" Robinson, stood next to the other Robinson, whose dancing feet had helped boost National League attendance to more than ten million in 1947, then the highest in its history. "I am sixty-nine years old," Bill Robinson said, "but I never thought I would live to see the day when I would stand face to face with Ty Cobb in Technicolor."

Jackie's and Rachel's mothers were flown in from California to be at Ebbets Field that day. "The first time my mother met Mr. Rickey," Jackie's sister Willa Mae recalls, "she was thanking him for signing Jack. And he said, 'Don't thank me, Mrs. Robinson. I have to thank you. If it had not been for you, there wouldn't be any Jackie.' " A small, stooped woman, Mallie Robinson stood near home plate and thrilled to the cheers for her son. "That was one of the most touching moments in Jack's career," recalls brother Mack, "to see Mother right there in the middle of the ceremony and all the accolades."

Playing in more games than any other Dodger in 1947, Robinson scored more runs than any other teammate, stole more bases than any other player in the National League, and wound up with a batting average of .297. *The Sporting News*, once doubtful of his ability, designated him Rookie of the Year. "He was rated solely as a freshman player in the big leagues," the baseball newspaper said, "on the basis of his hitting, his running, his defensive play, his team value." It was an extraordinary season for a man playing under unimaginable pressure.

The Dodgers won the pennant that year. It was the fifth time in six years that a team built by Branch Rickey had captured the National League flag.

"It occurred to Mr. Rickey," Dodson recalls, "that with the winning of the pennant, some of the Brooklyn black community leaders might have difficulty obtaining tickets to the World Series. Mr. Rickey inquired of his ticket manager if many blacks would be coming to the Series. 'Not many, Mr. Rickey,' the ticket manager responded. 'I've done a pretty good job on that.' It was a case where the policy on the top was not understood by those underneath. Mr. Rickey had to get the tickets personally and give them to the black leaders."

On September 30, 1947, the Yankees squared off against the Dodgers. It was the first World Series a black man ever played in. "That first game got to me," recalls Mack Robinson. "I was pulling and groaning and stretching and grunting for every step or slide or swing. I was playing it all right with Jack."

In the first game, Robinson flashed the razzle-dazzle style that had boggled National League pitchers all season. He walked in the first inning, and then stole second. He walked again in the third inning. This time, his dancing moves off first base so unnerved Yankee pitcher Spec Shea that he balked Robinson to second base.

Robinson's seven hits tied him with Reese for the club leadership in the Series. He also played errorless ball in the field and stole two bases. At bat, his performance overall was disappointing. He hit only .259. "We knew how to pitch to him," recalls Bill Bevens, who was one out away from the first no-hitter in World Series history in the third game, when Cookie Lavagetto doubled in two runs to win the game for the Dodgers. "We figured he had been a football player and his shoulders didn't get around that good. We didn't have any trouble with him. Later on he learned how to hit those pitches."

"We won that Series," notes Yogi Berra, "but we knew that with Robinson in Brooklyn, we'd be facing the Dodgers lots of times in the future."

THE MAHATMA

IN CHARGE

The 1947 World Series was the last hurrah for one of baseball's most colorful characters. Larry MacPhail, whose baseball roots went back to the St. Louis Cardinals' Columbus farm team, resigned from the Yankees and baseball in his greatest moment of glory. Exultant in victory, the redheaded Yankee president forgot his differences with his former boss over breaking baseball's color line. MacPhail approached Rickey with a conciliatory gesture "for old times' sake." Rickey rebuffed him. "I will be civil because people are watching," he said, "but I don't want you to ever speak to me again."

The extent of Rickey's enmity to MacPhail went beyond the Dodson's Committee on Unity and their differences on race relations. Rickey held MacPhail personally responsible for ruining Pete Reiser. During a Cardinal-Dodger game in 1942, the irrepressible Reiser crashed head first into a concrete wall attempting to make a catch. Cardinal doctors examined Reiser and advised rest. MacPhail thought the advice was a plot to keep the hard-hitting outfielder out of the Dodger lineup. He rushed Reiser back into service too soon. There was more damage; there were more rips and tears on the Reiser body. "Pistol Pete" went into the armed forces, and when he returned he was never the same. Rickey maintained that when he originally sent Reiser to MacPhail back in 1938, when he was to be submerged in the minors, he had entrusted MacPhail with a rare talent. MacPhail's negligence had ruined him. To Rickey, this was unforgivable.

In a speech at Wilberforce University in 1948, Rickey revealed another reason for his anger toward MacPhail. He charged that early in 1946, club owners voted 15–1 against admitting Negroes into major-league baseball "just yet." MacPhail was chairman of the policy committee that engineered the vote. The report in which the vote was contained was never published. MacPhail denied any anti-black commentary was included in the report; Rickey asserted it was. Indeed, he maintained that MacPhail made a speech accusing him of ruining baseball. MacPhail said there were enough blacks coming to see games, and if more came whites would stay away, creating a disaster for organized baseball. "Mr. Rickey, at first, wanted to answer MacPhail," Professor Dodson remembers, "but he later told me it was all water under the bridge and they can't pour it back."

One day after the 1947 World Series, MacPhail sold his interest in the Yankees to Del Webb and Dan Topping. Baseball was to hear from him no more. But Rickey pressed on.

Toward the end of the 1947 season, as the Dodgers surged for the pennant, Dixie Walker said, "No other player on this club with the possible exception of Bruce Walker has done more to put the Dodgers up in the race than Robinson has. He is everything Branch Rickey said he was when he came up from Montreal." Apologetic, Walker went to Rickey and told him that he no longer wished to be traded from the Dodgers. It was too late. In one of the best trades the master trader ever made, Walker was sent to Pittsburgh along with pitcher Hal Gregg for left-hander Preacher Roe and third baseman Billy Cox.

Elwin Charles Roe had won just four of nineteen decisions for the Pirates in 1947. Over the next six years as a member of the Dodgers Roe won ninety games and lost just thirty-three. Cox played third base for the Dodgers from 1948 to 1954. A skinny, sad-looking man, "he looked like a plucked chicken when he stripped down," recalls former Brooklyn Dodger publicist Irving Rudd. "It amazed everyone that he could find all that power to put on his throws when he went into the hole." Cox was perhaps the best-fielding third baseman of his time and an important ingredient in the winning ways of the Dodgers.

Throughout the 1947 season, Rickey insisted that Robinson be evaluated simply on his merits as a ballplayer. Hungry for data, for quotes, for new insights, reporters trailed after Robinson and his wife and child. "The way things are now," Rickey snapped at a press conference, "Robinson is a sideshow. Give him a chance. If I had my way about it, I would place a cordon of police protection around him so that he could be a ballplayer." "Mr. Rickey was paternal without being paternalistic," Rachel Robinson remembers.

The Dodgers received a tremendous amount of mail. Each one of the letters regarding Robinson was answered. There were many that were vile, disgusting tirades against Rickey and Robinson. These were answered in polite but firm language. Those who wrote negative letters and those who sent complimentary ones were all thanked for taking the time to write.

Hundreds of organizations clamored for a piece of Jackie Robinson, who was voted runner-up to Bing Crosby as the most popular man in America. There were more than five thousand social and commercial requests for personal appearances. Other groups beseeched Rickey to allow Robinson to work with them to help eliminate racial prejudice. Rickey's answer to all these requests was always a firm no. He was determined that the "noble experiment" not be commercialized, politicized, or overdramatized.

There was one instance when Rickey lifted his ban on personal appearances. A twelve-year-old boy named Eddie Hamlin had mistakenly tossed gasoline on a bonfire at a skating rink and was burned severely from head to foot. The boy came from a poor family who was unable to meet hospital expenses. The boy's idol was Jackie Robinson. Hospital authorities contacted the Dodgers. The youth, struggling to survive, would, they hoped, receive inspiration from a visit by the player he idolized.

Robinson came to the hospital and met with Eddie and gave him an autographed baseball and a pep talk. The visit was kept secret from the press; most of the hospital staff was not even aware of it. A few months after the visit, Eddie Hamlin was discharged from the hospital and headed toward complete recovery. The story of Jackie's visit to a burned boy would have made excellent news copy. But Rickey stood firm. "Judgment of Robinson was to be made by what he did on the baseball diamond and in no other way."

There was another hospital visit that could have produced much favorable publicity for Rickey and Durocher, but again the former Ohio schoolteacher felt the deed should be its own reward.

After the war ended, there were many veterans suffering from tuberculosis who were lodged in hospitals and rest homes. At that time, tuberculosis generally required removal to a sanitorium for rest. Publicist Irving Rudd used to invite sports people to visit the veterans to boost morale. Rudd asked Branch Rickey and Leo Durocher to accompany him to a hospital in Castle Point, near Beacon, New York. "They both agreed," Rudd recalls, "but they both insisted there be no press, no publicity. Leo was under suspension or had just come off it. He could have used some good press, but he insisted he wouldn't go if there was any press. The normal way we went on those visits was by station wagon. Rickey told me to meet him at Two fifteen Montague Street. We went up by chauffeured limousine. Nobody got paid a dime. I used to do it, and the other sports people did it because they cared.

"There were a couple of hundred men in a plain big room, no fancy auditorium with spotlights. Rickey began his talk in his gravelly voice. 'You know, men, I am one of you.' And then he went into a long story about being struck down with tuberculosis. He told the whole story, his primitive treatment, his long convalescence. He really related to them. 'I was there,' he barked. 'You men have to follow the instructions of your doctors and nurses.' Geez, it was a hushed time, this gravelly, big-browed guy talking to these guys in their own language. In those days tuberculosis was a rough thing, but he was giving them hope, a lot of hope. And he stunned everybody in the room, for it was the first time we had known about him and TB. He and Durocher were there for about three hours, and the evening ended with all of them talking baseball and giving out autographs."

There were those who called him a man of conscience; others called him a charlatan. Rickey took the characterizations in his stride and kept on building. On March 6, 1948, he traded Eddie Stanky to the Boston Braves, clearing the way for Robinson to take over at second base. Pee Wee Reese always joked that during all the time he was with Brooklyn he never purchased a house. "I was afraid with Mr. Rickey around I would be traded." On May 16, 1949, Bob Ramazzotti, "the new Pee Wee Reese," was traded to the Cubs for $25,000 and Henry Schenz.

Rickey signed Sam Jethroe, who had tried out with Robinson at the Fenway Park charade. Installed at Montreal, he stole eighty-nine bases in 1949. But in 1950 Rickey sold Jethroe to the Boston Braves for $100,000. "It was the first time in my life where I sold a man who may be better than what I have," the busy trader said. "I may have impoverished myself. But it seemed to me the move was necessary. I could not satisfy myself that, good as he is, he would make the ball club more likely to win another pennant. And by selling Jethroe to the Braves, I brought another Negro into the major-league baseball field." Jethroe came up to the majors as a twenty-eight-year-old rookie and lasted but four seasons.

Breaking baseball's color line enabled Branch Rickey to tap into a gold mine, but he elected not to monopolize the rich lode of talent in the Negro Leagues. Four players he did sign who became rookies of the year were Jackie Robinson (1947), Don Newcombe (1949), Joe Black (1952), and Junior Gilliam (1953). But there were others he passed up.

Monte Irvin could have been a Brooklyn Dodger. Larry Doby could have been a Brooklyn Dodger. Sam Jethroe could have been a Brooklyn Dodger. "Mr. Rickey wanted to spread the black players around," Mal Goode believes. "He saw his job to convince the other owners to integrate baseball. It took a long, long time." Installed as a special-assignment Dodger scout after the 1946 season to recommend other black prospects, Roy Campanella touted Irvin and Doby. "The Cleveland Indians are interested in Doby," Campanella remembers Rickey's explaining. "It is my fervent hope that every club in baseball sign a colored player." Cleveland signed Doby, who became the first black player in the American League.

Irvin was signed by Fresco Thompson of the Dodgers in the winter of 1946 in Puerto Rico. Mrs. Manley, owner of the Newark Eagles, Irvin's team, threatened legal action unless Rickey paid $5,000 for Irvin. It was a nominal price for the talented ballplayer, but "rather than get into any kind of hassle," recalls Irvin, "Mr. Rickey contacted Horace Stoneham and recommended that he sign me." And that was how Monte Irvin became a New York Giant.

"Mr. Rickey was basically a Christian man," notes

Goode. "And he firmly believed the treatment of the black man was a blot on the history of America. We'd talk and walk about his lawn, and he'd wear that little straw hat of his. 'I can't do something about racial bigotry in every field,' he told me, 'but I can certainly do something about it in the field of baseball.' "

There were times when even Rickey's reserve broke. One day in early spring he called Dr. Dodson. " 'I sometimes wish I had never gotten into this business of attempting to break the color line in baseball,' " he told Dodson, " 'but I wonder if you and Dr. [John] Johnson of the Unity Committee can spare a day and fly down with me to Newport News to meet Jackie and Rachel."

"When Mr. Rickey got aboard the plane he told me he had sent a contract to Jackie with the figure Jackie had earned the year before as a starting point," recalls Dodson. " 'Jackie snorted,' Mr. Rickey explained. 'He sent it back unsigned with some very unkind words. He's carried away by all the publicity and does not have his mind on baseball. He's been wined and dined across the country as a great hero. He's made the lard circuit. Because he's come into baseball late, Jackie wants to make his million quick because his playing years are short. I told him that he could make his million in three or four years if he concentrated on baseball and that he would also be a contributor to race relations, but the way he's doing it, it spelled disaster.

" 'He's tremendously overweight and involved in too many things to be totally concerned with baseball. I gave him the initial figure as a basis to start negotiations as I had always done with other players, but he has me over a barrel. The publicity and position he has make it possible for him to demand almost any salary he desires, but I don't expect to be exploited in any way. I want you to meet with Jackie and Rachel.' "

Dodson and Johnson obliged Rickey. "Jackie and Rachel were upset to begin at a salary in the second year that Jackie had ended with in the first year, but when we explained that it was just a starting point they were quite willing to sit down with Mr. Rickey. They all came to agreement that afternoon on the salary, but the problem as Mr. Rickey had suspected was far from solved. Jackie was some forty pounds overweight and terribly out of shape. One member of the Dodger organization said Jackie was 'nigger rich'— that he could not stand prosperity."

The Dodgers held spring training in Santo Domingo in the Dominican Republic in 1948, largely because Rickey had received a $50,000 guarantee from President Trujillo. Now reinstalled as Dodger manager, Leo Durocher came face to face with, in his phrase, "a fat-assed Robinson who looked like a blimp."

Robinson had lost some of the weight after the Dodson-Johnson meeting, but was still twenty-five pounds overweight. Durocher thought Robinson had sabotaged him. As Rickey once said of Durocher, "Leo is far from perfect. His judgment in handling different personalities is his biggest weakness." "The Lip" treated Robinson like a rookie, pushing him through punishing drills and exercises, ridiculing him in front of the press. Those long hot days in the Dominican Republic planted the seeds for enduring animosity between the two strong-willed men.

The 1948 season began badly for the Dodgers. Robinson was still shedding pounds, still fighting to get into shape. Campanella, the heir apparent at catcher, had been sent down to break the color line at St. Paul in the American Association. Bruce Edwards, the incumbent catcher, was hampered by a sore arm. Pressure grew to replace Durocher. The Dodgers lost one game 13–12, and Durocher was ejected from the contest. The ejection further strained relations between Durocher and Rickey, and between Durocher and Robinson.

Actress Laraine Day remembered the beginning of the end for her husband Durocher as Dodger manager. "I've just had a call from Rickey," said Leo. "He wants me to resign. I won't resign. He'll have to fire me."

Always unpredictable, Durocher goaded the Dodgers. Campanella was brought up from St. Paul. The club became more cohesive and started to win. "Now we'll see about re-signing," crowed Durocher.

While Durocher never did resign, Rickey made his "availability" known to New York Giant owner Horace Stoneham. On July 16, 1948, Durocher crossed town to become the manager of the "Jints"—the Dodgers' archrivals. It was one of many paradoxical personnel shifts the master trader had orchestrated during his long career. In another odd move in 1948, Rickey, who was impressed by an announcer broadcasting an Atlanta Crackers game, traded Cliff Dapper, a catcher on the Montreal Royals, to Atlanta. Dapper became the Atlanta manager, and the announcer, Ernie Harwell, joined the Dodgers.

Burt Shotton came back to manage the Dodgers, and Robinson, who had been below par with Durocher as manager, began to round into form. "It may have seemed to Leo," Robinson reflected later, "that I was goofing off for him and giving all I had for Shotton." The return to his 1947 playing form was actually due to Robinson's return to his previous season's playing weight, but Durocher bore a grudge.

The fierce Robinson and the fiery Durocher became the flash points in the frenzied rivalry between the Dodgers and Giants and their supporters. "They used to really go at it hot and heavy," remembers Irvin. "Durocher used to put his hands on the side of his head and yell out that Jackie was big-headed, swell-headed.

"One time Jackie went too far in answering back as far as Leo was concerned. 'I may be swell-headed, Leo, but at least I don't use my wife's perfume,' Jackie yelled." It was a not-too-subtle reference to Durocher's lavish use of sweet-smelling cologne.

"They both wanted to go at it. Leo saw red. Jackie saw red. They were both being restrained by their teams. They wanted to fight and fight right then. After that incident, there was a real, deep feud between them," notes Irvin.

The 1948 Dodgers finished in third place. Robinson's staggering start had been too much of a handicap. Rickey was able to take satisfaction in the pennant Clay Hopper won at Montreal, and the St. Paul pennant captured by Walt Alston. The two wholly owned Dodger minor-league affiliates met in the playoffs. It was only the second time in baseball history that such a match-up took place. Montreal, powered by Don Newcombe, was the victor. Bobby Bragan, another Rickey reclamation project, piloted Fort Worth all the way to the Little World Series but lost to Birmingham. A third Triple-A minor-league franchise was established in Hollywood with Bob Cobb, owner of the Brown Derby restaurant chain, and Vic Collins. In 1949, Hollywood, with its new working agreement with the Dodgers, won its first Pacific Coast League pennant since 1931.

Robinson finished the 1948 season with a .296 batting average and eighty-five RBIs. Seven times he was hit by pitches to lead the league. Once he was thrown out of a game. With Robinson and Campanella entrenched in the Dodger lineup, and with Newcombe poised to join them, those same club owners who had called Rickey complaining, "You're gonna kill baseball bringing that nigger in now," were now calling to ask, "Branch, do you know where I can get a couple of colored boys like Jackie and Campy and Newk?"

CHANGING ROLES

In 1949, in his third year with the Dodgers, Jackie Robinson the black pioneer became Jackie Robinson the ballplayer. No longer the lone black face on the baseball diamond, Robinson could at last show his superlative skills without the constant pressure of representing an entire race. The wraps came off, and he made use of every skill he possessed to let the flash and fire come through.

Branch Rickey knew how important it had been for Robinson to bank the competitive fires inside him. More than anyone else, Rickey knew how much Robinson had taken in his first two years. The time had come to let Jackie loose from the restraints Rickey had imposed on him. As Rickey later observed, "I realized the point would come when my almost filial relationship with Jackie would break with ill feeling if I did not issue an emancipation proclamation for him. I could see how the tensions had built up in him in two years, and that this young man had come through with courage far beyond what I had asked; yet, I knew that burning inside him was the same pride and determination that burned inside those Negro slaves a century earlier.

"I knew also that while the wisest policy for Robinson during those first two years was to turn the other cheek and not fight back, there were many in baseball who would not understand his lack of action. They could be made to respect only the fighting back, the things that are the signs of courage to men who know courage only in its physical sense. So I told Robinson that he was on his own. Then I sat back happily, knowing that, with the restraints removed, Robinson was going to show the National League a thing or two."

"There was always an understanding that the two of them had," notes Rachel Robinson. "Jack would go along with the program for a limited time. As he began to feel more and more in control of the situation, as he proved himself as a ballplayer, he knew it was time to be himself. It was hard for a man as assertive as Jack to contain his own rage, yet he felt that the end goal was so critical that there was no question that he would do it. And he knew he could do it even better if he could ventilate, express himself, use his own style."

In spring training in 1949, Robinson reported in excellent shape, primed for the new season. He had learned a lesson in 1948 about watching his weight and keeping in condition during the off-season. "They'd better be rough on me this year," he told a reporter, "because I'm sure going to be rough on them." The statement accentuated Robinson's new verbal ferocity and resulted in his being called in by Commissioner Ford Frick. A bit miffed because he did not feel a white player would have been singled out for the same statement, Robinson explained to Frick that he was no longer going to turn the other cheek, that if insults and threats were hurled at him, he was ready to give them back.

His new aggressiveness first surfaced in an incident with Dodger rookie pitcher Chris Van Cuyk. The six-foot, five-inch two hundred-pound hurler threw several fastballs at Robinson's head during an intra-squad game. The two shouted at each other, and nearly came to blows. Fortunately, other players got between them and calmed things down. The two incidents were signals, though, that number 42 was now finished with the "turn the other cheek" attitude that he had faithfully labored under for his first two seasons.

Now secure that his "experiment" had succeeded and that blacks were an accepted fact of baseball life, Rickey scheduled a three-game exhibition series against the Atlanta Crackers despite threats of racial violence. Dr. Samuel Green, grand dragon of the Ku Klux Klan, maintained that it was illegal for interracial baseball to be played in Georgia.

Rickey, who had avoided confrontations before, was furious and adamant. "The games will go on," he told reporters. "They have been scheduled, and the Dodgers will play!" Nearly 50,000 came out to see the three games. When Robinson came to bat in the first game, it was the first time that a black man had batted against the Atlanta Crackers. Most of the 15,119 fans, black and white, stood up and cheered. In the Sunday game, nearly 14,000 blacks came to the park. They overflowed the segregated section of the stands and stood a dozen deep in the outfield. There were no incidents. Robinson, who had not known what to expect, and had worried about snipers in the stands, was relieved. He was delighted to have played in an integrated contest in the state of his birth. "I wouldn't trade shoes with any man in the world," he said after the series ended. "I always had the feeling that a sports fan is a sports fan anyplace in America."

Now unburdened, Robinson's many talents unfurled day after day. Beginning a string of six straight .300 seasons, Robinson led the league in batting (.342) and stolen bases (37). He was second in RBIs (124) and hits (203). He was third in slugging percentage (.528), runs scored (122), and triples (12). He was fourth in doubles (38) and fifth in total bases (313). He also pounded 16 home runs and led all second basemen in double plays. At the end of the season he was named the National League's Most Valuable Player.

George Sisler, Rickey's old University of Michigan protégé, was the man the Mahatma picked to tutor Robinson.
Robinson gave him credit for his improved play in 1949.
"First he taught me to hit to right field instead of pulling
everything," said Robinson, "and then he taught me to play
the ball as it was hit."

Sisler's direction polished Robinson's hitting and fielding.
Other skills were innate. As a runner, he had an explosively
quick start, acceleration bred into his muscular body from
his days as a track star. He was able to move from a standing
position and by his second or third step streak ahead in full
flashing stride. He had an inborn ability to study a pitcher's
movement and spot a weakness or flaw. He had the ability to
run full speed to the next base and look back without losing
speed. He was a clever and calculating slider, adept at leaning or positioning his body to avoid the infielder's tag.

"Robinson was the only player I ever saw who could
completely turn a game around by himself," remembers Hall
of Famer Ralph Kiner. "His ability to run the bases, to in-
timidate the pitchers, to take the extra base, to hang in there
under the worst kind of pressure made him antagonize the
opposition to the benefit of his own team."

Some of his opponents began to feel anger, envy, and
frustration. In one game where the Dodgers were leading
the Phillies by a big score, Robinson came to bat. "Stick one
in his ear," screamed Schoolboy Rowe from the Philadelphia
dugout.

"That's a fine thing to say with the score the way it is,"
Robinson snapped at the Philadelphia catcher. At the end of
the inning, the catcher reported what Robinson had said to
Rowe.

"If he has anything to say," barked Rowe, "tell him to say
it to my face."

The next time Robinson came to bat, he turned full face
to the Phillie dugout. His loud, shrill voice repeated the
earlier remark. Rowe charged out of the dugout toward

Robinson. Players from both teams raced out and stepped between the two angry men. It was just one incident in a ten-year career, but it illustrated, in Stan Lomax's phrase, "Robinson's ability to get under the skin of the opposition, to make them chafe and become unsettled."

In July of 1949, Jackie Robinson became an internationally known figure; his name and his picture were featured in newspapers all over the world. He had become an adversary of Paul Robeson.

Robeson had issued a statement that, speaking as a black man, he knew that American Negroes would not fight on the side of the United States in a war against the Soviet Union. The statement was made in the climate of strained Cold War relations between America and the USSR.

Growing up in Princeton, New Jersey, Robeson recalled how whites pushed blacks off the sidewalk. Later, as captain of the Rutgers football team, he was subjected to the humiliation of having to sit on the bench when his college played southern teams. A Phi Beta Kappa law student, he ran into discrimination when he sought employment with white firms. He became a noted singer and again found that he was discriminated against and forced to stay in segregated housing while on road tours. In 1931, Robeson left the United States and settled in England and later moved to the Soviet Union to educate his son. He became a controversial fighter for civil rights and a staunch supporter of what he believed was the "freedom and dignity of the Communist cause."

Congressman John S. Wood of Georgia sent out invitations to prominent blacks requesting that they testify before the House Un-American Activities Committee to "give the lie to statements by Paul Robeson." Robinson was one of those who received an invitation.

Ironically, it was Robeson who had met with Commissioner Landis back in 1943 requesting that blacks be permitted to play major-league baseball. And it was Robeson who had carried a placard as a member of the "End Jim Crow in Baseball" committee in 1945 and picketed the New York Yankees' season opener. Robinson's decision to testify was made with a certain amount of ambivalence, but he finally felt certain that what Robeson had said demanded a response.

Robinson's speech to the House Un-American Activities Committee was made on July 18, 1949. It hit hard at the point that one black person speaking in Paris did not speak for an entire race. Robinson concluded his speech with these words:

"I can't speak for any fifteen million people any more than any other person can, but I know that I've got too much invested for my wife and child and myself in the future of this country, and I and other Americans of many races and faiths have too much invested in our country's welfare, for any of us to throw it away because of a siren song sung in bass.

"I am a religious man. Therefore I cherish America, where I am free to worship as I please, a privilege which some countries do not give. And I suspect that nine hundred and ninety-nine out of almost any thousand colored Americans you meet will tell you the same thing.

"But that doesn't mean that we're going to stop fighting race discrimination in this country until we've got it licked. It means that we're going to fight it all the harder because our stake in the future is so big. We can win our fight without the Communists, and we don't want their help."

Robinson's speech drew unanimous raves. Newspaper headlines proclaimed: "An American Speaks" . . . "Negro Loyalty" . . . "True Hero" . . . "Jackie Bats .1000 in Probe of Reds" . . . "The Right Slant" . . . "World Proud of Robinson" . . . "VFW Cites Robinson."

A *New York Daily News* editorial on July 20, 1949, entitled "Quite a Man, This Robinson," was typical of the favorable press reaction: "We imagine Monday, July 18,

1949, will go down in Jackie Robinson's memory book, if he keeps such a thing, as a red letter day. Mr. Robinson is the far-famed Negro second baseman of the Brooklyn Dodgers ball team. On this particular Monday, he went to Washington. . . . More than likely there was some press agentry involved, but for all that Mr. Robinson made a powerful and moving statement of his views."

"Mr. Rickey was consulted by Jackie," recalls Dan Dodson, "for help with his speech. . . . Mr. Rickey gave Jackie a speech draft which was very rough and contained words in it like 'a person could not be horse-whipped.' I tried to change the pattern of it to use a slightly different approach. Then Mr. Rickey suggested that another black would be most helpful for what Jackie had to say. Jackie got his own counsel from Lester Granger of the Urban League and others. The speech he finally came up with did not include any of the material I or Mr. Rickey had presented. It turned out to be a better statement than ours."

Years later, in 1960, however, Robinson saw the Robeson controversy differently. "I have grown wiser and closer to painful truths about America's destructiveness," he said. "I do have an increased respect for Paul Robeson. In those days I had much more faith in the ultimate justice of the American white man than I have today. I would reject such an invitation [to testify before the House Un-American Activities Committee] if offered now."

But in 1949 Jackie Robinson was the pioneer, the star of stars. With each season that passed, the grandson of a slave became one of the most famous men in America. His voice, his walk, his batting stance, his name, and what he represented were part of American history's messenger and the future's legacy. Gradually, he seized the opportunities to capitalize on his fame.

Robinson's first-year salary with the Dodgers was $5,000, raised to $12,500 in 1948. In 1950, he was paid

$35,000—the top salary to that point in Dodger history. In those early years you could purchase a television set from Jackie Robinson in Rego Park, Queens. He worked during the off-season for salary and commission three nights a week at the Sunset Appliance Store. It was reported that the Robinsons owned a sixteen-inch television, and that three-year-old Jackie Jr.'s favorite programs starred Howdy Doody, Mr. I. Magination, and Farmer Gray.

Robinson tried a stint as a sports commentator for radio station WMCA in New York City, and opened the Jackie Robinson Department Store at 111 West 125th Street in Harlem. It was an outlet for "good-quality clothes with Jackie's name on the label," notes Irving Rudd.

There were commercial tie-ins, with Jackie Robinson jackets that sold for $6.95 and caps that cost 98¢. One could also buy Jackie Robinson polo shirts, sports shirts, and tee-shirts. He endorsed Borden's Evaporated Milk and Bond Bread. A black trailblazer on the playing field, he was also the first black sports star to be conspicuously featured in the consumer marketplace.

After Robinson's glorious 1949 season, screenwriter Lawrence Taylor wrote a movie script for *The Jackie Robinson Story*. It was rejected by several studios. No one was willing to take a chance on a film with a black hero. Eagle-Lion finally picked up the project and sent a copy of the script to Branch Rickey. He pledged cooperation if the script were revised to include more of the hardships that Jackie had endured.

Everyone agreed that no one could play the role of Jackie Robinson as well as Robinson himself. Three weeks of production time were alloted for the low-budget film. Near the end of the production schedule, they shot day and night. "The way they had me running bases," Robinson recalled, "I never had any spring training in which I worked any harder." Rickey was cooperative but adamant that his star ballplayer not miss a single minute of spring training.

On May 17, 1950, *The Jackie Robinson Story* premiered at the Astor Theater in Manhattan. Nine days before, the cover of *Life* magazine had a picture of Jackie Robinson under the headline: "Star Ballplayer Stars in a Movie." Minor Watson had the Branch Rickey role. Ruby Dee played Rachel. Jackie received $50,000 plus a share of the film's profits; 5 percent of the movie's profits went to the National League players' fund.

Rickey was Robinson's mentor and confidant through these years, buttressing Robinson in his moments of doubt, shielding him from opportunists and critics whenever possible, counseling him with wisdom gained from his long years of experience with all types of men. "We could always call Mr. Rickey on the phone; he was always available to us," said Rachel. "It wasn't as if he had just thrust Jack into a situation and left him to fend for himself. He took responsibility."

Perhaps the bond of breaking baseball's color line made their relationship something special. But it was Rickey's style to watch over all his players. Back then the relationship of the player to the team and the team to the player involved closeness and loyalty. Executives like Rickey considered it their responsibility to involve themselves in many aspects of their players' lives. "Imbued as I am with the virtues of connubial bliss," he once said, "I naturally take pleasure in seeing happily married ballplayers." He not only took pleasure in seeing his players happily married, but he did all he could to lead them to the altar.

Rickey was always concerned with what his players did when they were not on the ballfield. This sometimes became a problem in the off-season, when he insisted on keeping tabs on their whereabouts. Irving Rudd recalls an encounter involving Rickey and one of his players.

"After Don Newcombe won the 1949 Rookie of the Year award, the Buddy Lee Clothing Store in Brooklyn hired him as a greeter. His duties were to shake hands with everyone who came into the store and then suggest that they purchase a half-dozen suits, or some other items of the store's ample stock. I was hired to publicize the fact that Newk was working there weekends. I did this for about two or three weeks," recalls Rudd.

"Newk came up with the nickname 'Meat' for me. I never knew why. After my third week of working with him he said, 'Hey, Meat, how'd you like to be my manager? I'll give you ten percent.'

"I wondered about it," continues Rudd. "I thought, ten percent of what? Black guys and gals weren't even on television much back then. He was the hottest rookie around, but he wasn't in great demand. He really wanted me as a screener to fend off characters and maybe get him a few bucks for a speaking engagement here or there. Fifty bucks back then was a big touch, a good touch. Today, even a guy batting one forty-six wants five hundred dollars for an appearance.

"I got Newk some endorsements—Jeris hair tonic, Champ hats, some black insurance company—about ten thousand dollars' worth of endorsements, which was staggering back then, and then I was approached to book him into a series of exhibition matches as a wrestling referee. We were going to travel about the country. I had to meet with Rickey to get his approval.

"I went down to Montague Street, and Rickey was sitting behind that desk, all big, bushy eyebrows, brandishing his cigar.

" 'All right, Irving,' he said in that great cavernous, oratorical voice. 'I trust you. You're a clean young man. I know your reputation.'

"He was going on. Sometimes I thought if you asked him what time it was, he would tell you how to make a watch.

" 'Go now,' he said, 'with Mr. Newcombe, and sin no

more. But remember, I reserve the right momentarily to cancel this tour at any time if I feel it is getting out of hand or not projecting the proper image for myself, for Mr. Newcombe, or for the Brooklyn Dodgers.' "

Rudd left and worked out the details for creating the proper image for his new project. A warm-up jacket was purchased, and across its front were the words: "Don Newcombe, Referee." The huge Dodger right-hander was then supplied with some basic instructions in the art of being a wrestling official. "We trained him," recalls Rudd, "always to stay near the head of the guy at the bottom—that was the safest spot in the ring. He was a valuable property, and we were concerned about his getting hurt."

The tour proceeded in a crazy-quilt pattern, moving from city to city. In Washington, as the small, slight Rudd and the tall, broad Newcombe were preparing to leave and go by sleeper to North Adams, Massachusetts, a reporter asked Newcombe, "Don, don't you think you're worth more money than the Dodgers are paying you?"

"I don't think nothin' " is the phrase Rudd recalls Newcombe used in response. "He was a very polite guy," adds Rudd. "We arrived in the sleeper at Grand Central Station in New York City and were out in the street hopping into a cab to go to Penn Station to catch the train to North Adams. Newk had grabbed a newspaper just before we got into the cab.

" 'Well, Meat,' he said to me, 'I don't think this tour of ours is going to last very much longer.'

"What's the matter?" Rudd asked. Newcombe handed the newspaper to the surprised Rudd. There was a picture of the Dodger hurler in his pitching pose under the headline "Won't Pitch, Unless I Get Twenty G's—Says Newk." He had been misquoted. The headline was pure fiction.

Arriving at their hotel in North Adams and entering their room, the duo had barely settled down when their telephone rang.

"Irving, Harold Parrot," Rudd recalls the ominous voice of an aide on the other end of the phone. "Mr. Rickey would like to speak to you."

"Hello, Irving," Rickey said. "You do recall what I told you when we sat in my office at Two fifteen Montague Street."

"And then," Rudd recalls, "it was blah, blah, and blah, blah, and blah, blah and 'Irving, you have to call the tour back now!'

"Mr. Rickey," said the struggling Rudd, "I presume that you are calling me because of the newspaper story this morning. Newk never said that . . ."

"The tour," Rickey interjected, "must be ended!"

"But . . ."

"It cannot go on any further."

"But . . . but . . ."

At this point Newcombe, who began his career in 1944 as a seventeen-year-old with the Newark Eagles and claimed that major-league baseball didn't interest him until Jackie Robinson came along, grabbed the telephone.

"Meat," Newcombe told Rudd, "don't argue with the man. Yeah, Mr. Rickey. Yeah, Mr. Rickey. Yeah, Mr. Rickey. We'll take the train right home today, Mr. Rickey."

With Newcombe, with Robinson, with the other players on the Brooklyn Dodgers, Rickey's mandates were followed. His age, his experience, his reputation earned him influence, power, and respect among the players. He was the boss. Beyond Rickey's powerful personality was the strength of his position as general manager. In those days players either obeyed general managers or found themselves playing ball for other teams—or playing not at all. Newk had no alternative but to yield to Rickey. Yet for all his power over the players, in the corporate in-fighting for control of the Dodgers, Rickey remained the abstemious midwesterner, the outsider, the loner.

In mid-July of 1950, John L. Smith, vice-president and

part owner of the Dodgers, died. His death created a bitter power struggle between Branch Rickey and Walter O'Malley. Smith's widow and the Brooklyn Trust Company became co-executors of the $4-million estate. Control of Mrs. Smith's stock passed to the Brooklyn Trust. O'Malley, firmly entrenched in the Irish Catholic Brooklyn political power bloc that had influence in utilities, insurance companies, and banking, was now able to control two of the three votes on the Dodgers.

Youthful, ambitious, O'Malley is remembered by Irving Rudd as "a great guy—avuncular, cheerful, courteous, but no bucks. No self-respecting Jewish kid should ever work for someone like that. . . . It was Brooklyn Union Gas Company, no-bucks wages."

With O'Malley in control, Rickey was in a difficult position. Mired in a tough pennant race, he was frustrated by a shortage of pitching. His plan to buy St. Louis southpaw Howie Pollet, a twenty-game winner in 1949, for $600,000 had been spurned by the Cardinals. Rickey was in debt to bankers for his share of the Dodgers, and his five-year contract was about to expire with no indication that it would be renewed. "I have tried repeatedly," Rickey told members of the Dodgers board of directors, "and without success to have my contract introduced and considered by the bank."

The harried executive, realizing his efforts to renegotiate his contract were futile, proceeded to arrange for the sale of his Dodger stock. An ownership clause gave him the option to sell his stock back to the other shareholders at cost. However, he had no intention of exercising this option, since Dodger stock had tripled in value during his tenure. He reached out, as he had so many times in the past, to his network of friends. John K. Galbreath, an Ohio Wesleyan fraternity brother and president of the Pittsburgh Pirates, arranged a meeting between Rickey and William Zeckendorf, a New York City real-estate tycoon.

An agreement was reached. Zeckendorf pledged himself

to purchase Rickey's stock for $1 million. The offer was good for ninety days. "If your partners meet the offer," Zeckendorf informed Rickey, "you will have to pay me fifty thousand dollars for tying up my funds."

O'Malley was livid. Determined not to let any outsiders into the Dodgers' inner circle, he met the offer. Zeckendorf was not let in. Rickey was let out.

On October 28, 1950, a press conference was held at the Hotel Bossert in Brooklyn, just a few blocks away from the Montague Street office of the Dodgers, where Rickey had smoked his cigars and met with Jackie Robinson, Roy Campanella, Don Newcombe, and thousands of other players, executives, reporters.

"Comest thou here to see the reed driven in the wind?" Rickey's booming voice greeted the press. His eight years with the Dodgers at an end, Rickey announced his resignation and added, "It is my duty and privilege to introduce the new president of the Dodgers, a man of youth, courage, enterprise, and desire." A great deal of stress was placed on the last word.

The forty-seven-year-old O'Malley faced reporters. "I would like to say that for the past seven years that I have been associated with Mr. Rickey, I have developed the warmest possible feelings for him as a man. I do not know of anyone who can approach Mr. Rickey in the realm of executive baseball ability. I am terribly sorry and hurt personally that we will now have to face his resignation."

It was a polite passing of power. The emnity that existed was not for public display. The bitter dislike that both men felt for each other was carefully masked. O'Malley had won the battle, but it had been Rickey who had transformed a struggling Dodger franchise not only into a powerhouse team on the field but also into a thriving economic enterprise.

The 1950 Brooklyn organization had 635 players dispersed among twenty-five teams, in contrast to 250 players in 1943, 150 of whom were in the armed forces. Three minor-league franchises were totally owned; Montreal was valued at $1 million, Fort Worth at $400,000, and St. Paul at $350,000. The 1943 Dodgers was a team in debt; the 1950 Dodgers had a capital surplus of $100,000, available cash of almost $900,000, and an earned surplus of $2.6 million. Rickey had diligently supervised Brooklyn's balance sheet.

SPEAKING OUT

Rickey's departure from the Dodgers left a huge void. Perhaps none of the players felt it as profoundly as Jackie Robinson. "I never had any difficulties with the Dodger organization until Branch Rickey left," Robinson noted.

With Rickey's exit, his title of general manager was never to be used again in the Dodger organization. Buzzy Bavasi, Montreal general manager from 1948 to 1950, took over most of Rickey's functions, but not his title. Mention of Rickey's name in Dodger circles was officially forbidden. Violators were subject to a one-dollar fine that was allegedly deposited in an office pool. Anti-Rickey revisionism was in vogue under O'Malley. "That whole Galbreath-Zeckendorf thing made O'Malley real bitter," remembers Lee Scott. "And that's one of the reasons when Rickey went to the Pirates that Brooklyn never booked exhibition games with Pittsburgh. O'Malley said, 'I don't want to have anything to do with him. I won't play his team if I don't have to.' "

Robinson was distressed by the purge of many of Rickey's aides and the negative feelings openly expressed about him by O'Malley. When Robinson defended Rickey in O'Malley's presence, the former Brooklyn lawyer was miffed. "I will always defend Mr. Rickey," Robinson told O'Malley.

"I owe him a debt of gratitude. I will always speak out with the utmost praise for the man."

Robinson commented that he was not "O'Malley's kind of black; Campanella was." During the 1950s, the Supreme Court ruling outlawing segregation in schools precipitated bombings of churches in the Miami area. Campanella expressed the opinion that the trouble was caused by "Negroes wanting too much, too soon. They should stop pressing." Robinson flailed out at the racist behavior, further alienating O'Malley, who saw a more limited, more circumspect role for an athlete than that of civil rights spokesman.

Next to Robinson, Roy Campanella was perhaps the most famous black baseball player of the period. There were, however, marked differences in background and personality between the two teammates. Campanella had had little formal schooling, and had begun his pro career at the age of fifteen with the Baltimore Elite Giants. He was fond of telling about the old days, when he caught both ends of a doubleheader and then slept on a bus before catching another doubleheader the next day in a town a few hundred miles away.

"I remember when I played not one game, not two games, but three games in one day, and all I got was a dollar fifty," says Campy, who hit more home runs than any other catcher in Dodger history. "Being up in the big leagues is heaven. Baseball had been good to me. I can't complain. I don't want to cause any trouble. I'm not a man for controversies. I shy away from them like the plague."

It was in this respect that the differences between Robinson and Campanella were most pronounced. A story told by Irving Rudd illustrates Campanella's attitude toward Robinson's increasing outspokenness in racial matters.

"An organizer came to a meeting in some backwoods town in Georgia. 'You must understand,' he said, 'we blacks must stand up for all our rights. Don't let the sheriff cow you. Don't let the whites bully you.'

"An old pappy guy in the back raised his hand to speak. 'Yessir, mister organizer. I dern lissin' to you speak an' I jest git the feelin' you blacks are gonna git us niggers killed!' "

Part of the Robinson-Campanella conflict grew out of the "old pappy guy" attitude. Part of it was rooted in the fact that Campanella felt obliged to perform as Branch Rickey advised; Robinson ultimately responded to his own instincts and to the years of Mallie's teachings to defend his rights and be unashamed of who and what he was.

"We had many meetings with Mr. Rickey," recalls Campanella. "Jackie and I were to avoid arguments on the field. We were not to get put out of ballgames. Not only would we hurt the issue, we hurt our team, and our team couldn't replace us in the positions we played. I was put out of two games in my career. I would squawk if I had a squawk comin', but I knew how to squawk as Mr. Rickey taught me.

"One day Mr. Rickey had Jackie and me in his office. He said, 'I have stuck my neck out of the window for you fellows. Please don't let them chop it off.' And silently within myself I took a vow. I said to Mr. Rickey, 'I would never do anything to harm this situation.'

"Jackie was a politician, wanted to be a politician. I didn't. I would exercise my vote and urge all blacks to exercise their vote, but I'd be darned if I'd get up on a soapbox and preach for one party or another. Jackie was a Republican. I was a Democrat. Mr. Rickey never wanted us to get into politics. He asked us, 'Please don't ever say vote for this person, vote for that person.' I took this to heart. Jackie didn't. Mr. Rickey didn't see eye to eye with Jackie on this."

Robinson's increased militancy, his public stands, his civil rights involvement, his goading of players like Campanella to become more racially conscious, his assertiveness on the playing field—all of this made him a controversial figure. "When Ted Williams opened his mouth," Willa Mae notes, "nobody made much of a fuss. But because my brother Jack was black and the first one to break the color line, everyone got excited. He had a right to his opinion." He seemed to have an opinion about everything, and everybody seemed to have an opinion about him.

Monte Irvin shared with Jackie Robinson the bond of being black pioneers in New York City baseball in the golden age of the sport. "We used to talk superficially, nothing about nothing," the handsome Irvin recalls. "And then when we found ourselves on the ballfield, we tried to beat each other's brains out, which is the way it should be.

"In the early years we used to go out barnstorming after ths season and play many exhibition games. Wherever we went, he was the man. People did not pay much attention to anybody but Jackie. He was the one that had broken the color line. Again it's a natural thing to feel a little jealousy, to feel left out. I'm talking about Larry Doby, about Don Newcombe, about Roy Campanella, about myself. We started to call Jackie 'Mr. America' to kid him a little. He didn't appreciate that at all."

There were those who did not appreciate his outspoken views. "Most players," Irvin notes, "thought Jackie was interjecting himself into situations where he shouldn't have been. He was not a politician. He was not a spokesman for anybody. Here he was assuming that role. Most thought he was setting himself up as a leader and some thought, Don't think for me, and tell me what I should do. Since he was the first, maybe he thought he had the responsibility, but most of the black baseball players thought he was setting himself up as spokesman for the entire Negro race."

There was one moment in all the supercharged moments of Brooklyn Dodger–New York Giant confrontations that Irvin still feels somewhat bitter about. Sal Maglie was toying with the Dodgers at Ebbets Field, shaving the plate, throwing the ball dangerously close to each batter.

"We've got to do something about that guy throwing at us," Reese told Robinson. "If we don't, somebody's going to get hurt," continued Reese, the only captain the Brooklyn Dodgers ever had. "When you come up next time, Jack, drop one down the first-base line and try to dump Maglie on his butt."

Jackie Robinson was a baseball player on a ballfield, but he was also a gladiator in an arena. He came to bat and deftly dropped a bunt down the first-base line. The crafty Maglie stayed on the mound. He was unwilling to plant his body in front of an impassioned Robinson charging down the line. Giant second baseman Davey Williams covered first. Robinson barreled into him, sending the smaller player sprawling hurt onto the grass. Robinson was surprised it was Williams he had bowled over and not Maglie, but running with his head down, Jackie would have gone through any obstacle to reach base safely.

"Williams got in the way," Robinson explained later. "He had a chance to get out of the way, but he just stood there right on the base. It was too bad, but I knocked him over. He had a Giant uniform on. That's what happens."

"We looked upon it as dirty baseball," recalls Irvin. "It was a cheap shot. In fact, it nearly ruined Davey's career. [Williams, badly shaken up, was removed from the game. He suffered a spinal injury.] When Robinson did it, Durocher called us down underneath the dugout. He was furious. 'Let's give it back to him,' he said. He looked at Hank Thompson and me. 'How do you guys feel about it?' We agreed with Leo. I said, 'We've got Giants written across our uniforms and that's what counts.' "

Two innings later, Alvin Dark slugged the ball up the alley in left field. It was an easy double for the Giant shortstop, but Robinson was playing third base, so Dark streaked around second straight toward third. Reese's relay throw hit the dirt in front of third base as Dark left his feet and launched into a slide. "Dark jumped at Jackie," recalls Irvin. "He was going to spike him, to give it back to him." At the last instant, Robinson stepped back and slammed the ball against the Giant shortstop's nose. The ball bounced off and Dark was safe. "I would have torn his face up," said Robinson, "but as it turned out I'm glad it didn't happen that way. I admired Dark for what he did after I ran down Williams."

Irvin observes: "Jackie knew what Dark was doing, but he kinda laughed and the tension was off a little bit, but it was a tough moment. It could have been a real nasty thing if there had been a fight between them. There might have been a riot."

The Dodgers won the game, and Robinson said afterward, "I've always admired Al [Dark], despite his racial stands. I think he really believed that white people were put on this earth to take care of black people."

"Some of the problems Jackie had," observes Irvin, "he created for himself. Jackie probably had a little rougher time than anybody else would have had because of the aggressive, abrasive nature that he had. If Campanella had been first, he would not have had as rough a time. Campanella is talkative, gregarious, he's likable. Jackie was not. It got to the point near the end where some of Jackie's teammates didn't even like him."

Robinson's former teammate Ben Wade takes a more solicitous view. "If some didn't like Robinson," says Wade, "it was for no other reason than he was black. He took it for a long time. Right at the end of his career he said, 'I've taken it long enough; now I'm gonna get back and say what I think.' He said some things that I didn't like, but he certainly had the right to say them."

Stan Lomax, who was there at the start and at the end, was able to see the change in Robinson. "In his last few years," notes Lomax, "he was paying off people for those indignities that happened to him whether they were there when they happened or not. He got pretty short-tempered. I wasn't bothered. I knew the handicap under which he started . . . he was paying off debts . . . and maybe we should balance things."

Aggressiveness on and off the field made him a mark as the mild-mannered, soft-spoken, self-effacing image was replaced by one that was determined, outspoken, socially conscious. The code words used to describe him were "hothead," "crusader," "troublemaker," "pop-off." The hidden definition for these labels was clearly understood by Robinson.

In 1953, he appeared on "Youth Wants to Know," a program moderated by Faye Emerson. Responding to a question about why there were no black players on the New York Yankees, Robinson said, "I have always felt deep in my heart that the Yankees for years have been giving Negroes the runaround." At the time there were seven major-league teams with a total of twenty-three black players. The Robinson comment aroused a lot of people and stirred up much controversy. A Cleveland columnist called him a "rabble-rouser" and a "self-proclaimed soapbox orator." Robinson did not step back. "I've a right to my opinions. I'm a human being. I have a right to fight back," he said. "I will not retract my statement that I feel the New York Yankee management is prejudiced against black ballplayers."

Many times his fights were with the press. Some sportswriters told him that his attitudes would cost him awards. His response was that any trophy won for being a "good kid" would be of no value to him.

"He would get some of the press to feel uncomfortable by bringing up social issues," Rachel notes. "They'd say, 'What are you bringing this up for when I'm trying to talk to you about the game, about the score?' It was a cultural conflict. They were white. He was black. He mistrusted what they could do to him. They mistrusted him. He would challenge them and strike out at them. It was normal, a normal thing surrounding a person doing anything not within the status quo."

"It was sad the way he had to take shit, real shit, from people most of whom he could have broken in half," recalls

Irving Rudd. "Robinson was a man among men, a powerful man, an intellectual . . . who had at first to take being called a nigger by some fucking imbecile. He had to release some of those frustrations later . . . and when he did there were always those who waited to find fault with him."

Throughout his career, there were the phone calls and the visits back to Pasadena. "All along," remembers Mack, "we knew Jack had a tremendous burden to carry, but we knew he would succeed. We never kept a scrapbook, but we strained for every scrap of information we could get about him. We listened to the radio broadcasts, the re-creations, and we read all the newspaper stories about him. . . . Seeing him play made me very proud, made the whole family very proud. You couldn't go around with your chest pushed out saying 'that's my brother.' You'd lose a certain amount of respect . . . but we were proud, real proud. Although we used to go and see Satchel Paige and others play, this was different."

Willa Mae remembers the phone calls and the visits. "When he came back to Pasadena after each season, he never forgot to go and see the old people. He loved them and they loved him. He would call and he would say, 'I'm going to be over for three hours. Get the Pepper Street Gang. Have them come over. I want to be with them again.'"

Mallie Robinson worked as a domestic until Jack's entrance into baseball. Then she stopped. "Jack wanted to move her to another house," recalls Willa Mae, "another location, but she wouldn't move."

"When he called or came over, he used to talk sometimes about the things that had been done or said to him." Willa Mae learned about the cold sweats, the indignities, the sleepless nights. "They took their toll on him," she recalls. "He said that if it had not been for his people, that he was doing it for his people, he would have quit after that first year. It was really too much for any human being to take."

Sidney Heard would sit with his childhood friend on the stoop in the California evenings and muse about old times and learn about the people in Brooklyn and what Ebbets Field was like. "Jack did a lot of talking about Rickey. He used to tell us how he loved Branch Rickey; he used to tell us how Branch Rickey was the only father he ever remembered."

"Jack would talk to Mother and ask her to pray for him, to pray for all of the Dodgers," remembers Willa Mae. "And how she did. She was called the praying mother for the whole team. She went to church every Sunday and prayed. It wasn't just Rickey and the ballplayers that helped Jack. It was the Lord working through him.

"My mother was always concerned about Jack, but she was worried about Pee Wee [Reese], too. My mother prayed for Jack, and she prayed for Pee Wee. I always prayed for Pee Wee, too."

The family was deeply moved by an incident in Cincinnati early in Jackie's career. The ballpark was jammed, and thousands of country people had come down from the hills of Kentucky. The atmosphere was racially charged. When the top of the first inning ended, the Dodgers took the field. Reese stopped to talk to Robinson and placed his right arm around the black man's shoulder. The gesture triggered absolute silence in the stands.

Much has been made of that incident as the one that symbolized the Reese-Robinson friendship. Much has been made of the gesture of the white arm on the black shoulder. Reese today claims he does not even remember doing anything. "I put myself in Jackie's shoes," says Reese. "I think of what it must have been like for him. I think of myself trying to make it in an all-black league. I know I couldn't have done it. I remember people in the stands calling Robinson a watermelon-eater. I never went up to get anybody for saying that because Jackie Robinson could take care of himself. I know he always talked a lot about my putting my arm around his shoulder in Cincinnati, but I don't even remember doing it."

Rachel Robinson admits she is as subject to the myths that had developed as anyone else. Like Reese, she intimates that the media and the public at the time sought to come up with symbols that fit their own needs. "Pee Wee was a good working colleague, a good team man," she says. "He was able to put aside the racial prejudice that allegedly was in his family. We were friendly with the Reeses, the Hodgeses, the Erskines, the black players and their families, especially."

On the playing field, Robinson was a part of it all. Off the field, those who knew him saw him as a complicated man, set apart from his colleagues. "There was respect, but also a lot of ambivalence in his relationship with the other blacks on the Dodgers," Irving Rudd recalls. "They were not home-and-home visitors."

For the Robinsons, home at the start was the tiny spot at the McAlpin Hotel in Manhattan, then an apartment at Bainbridge Street in Brooklyn. As the Robinson family grew, their need for space grew. The Robinsons moved from their tiny apartment to 5224 Tilden Avenue in the East Flatbush section of Brooklyn, not too far from Ebbets Field. A daughter, Sharon, was born on January 13, 1950, and on May 14, 1952, a second son, David, was born. There was another move to a larger house on 177th Street in St. Albans, Queens. Some of the Robinsons' neighbors were Roy Campanella, Ella Fitzgerald, and Count Basie.

While Robinson may not have been much of a socializer and while he may have had his differences with some of the black players on the Dodgers, he made a difference in their careers and their lives. "The drunks at Toots Shor would talk about stand-up guys," Irving Rudd recalls. "What they meant was that if you stood a guy up against the bar and he didn't fall down, he was a stand-up guy. But Robinson really was a stand-up guy. What a firm friend to have."

"I was pitching one day in Pittsburgh," recalls Don Newcombe. "I had an eleven-run lead. I let up a little and loaded the bases. Ralph Kiner was coming up. Jackie came over from second base to talk to me. 'If you don't want to pitch,' he shouted, 'go back to the hotel. Get the heck out of here.' I got so mad I struck out Kiner and got out of the inning. The next day Jackie told me, 'The only time you pitch good is when you get mad. That's why I said what I did. From now on I'm going to keep you mad.' And whenever I needed it, he got on me."

Robinson used the opposite approach with Joe Black. "It was the first time I ever pitched in St. Louis," recalls Black. "Stan Musial was at bat. A voice in the Cardinal dugout called out, 'Stan, you shouldn't have any trouble seeing that white ball against that black background.' I was furious. Robinson called time. 'I know you want to punch that guy in the mouth,' he said. 'Forget it. Pitch.' That calmed me down. I got Stan out and pitched a good game. Later Stan apologized for what his teammate had said."

Robinson felt an obligation to all his teammates, the white players as well as the blacks, the average ones as well as the stars. "I wasn't a star when I pitched for the Dodgers," recalls Ed Roebuck, "and they had so many stars on that team that I was almost in awe of them. But Jackie—who *was* the Brooklyn Dodgers—made me feel more at home. He'd come out to the mound. He knew how I felt. 'C'mon, Ed,' he would say. 'You can do it. You can pitch up here. We all know you can.' "

Robinson also felt an obligation to all black players, not just his teammates. Even Willie Mays sometimes received advice. "Jackie would call me up at night at home and give me little tips, how to get the jump on certain pitchers, but not the Dodgers," explained Mays. Of course, Robinson's concern for the young Mays didn't get in the way of his competitive drive. Once the Giant center fielder crashed into the wall at Ebbets Field going after a line drive and collapsed on the dirt warning track. "The next thing I knew," recalled Mays, "Jackie was out there, turning me over, checking to see if the ball had dropped out of my glove."

In 1951, the Giants, propelled by the twenty-year-old Willie Mays, and the Dodgers, powered by thirty-two-year-old Jackie Robinson, battled through 153 games of the 154-game schedule. On the final day of the season, the two teams were tied for first place. It was déjà vu for Brooklyn. Knocked out of the pennant by the Phillies on the last day of the 1950 season, the Dodgers were again pitted against Philadelphia on the final day of the 1951 season. "What happened on that day," Rachel recalls, "always ranked as one of Jack's biggest thrills in baseball."

In the seventh inning of their game, the Dodgers received the news that the Giants, behind Larry Jansen, had nipped Warren Spahn and the Braves, 3–2. It was the seventh straight win for the Giants, and clinched at least a tie for the pennant.

Stan Lomax went into the Giant dressing room anxious to "get something on tape for my radio show, to get one or two of the Giants to say 'We won it all; we won the pennant.' They would not say anything. One of them explained, 'The Dodgers are still playing in Philadelphia—Robinson is there—anything can happen.' "

The Dodgers scored three times in the eighth inning to tie up their game, 8–8. More than thirty-one thousand watched the action play out as darkness descended over Philadelphia. Sunday blue laws prohibited them from turning on the lights.

In the bottom of the twelfth inning, with the score still tied, Eddie Waitkus of the Phillies slammed a low liner over second base. Robinson, moving with the crack of the bat, made a lunging, bellyflopping grab of the drive to stave off the threat. Jackie's elbows were jammed into his chest and he lost consciousness for a few moments, but he held on to the ball. Another player at that point would have left the game, but Robinson, shaken and smarting, stayed.

"I was on third base," remembers Robin Roberts, who was pitching against the Dodgers that day. "Robinson dove for the ball. I still think that he trapped the ball. I touched home and thought the game was over, but I was told by the umpire that Jackie had caught the ball. Years later I met Robinson at a dinner and asked him if he really caught the ball. He smiled and asked me, 'What'd the umpire say?' "

In the top of the fourteenth inning, with the score still tied, Robinson came to bat. There were two out. He slammed Roberts's pitch into the upper left-field stands for a home run. Deliriously happy, his Dodger teammates hoisted him onto their shoulders. The game-saving catch of the Waitkus liner and the game-winning home run by number 42 set the stage for the second playoff in National League history. Robinson, who had batted .338 and recorded his fifth straight year of thirty or more doubles, had been a Montreal Royal when Brooklyn and St. Louis met in the first playoff in 1946.

The Giants and Dodgers split the first two games of the playoff. After seven innings of the third and final game, the score was tied, 1–1. Newcombe announced in the Brooklyn dugout that he was too exhausted to continue. "We're all tired," Robinson exploded at the huge pitcher. "You've got two more innings to go—six outs. You just go out there and pitch!"

The Dodgers scored three times in the top of the eighth inning. Robinson's fury seemed to spur Newcombe on. He struck out the side in the bottom of the eighth inning, but he faltered in the ninth. The Giants scored once. With runners on second and third base, Newcombe exited and Ralph Branca came in to relieve.

On the job, in schoolrooms, in prisons, on car radios, and in candy stores, New York City was plugged into the war between the two historic rivals, the Jints and the Bums.

The precise moment was 3:58 P.M., October 3, 1951. Bobby Thomson smashed a home run over the wall in left field, less than 315 feet from home plate. Thomson's "Shot Heard 'Round the World" gave the Giants a stunning come-from-behind pennant victory. An instant before, the huge Polo Grounds crowd had been mesmerized by Branca pitching to Thomson. Now thousands were climbing out onto the playing field. "Holy hell broke loose all over," recalls former Giant Wes Westrum. Only Jackie Robinson of the Brooklyn defenders in the field remained at his position. Hands on hips, a scowl on his face, he waited and watched to make sure that Thomson, trotting out the home run, touched every base. "That was so characteristic of Jack," observes Rachel Robinson. "It was typical of his need to win."

Even when Robinson tried to relax, his competitive instinct asserted itself. Irving Rudd recalls one winter weekend in 1954 spent with Robinson. "My wife Gertrude and I and Jackie and Rachel were up in Grossinger's Hotel in the Catskills," he remembers. "We were all near the ice-skating house, where there was also a toboggan ride.

" 'Hey, Jack,' I said, 'Let's hit the toboggan!'

"He gives me a withering look. 'Who you racing against?' he asks. 'You skate?'

" 'Not very well.'

" 'C'mon,' he says, 'let's go skating anyway.'

"I said okay, and we all go to the ice house. We put skates on. The wives go to the rail to watch. He goes out on the ice and proceeds to lose his balance and fall flat on his back. Geeeez! The image of [Walter] O'Malley came into my head. I just blew my job. He fractured something, and why didn't I stop him from skating? He gets up . . . brushes himself off.

" 'C'mon, Irv, let's race!' He gives me that big smile.

"So the two of us go like two drunks around the rink at Grossinger's. He's flopping on his knees, I'm sliding on my ass. We get up and keep going and flopping and going, and he beats me by five yards.

" 'Let's do it again,' he says.

"Around we go. This time he beats me by about twenty yards.

" 'One more time,' he says.

"One more time we go. By the third time around he is really skating. He's such a natural, gifted athlete, he's skating like a guy who has been at it for weeks. It's no contest. He almost lapped the field on me . . . that was it. Now there's a crowd around me and they're cheering. He puts his arms around me. He wasn't a demonstrative man. 'Irv,' he says, 'am I glad you were here this weekend. I had to beat someone before I went home!' "

WINDING DOWN

On November 6, 1950, after having carefully evaluated all employment possibilities with his circle of loyalists and his family, Rickey moved on to Pittsburgh. "He saw it as a challenge," explains Mal Goode. "It was a last-place team, and the idea of getting lots of kids and building a third National League power was very appealing to him."

Installed as executive vice-president and general manager of the Pirates by his old college friend John Galbreath, Rickey was granted total freedom to do as he wished to rejuvenate the hapless team.

"Rickey's Boys" followed him to the new challenge. George Sisler came along to head the "Buc's" scouting department. Ironically, it was George's son, Dick, who had hammered a home run on the last day of the 1950 season to defeat the Dodgers and give the Phillies the pennant.

Branch Rickey, Jr., was placed in charge of the Pirate farm system. Milt Stock and Clyde Sukeforth, former Brooklyn coaches, came over to help. Bob Cobb, owner of the Hollywood team in the Pacific Coast League, ended his working agreement with the Dodgers. "I don't know Mr. Rickey's plans," Cobb said when Rickey was removed as

Brooklyn general manager, "or even if he's continuing in the baseball business. I'm going to follow him even if he goes into the laundry business. I'll fill the Hollywood park with washing machines and get a working agreement with him. I'm a Rickey man to the finish."

The sixty-nine-year-old Rickey sold his farm in Chesterton, Maryland, along with its duck blinds and its pits for shooting wild geese. Across the Allegheny River from Pittsburgh, in Fox Chapel Township, he purchased one hundred acres with a large house. He contracted for the building of a combination stable and barn to house ponies for his grandchildren. With his usual thoroughness, he sent scouts east, west, north, and south to focus on new sources of talent. The commitment was made to spend money and to go after black and Hispanic youths.

One of his first actions was to claim a player from the Brooklyn Dodger farm system whom Rickey had signed to a complicated minor-league bonus arrangement. The Dodgers tried to hide him in the low minors, but Rickey knew all about him and claimed him for a sum of $8,000. His name was Roberto Clemente. He would join the Pirates in 1955 and star in their outfield until his tragic death in 1972.

The entire Pittsburgh farm system was overhauled. Sweeping changes were made in the Pirate roster. Veteran players were discarded, and a brigade of "bonus babies" began to take their place. Rickey described the bonus system as insanity, but realized that the only way to build the Pittsburgh team was from the ground up. His five-year plan, begun in 1951, was disrupted by the Korean War. High school and college youths that he had signed were taken into the armed forces. "Things cannot be considered normal," he said, "and it will not be possible to make the progress desired until our boys start to come out of the service as fast as they are now going in." At one point, 174 players in the Pittsburgh organization were in the armed forces.

Rickey looked on with mixed emotions as the 1952 Dodgers won 96 games and the National League pennant. They followed this by winning 105 games and another pennant in 1953. Their star-studded lineup was Rickey's legacy: Pee Wee Reese, Billy Cox, Gil Hodges, Jackie Robinson, Duke Snider, Carl Furillo, Roy Campanella, Preacher Roe, Don Newcombe, Carl Erskine. Robinson batted over .300 both seasons; a second baseman in 1952, he switched to left field in 1953 with the arrival of Junior Gilliam, another Rickey product.

Proud of the Dodger team he had built, Rickey scuffled about attempting to improve the Pirates. He had very little to work with; they had the home-run-hitting Ralph Kiner, but not much else. By 1952, Rickey's spending had exceeded the profits of the Pirates. John Galbreath's private funds were used to make up the deficit. Other stockholders refused to contribute. In spring training that year, Rickey sent Galbreath a letter citing twenty reasons why Ralph Kiner should be traded. "This relates only to his baseball value," the Mahatma said, "and certainly not to his personality. He is one of the nicest boys I've ever met, but Ralph satisfies my requirements in only one respect—as a home run hitter. To me, that isn't enough."

Kiner, today a broadcaster for the New York Mets, recalls the first time he met Branch Rickey in contract negotiations, in 1952. "He was extremely difficult. There was a saying that he had all the money and all the ballplayers and he never let the two get together."

Kiner was the 1952 National League home run leader with thirty-seven. "Rickey offered me a twenty-five percent cut in salary," the affable Kiner recalls. "That was the maximum cut allowed at the time. I held out for two weeks, and I ended up getting a shade more than he first offered. He more or less told me to take it or leave it. . . . I couldn't have left it," jokes Kiner. "I would have had to go to work for a living."

The 1952 Pirates finished in last place, fifty-four and a half games behind the Dodgers. Kiner led the league in home runs for the seventh straight season. The Braves offered Rickey seven players and $150,000 for Kiner. Rickey was not permitted to make the trade. "You've got to win the pennant without Kiner or contend for it with him," a Pittsburgh official warned Rickey. "You can't trade him now." Kiner was an institution at Forbes Field. Even when the Bucs were hopelessly out of a game, fans would linger just to see Kiner bat one more time, hoping to see him hit one more home run.

With the franchise losing both games and money, Rickey borrowed $200,000 against future earnings and plowed it back into Pittsburgh stock. "It's not a good buy now," he said, "but it may be if I work hard enough. I've just got to work to make it worth more." Investment in the future was a way of life for Rickey. He had organized a corporation for the production of fiberglass batting helmets, the American Baseball Cap Company, and involved friends and relatives in the venture. All of them lost money that first year of 1952, but five years later the helmet was standard equipment in the major leagues. Three hundred thousand helmets were produced in 1957, and the corporation made a substantial profit.

In 1953, the man who had traded Dizzy Dean and Rogers Hornsby and Dixie Walker traded Ralph Kiner. The slugging outfielder moved on to the Cubs, along with catcher Joe Garagiola, pitcher Howie Pollet, and infielder George Metkovitch. The Bucs received pitcher Bob Schultz, catcher Toby Atwell, first baseman Preston Ward, infielder Gene Freese, outfielders Gene Hermanski and Bob Addis, and $100,000.

"It was a typical Branch Rickey operation," notes Kiner. "I found out about the trade from manager Fred Haney. In fact, we took batting practice in Pittsburgh Pirate uniforms and the trade was consummated after batting practice. We moved next door to the Chicago Cub dressing room in Forbes Field and changed uniforms. I don't think I ever talked to Branch Rickey after that."

Joe Garagiola remembers the trade with a certain degree of humor. The wisecracking announcer recalled that a couple of days before the trade Rickey greeted him on the playing field: "We've got big plans for you, Joe, big plans."

With Ralph Kiner gone, and no real rooting interest left, attendance at Forbes Field dropped below six hundred thousand for the first time in a decade. The 1953 Pirates scored the fewest runs of any team in the league, recorded the lowest team batting average, and gave up more than five runs a game.

Frustrated by the ineptitude of the Pirates, and not totally enamored with manager Fred Haney, Rickey looked over to the Brooklyn organization for a new pilot. He attempted to obtain Pee Wee Reese, but was told the little shortstop was not available. His next choice was Walter Alston, a manager in the Dodger farm system for thirteen seasons, but O'Malley had plans of his own for the native of Darrtown, Ohio.

When the 1953 season ended, Charlie Dressen, who had replaced Burt Shotton as Dodger manager, demanded a two-year contract. He argued that he had won two straight pennants, 298 games in three seasons, that Durocher had just signed a three-year contract with the Giants and that his record was better than Durocher's.

O'Malley was not impressed with Dressen's arguments for job security. In Alston, the man Rickey had praised so highly, he found a man who would be content with a one-year contract. He replaced Dressen with Alston, signing him to the first of twenty-three consecutive one-year contracts to manage the Dodgers.

The dour, taciturn Alston was a bland counterpoint to the effervescent Dressen, the man they called "Jolly Cholly." Alston was an O'Malley man; Dressen was openly for Jackie

Robinson. "Give me nine guys like Jackie Robinson," he had said, "and I'd never lose."

With Rickey struggling at Pittsburgh and with Dressen gone, Robinson became involved in contentious coexistence with the two Walters, neither of whom was his type of man.

There were also many differences of opinion between Robinson and Buzzy Bavasi, who had taken over most of Rickey's duties. Bavasi had his own ideas about how to motivate his players. "One night Bavasi came into the Dodger dugout," recalls Irving Rudd, "and he started to berate the players as a whole. He called them a bunch of ingrates, a bunch of dogs, etc. Robinson was livid. 'I hope you're smiling when you say that, Buzzy,' he said. Bavasi clammed up, but you could see the tension and the friction between the two of them."

The friction between Alston and Robinson was even more evident. In a 1954 game, Duke Snider pounded the ball into the left-field stands as the Dodgers played the Cubs at Wrigley Field. The ball came back onto the field. Umpire Bill Stewart ruled that the ball had hit the wall and awarded Snider a double. Robinson thought a fan had touched the ball and that Snider should have been given a home run. Screaming and in a rage, Robinson raced out of the Dodger dugout to protest. Alston stood near the third-base coach's box, hands on hips, staring at Robinson. Number 42's rhubarb with Stewart lasted several minutes, but the umpire would not change his decision. Robinson went back to the dugout.

Later a teammate told Robinson that Alston had expressed anger at what he called "Jackie's temper tantrum."

"The team might be moving somewhere," snapped Robinson, "if Alston had not been standing on third base like a wooden Indian. The run meant something in a close game like that, so whether or not I was right or wrong, it paid to protest to the umpire . . . but not according to Alston. What kind of a manager is that?"

The following day a newspaper photo revealed that Robinson had been correct. A fan had touched the ball. The "wooden Indian" comments also appeared in the newspapers. The Robinson-Alston rift widened.

In spring training, and throughout the exhibition season in 1955, Robinson rode the Dodger bench. Alston was evasive about his plans for number 42. Robinson was frustrated. He had batted .311 in 1954, alternating between third base and the outfield. He went to *New York Daily News* reporter Dick Young and made inquiries about Alston's plans. Robinson's query proved to be a mistake. Alston heard about it.

At a team meeting, Alston went into a long tirade about cowardly players who went to the press. Robinson shouted that if there was better communication between Alston and his players there would be need to go to outside sources.

Alston was enraged. Both men began to shout at each other. They were ready to fight and would have fought had it not been for Gil Hodges. The muscular Dodger first baseman seized Jackie's arms. "Cool down, buddy," he said. "It's not worth fighting about. Take it out on the other teams."

It was very hard for Robinson to take it out on the opposition in 1955. It was a season of nagging injuries, reduced playing time, and acrimonious exchanges with Alston and O'Malley. It was a year of discontent and frustration that saw his batting average drop to .256.

The slogan of Brooklyn fans after each World Series defeat by the New York Yankees had always been "Wait 'Till Next Year." The slogan was becoming a way of life for the fans of "Dem Bums," and for Robinson; it was a nettling, unsettling frustration to lose year after year to the Yankees. Robinson's Dodgers were defeated by the Bronx Bombers in 1947, 1949, 1952, and 1953.

As the Yankees and Dodgers squared off once again in the 1955 World Series, "this year" it seemed the Brooks had the talent to prevail. They had stolen more bases, scored more runs, and hit more home runs than any other team in the National League in 1955: they had the highest team batting average and the top slugging percentage; their pitching staff had the most saves, the most strikeouts, and the best earned-run average. Snider, Hodges, and Campanella each drove in more than a hundred runs. Snider, Furillo, and Campanella each batted over .300. The talent was there, but so was the Yankee hex.

Robinson missed almost one-third of the Dodgers' games in 1955, had just sixteen extra-base hits, drove in only thirty-six runs. Fans and sportswriters did not view him as much of a factor in the World Series. He was dubbed "the old gray fat man," by some writers, for his gray hair and the paunch about his middle. His legs ached from the all the years of football and baseball, all the turns and tumbles and twists. His exceptional speed belonged to memory.

Whitey Ford opposed Don Newcombe in the first game of the World Series on September 28, 1955. In the top of the eighth inning, the Yankees were ahead, 6–4. There were two men out. Robinson was the runner at third base. His speed may have belonged to memory, but he still had desire. He stole home! "I took off and didn't care whether I made it or not," Robinson said later. "I was tired of waiting." The Yankees won the game 6–5, but the Dodgers were given a huge psychological lift by Robinson's steal of home.

Her brother's dramatics in that first game of the 1955 Series will always remain as Willa Mae Walker's greatest baseball thrill. "Yogi [Berra] always bragged about what Jack couldn't do against him. He said, 'Nobody, not even Jackie Robinson, will steal home on me.' So Jackie tried it. Years later the two got together and Yogi said he never touched Jackie at home plate, and Jackie said he never touched home plate."

The Yankees swept the second game at Yankee Stadium, and once again it looked as if the Dodgers would have to "wait 'till next year."

The third game was played at Ebbets Field before

34,209. Johnny Podres, pitching for the Dodgers on his twenty-third birthday, faced Bob Turley of the Yankees. The record shows that Podres yielded seven hits and struck out seven and that Campanella collected three hits and three RBIs to power the 8–3 Dodger victory. The box score doesn't show how Jackie Robinson triggered Brooklyn's win.

With the score tied, 2–2, he singled. Darting back and forth off first base, he so unnerved Turley that the Yankee hurler hit Sandy Amoros with a pitch. Podres came to bat. Again Robinson leaned, laughed, and taunted Turley. Podres dumped the ball down and reached first base safely on a bunt. Robinson was now on third base, Amoros was on second, and Podres was on first. Turley checked the runners. Ebbets Field was like an echo chamber of howls and squeals. Robinson feigned a dart toward home. Berra screamed to Turley to concentrate on the batter, not Robinson. The batter, Junior Gilliam, walked on four straight pitches. It was as if Turley had pitched to Robinson and not to Gilliam. Number 42 crossed the plate with a big smile on his face. The Dodgers led 3–2.

Casey Stengel was angry. He took Turley out and replaced him with Tom Morgan, who walked Reese, and the Dodgers led 4–2. Incredibly, two runs had been scored off the vaunted Yankee pitching staff, and the only ball that had been hit out of the infield was the lead-off single by Robinson.

The game moved along to the seventh inning, and the Dodgers were leading 6–3. The Dodger faithful were well aware that every run counted with the Yankee batting power at work in their small ballpark.

Robinson slammed a Tom Sturdivant pitch off the screen in left field. Elston Howard fielded the ball cleanly and saw Robinson make a wide turn past second base. Robinson changed gears and apparently was making a retreat back to second base. Howard made a fundamental error by throwing behind the runner, firing the ball into second in an attempt to cut off what he thought was Robinson's retreat. As the ball came in, Robinson lit out for third base. He slid safely into third, beating Billy Martin's relay throw. A single by Sandy Amoros brought Robinson home with another run, an insurance run.

"The way Howard fielded the ball," Robinson explained later to reporters, "I knew he would go through with his intention to throw to second, so I took off. If Irv Noren [the Yankees' regular left fielder] was out there, I would've held up, because Noren could pretend to throw to one base and throw to another. A couple of years ago no slide would have been necessary. . . . That was quite a burst of speed by a gray, fat man, wasn't it?"

The Dodgers went on to win games four and five of the Series. The Yankees won the sixth game, tying the Series at three games apiece. On October 4, 1955, Johnny Podres, who had been a fifteen-year-old living in Witherbee, New York, when Jackie Robinson broke baseball's color line, spaced out eight hits to defeat the Yankees 2–0 and give Brooklyn its only World Championship ever.

Robinson had batted an anemic .182 in the Series, but his four hits and five runs scored had come in the clutch. "He comes to win," Durocher had said of him. "Robinson comes to beat you." The kudos were for Podres and Amoros, Snider and Hodges and Campanella, but an old man in Pittsburgh, who had put most of the Brooklyn team together, knew how much number 42 had contributed to the Dodger victory just by being on the team.

The man who *Time* magazine said "talks like an evangelist in a voice that exploits the whisper as aptly as the roar" was delighted with the results of the 1955 World Series. His own Pittsburgh Pirates, however, brought him little joy that year. The Pirates had finished in last place, 38½ games behind the Dodgers.

The year before, mortgaging the present for the future, Rickey kept trading, bringing bodies and cash to the Pirates.

Danny O'Connell was sent to Milwaukee for six players and $200,000; Murray Dickson was dispatched to the Phillies for two players and $72,500.

Ironically, while O'Malley stood smugly at the summit in Brooklyn, presiding over the powerful Dodgers that were built by Rickey, competitive and financial disaster in Pittsburgh led to Rickey's departure after five years as Pirate general manager.

Forging a new dynasty in the city of steel had been difficult. The Pirates had finished in the cellar in four of Rickey's five years with the club, but Rickey perceived the sparks of the future. Vernon Law and Bob Friend were the heart of an improving pitching staff. Friend led the league in earned-run average, quite an accomplishment for a pitcher on a last-place team. Dale Long and Frank Thomas combined for forty-one home runs, and a rookie from Carolina, Puerto Rico, who would star for the Pirates for the next eighteen years, took over in right field. Roberto Clemente would one day rank with other Rickey products like Jackie Robinson and Stan Musial.

Joe L. Brown, the son of the famous comedian Joe E. Brown, took over for the seventy-five-year-old Rickey. "Joe Brown," Mal Goode points out, "was a real Rickey protégé and the nearest thing to Rickey on the race problem. There were no blacks when Rickey came to Pittsburgh. In 1954, Curt Roberts was on the Pirate roster, the first black player the team ever had. Brown didn't care if you were a bull moose; if you were able to play ball you played for Pittsburgh."

With Brown on the scene, Rickey continued in semi-retirement as chairman of the board of the Bucs. Freed from the laborious daily details of running the team, the Deacon spread his activities out into other areas.

There was more time for family. Like some wizened patriarch, he presided over festive family gatherings at Fox Chapel. He delighted in being with his six children and their spouses, and seeing his sixteen grandchildren cavort atop the ponies that had been raised for their enjoyment.

There was more time for politics. Throughout his life, Rickey had been offered opportunities to run for the United States Senate, and then the governorship in Missouri. Baseball always claimed his first loyalty, although he was a dedicated Republican. In the summer of 1956, he hit the campaign trail on behalf of the presidential candidacy of Dwight D. Eisenhower, a man whom he admired and who was a good friend.

While Rickey was loosening his involvement with baseball in Pittsburgh, Jackie Robinson's career was winding down in Brooklyn.

Reduced by injuries, by age, by time to a utility role, Jackie played seventy-two games at third base, twenty-two games at second base, nine games at first base, and two games in the outfield in 1956. He batted .275.

Duke Snider recalls Robinson's presence in a game in that 1956 season. The man they affectionately called "The Duke of Flatbush" was at bat in the top of the ninth inning at Wrigley Field. The Dodgers were tied, 2–2, with the Cubs. Sam Jones, a black pitcher, was on the mound for Chicago. "Jackie was on deck," recalls Snider, "yelling at Jones in that high voice he had. 'Sam, you're no good. . . . I'm going to beat you. . . . You've got no guts.' I hit a high pop-up, and now it's Jackie's turn. He's still taunting Sam and yelling. Sam is getting madder and madder. He hits Jackie with a pitch and now Jackie is on first. It's the last thing Sam wanted.

"Jackie is dancing around and yelling at Sam, and Sam keeps throwing over to first and yelling louder and louder. Sam gets so mad he throws the ball right at Jackie. Jackie ducks and the ball sails down to the bullpen in the right-field corner, and Jackie goes all the way to third. Sam is fit to be tied. Jackie is still yelling and laughing and dancing up the line. 'Sam, I'm gonna beat you, you've got no guts.'

Jackie is infuriating him. Well, Sam is looking at Jackie and cursing at him and paying him more attention than the batter and he throws the next pitch into the dirt. It's a short passed ball, and here comes Jackie charging down the line and sliding and it's three to two Brooklyn and we win another. Yeah, even after all those years, that Jackie was somethin' else."

In the last World Series Jackie Robinson ever played in, "Dem Bums" went to the seventh game before losing once again to the New York Yankees while pickets milled about the Dodger office at 215 Montague Street carrying signs that announced: "O'Malley—Biggest Bum of Them All," and "Keep the Dodgers in Brooklyn."

O'Malley had begun to dispose of properties in anticipation of the move of the Dodgers to Los Angeles. Ebbets Field was sold in October to a Brooklyn real-estate developer. Shortly thereafter, the ballpark of the Montreal Royals was sold. And then, incredibly, on December 13, 1956, Jackie Robinson, who was for so many years the symbol and the style of the Brooklyn Dodgers, was sold to the New York Giants for $35,000 and pitcher Dick Littlefield.

"Giants Get Robinson But He May Not Play" was the headline in the *New York Post*. Willa Mae, the sister he always confided in, maintains that "from the moment Jack became a major-league player, he never stopped looking for other employment opportunities. He never knew whether he was going to make it at first and then later how long it was going to last. He had already made up his mind that 1956 was going to be his last year in baseball."

The trade was made while Robinson was negotiating with *Look* magazine for his official and exclusive retirement story. Pressed by reporters for weeks for a commitment as to whether or not he would join the Giants, Robinson remained evasive. In January 1957, Jackie Robinson announced his official retirement from baseball in an article in *Look*. "My legs are gone and I know it," he wrote. "The ball club needs rebuilding. It needs youth. It doesn't need me. It would be unfair to the Giant owners to take their money."

Mal Goode is still bitter at the way the Dodgers disposed of his friend. "They treated him like an old shoe," says Goode. "I called him and asked him to play one more year, one more year with Willie Mays. 'I just want to see the two of you negotiating a double steal; play one more year, Jackie.'

" 'I'm not going to do it, Mal,' he said. 'Horace Stoneham offered me sixty-five, seventy thousand dollars—finally he handed me a blank check and told me to put in what I wanted for one year. I told him nothing doing. I wasn't going to play anymore.'

"That was Jackie," continues Goode. "He was a man of principle. He could have put one hundred thousand dollars down on that check and Stoneham would have paid him and he would have been happy to pay him. Stoneham was smart enough to know what Willie Mays and Jackie Robinson together would have done in drawing power. My God, it would've been a couple of million dollars in extra income. The Giants would have made a fortune with him on their team."

The end came in a blaze of controversy. Buzzy Bavasi charged that Robinson's retirement story was written only to enable Jackie to extract more money from the Giants.

"Personally," Robinson said, "I felt that Bavasi and some of the writers resented the fact that I had outsmarted baseball before baseball had outsmarted me. After Buzzy said that, there was no way I'd ever play again."

Rachel Robinson looks back over the years to put her husband's decision in perspective. "Jack was a person of extreme loyalty and devotion to family, to friends, to his team. When you have a person like that, they can't make changes that easily. He had always made up his mind that he would never play for any team but the Dodgers . . . and that coupled with the fact that he did not want to play anymore. He had looked for a way out of baseball for two years prior to the trade. The last couple of years he had trouble getting in shape. . . . He wanted to get into business, get on with the business of living. . . . He just didn't see the sports arena as the place. It just could never have been."

But what had been was past forgetting: the little mincing steps he took entering the batter's box; the erect and almost military batting stance—elbows high, feet rather close together, arms extended out from the body; the bat, poised and still, raised high above the right shoulder; the tension, the chopping swing of a man who appeared to be musclebound; the wide, sloped shoulders and the strong, heavy legs; the runner's walk—toes turned in, pigeon-toed gait; the top-heavy torso and the broad behind; the sensitive face and the wide forehead; the full mouth, the defined and determined chin, and the deep-set wide and flashing fierce eyes focused with twenty-twenty vision enabling him to pick up the ball and whip it where he willed.

Roy Campanella sits in his wheelchair in his modern home in Woodland Hills, California, not far from Dodger Stadium. All the differences with number 42 are like stones smoothed by the running stream of time. "Jack was one of the only cleanup hitters who wasn't a home run hitter. He was a line-drive hitter. He could bunt a man in from third, and it was impossible to throw him out, but the runner on third with two outs had to be alert to score. He could get the base hit when you needed it. He could steal a base when you needed it. He could make the fielding play when you needed it. Jackie could beat you every way there was to beat you. I have never had a teammate who could do all the things that Jackie Robinson could do. I could extend it even further —I have never seen a ballplayer that could do all the things that Jackie Robinson did. Except that he didn't get the opportunity at a really young age. He could've been twice as good. He could think so much faster than anybody I ever played with or against . . . he was two steps and one thought ahead of anyone else."

THE FINAL YEARS

The public image of Jackie Robinson in retirement from baseball was that of a heavyset, gray-haired man in a business suit. Reports of his diabetes provoked many reactions in those close to him.

"Jack told me, 'As soon as I get out of baseball, I'm going to find out what is wrong with me,' " Willa Mae recalls. "In the first week or two after he got out of baseball, he had to go having shots and all. He went into a diabetic coma and was in it for two weeks and more."

Sidney Heard remembers, "As kids we were prone to injuries 'cause we used to play hard. I noticed that when Jack did have an abrasion or scratch, it took an awful long time to heal. Our parents used to talk about how long that sore used to stay on Jack. We used to take dirt and put it on the wound and we'd heal, but he never did heal quick."

Robinson coped with the diabetes as best he could and went on with the business of living. Still very much a celebrity, he was employed as a vice-president for Chock Full O'Nuts—the community-oriented fast-food chain that employed many blacks.

Jerry Lewis, who today is the director of the Jackie Robinson Foundation, was a Korean War veteran in 1959 and one of the few black students at Columbia University. "My friends and I used to go to Chock Full O'Nuts at One hundred sixteenth Street and Broadway. It was there I met Jackie Robinson. He would come to the restaurant every Thursday as vice-president of personnel and we would talk. When I was a kid, he was my idol, my role model, and here he was in the flesh. He was an ebony giant with a gentle voice, and he always had time to talk to me and the others there. He made me feel I was somebody. He was a man of class who gave me hope before the hard civil rights movement."

Robinson became involved with Nelson Rockefeller. Their first contact came as a result of the Chock Full O'Nuts advertising jingle. Annoyed by the phrase "better coffee Rockefeller's money can't buy," Rockefeller sought to have the reference to his family deleted. He met with Robinson and Bill Black, chairman of the board of the company. The jingle remained as it was; nonetheless, Rockefeller and Robinson established a personal relationship that resulted in their working together often in the years to come.

Rachel went back to college and received her master's degree in psychiatric nursing. The children, Jack Jr., Sharon, and David, moved through their school years and childhood friendships and Little League games. Jack spread himself into other interests. There was a syndicated newspaper column, community and political activities, and friends.

"With success, there comes a change," notes Sidney Heard. "Jack changed, but not to us. I have a letter from him where he planned to get involved with the Gibraltar Savings Bank. It didn't pan out, but he told me to tell the gang that when it was going good, he would buy shares for all of us and let us pay him back later. He was not going to take any money from us."

Writer Leonard Gross and his wife were close friends of the Robinsons. Gross tells a story that illustrates how Robinson "never took part in what he didn't understand." Rachel and Mrs. Gross shared a season box at the New York Philharmonic. Jack called Gross one day offering him tickets to a special performance.

"What's the program?" Gross asked.

"Is there somebody named Bernstein?"

"Yes," said Gross.

"Well, he's in it."

ABC news correspondent Mal Goode remembers all the dinner-table conversations and visits. "We spent a lot of time together talking about politics and sports and the race issue. He was always full of fight." The love that Jackie and Rachel had for each other still impresses Goode, along with the respect they had for each other's accomplishments and differences. "Rachel was the backbone of his family," notes Goode. "Jack counted on her heavily. When he was playing ball, he was on the road a lot, in different cities. It was lonely, and people were after him all the time. But Jack never did anything to embarrass Rachel. Jack's life was his family; he always felt he owed something to his family first."

"When we were younger," recalls his daughter Sharon, "he had to travel a lot. He never stayed away long, and when he returned, the family was his focal point. We sat at the dinner table, taking it all in from this giant of a man who was also our father."

His son David still feels his father's presence. "The sound of the footsteps down the carpeted hall stopping at your door; the words were never long, never needed to be. . . . The grits were always made before I got up. I wouldn't know when he made them or where he was, but by the time I reached the kitchen, they were there, hot on the stove. You were never asked twice to do a chore. If the grass had not been cut by Saturday morning, it was the sound of his tractor as you lay in bed that spoke his message: You had not done your job. But I never got a beating from him, and I never saw him angry."

"He never forgot where he came from," recalls Goode, "although he was sometimes kind of surprised at how far he had come. Once President Eisenhower crossed a crowded ballroom and approached him. 'I couldn't believe it,' Jackie told me. 'The president did it because he wanted to shake my hand.'"

The Robinsons were now serenely settled in a twelve-room redwood and fieldstone house set on a five-acre tract in North Stamford, Connecticut. Built on two terraced levels, it overlooked a private lake and was surrounded by tall New England pine trees. When Jackie, Rachel, and their three children had first moved to Connecticut, some blacks criticized them for living in a white enclave. Some whites sounded off in muted echoes of their Pepper Street counterparts those long years ago. But aside from one incident involving a private golf club, the Robinsons were an accepted part of the Stamford community.

Recommended for membership in that private golf club, Robinson learned that some members had registered objections. He declined membership and chose instead to play the public course in Stamford with its two-hour wait on weekends.

He never used caddies. His swing was fast and came out of a small arc. Delayed wrist action, with cocked wrists suddenly uncorked on the downswing, enabled him to get all his power into his drives. The most he ever wagered was a dollar or two, but he always played all-out. He loved to compete.

Baseball was behind him. Red Schoendienst recalls meeting Robinson on a Manhattan street. "He told me that he didn't miss the game one bit. That surprised me."

When the wrecker's ball began to demolish Ebbets Field, a reporter asked Robinson for his reaction. "They need those apartments that are going up in its place," he said. "I don't feel anything. They need those apartments more than they need a monument to the memory of baseball. I've had my thrills."

After 1956, baseball became merely ritualistic for Robinson, but for Rickey, the ritual of his life remained baseball. While the owl-faced executive could remark it was ridiculous for someone trained in law to devote himself to "something as cosmically unimportant as a game," nonetheless, he did. Baseball was Branch Rickey's love, passion, obsession.

He gave of his time to political causes. He devoted much effort to the civil rights movement, and in 1957 accepted an appointment as co-chairman of the President's Committee on Government Employment Policy—a primitive precursor of the Equal Employment Opportunity Commission. But these things were peripheral. Baseball, for Rickey, was where it had always been—the center of his life.

Now with an additional prop, a cane that complemented the bow tie, the horn-rimmed glasses, and the big cigar, he enjoyed his role as baseball's elder statesman. With half a century of his life involved in the national pastime, he felt a responsibility to speak out on its status and direction. The announcement of the move of the Dodgers and Giants to California dismayed him. Rickey was highly critical of the franchise shifts and took some potshots at his old adversary Walter O'Malley. He argued that major-league baseball had a responsibility to keep National League baseball in New York City.

"It was a crime against a community of three million people to move the Dodgers," Rickey charged. "Not that the move was unlawful, since people have the right to do as they please with their property. But a baseball club in any city in America is a quasi-public institution, and in Brooklyn the Dodgers were public without the 'quasi.' Not even a succeeding generation could forget or forgive the removal of the Dodgers to California. Oh, my, what a team they were!"

On January 28, 1958, Roy Campanella, bulwark of that team, was severely injured in an automobile accident. He had been set to move with the Dodgers to Los Angeles. The accident subjected the three-time National League Most Valuable Player to the agonies of multiple operations and rehabilitation treatments. He remains paralyzed from the waist down and is barely able to use his arms. Campy was placed in the Rusk Institute for rehabilitation treatment. In August 1958, the once-powerful slugger was given permission to receive visitors for the first time.

A stooped figure leaning on a cane entered Campanella's room. It was early morning. The visitor had once had a deadly fear of flying in airplanes until he was cured by going up in an open-cockpit plane in the 1930s. Branch Rickey had suffered a heart attack just three weeks before. He had been told by doctors to remain in bed for three months, but when he learned that his old catcher could have visitors, he climbed aboard a plane. He wanted to be one of the first visitors.

"Well, Campy, how are you feeling?" The familiar voice was low. "It appears that the two of us have been having our troubles."

Campanella's eyes blinked. "Mr. Rickey, I wasn't that good, but now that I see you, I feel just fine." He smiled. "How are you?"

"There's nothing much wrong with me," Rickey responded in a stronger voice, "just a little battle with the old pump. These doctors, Campy, they can be a lot of trouble. But they do know what they are doing. You must follow their advice. Campy, tell me what they have you going through."

Campanella went into much detail explaining the extensive and complex exercise program he was undergoing.

"Exercise like that," Rickey said with the old conviction Campanella remembered from so many talks in the Montague Street office, "has got to help you. It's like a bruised finger on a ballplayer. The player is told to soak it in hot water for long periods of time, but instead of giving it a half hour of soaking, he gives it only five minutes and thinks he has met his responsibility.

"Don't do what some ballplayers do, Campy. Never give it less than what they ask. Continue to do more, and I know that when I see you the next time, I'll bet you a quarter that you'll be able to grab my hand instead of my having to reach out for yours."

Campanella still remembers the visit. "It made me feel wonderful," he says. "That Branch Rickey just about determined my future. He was as close a personal friend as anyone I've ever had in my life. He was someone special, someone as close to me as my own father."

The following year, there was a reunion of the Gashouse Gang in St. Louis. The twenty-fifth anniversary dinner of the 1934 team was a much more lighthearted get-together for Rickey than the one he had with Campanella. The seventy-eight-year-old Rickey praised Leo Durocher for "having the most fertile talent in the world for making a bad situation infinitely worse." Continuing his wry commentary about the old Cardinals, he said, "Why, they loved the game so much, by Judas Priest, I believe those boys would have played for nothing."

"By John Brown," Pepper Martin cut in, "thanks to you, Mr. Rickey, we almost did!"

Rickey was not the only man protesting the National League's abandonment of New York. William Shea, a Manhattan attorney, was appointed by Mayor Robert F. Wagner to head a committee to bring National League baseball back to New York City. Shea had first met Rickey when Shea was a young attorney working for the Brooklyn Trust Company. They had stayed in touch over the years.

"One of my first plans," Shea recalls, "was to have Mr. Rickey bring Pittsburgh into Ebbets Field and occupy it while we were in the process of building a new stadium.

That did not pan out." Things, though, were beginning to "pan out" with the Pirates. The 1958 team finished in second place. The young talent that Rickey had signed and nurtured was maturing.

In 1959, Rickey resigned as Pirate chairman of the board. "He gave up a very fine contract with Pittsburgh," says Shea. "He came over to work with us for expansion at a personal financial loss. He felt the need for expansion to give more players a chance to play, to make baseball more competitive."

The gregarious New York lawyer and the sagacious former Latin instructor formed an imposing duo. The two men were together continuously from 1958 to 1961. "We spent much time in Washington lobbying to prevent the Senate from adopting legislation that was passed in the House that would have banned any baseball expansion except by existing leagues," recalls Shea. "Mr. Rickey was always on the go. He had a heart condition, and he was always taking pills. He had several heart attacks, but he kept going forward all the time. I don't know how the man was able to do so much at his age. I don't think I ever worked harder in my life than the times I worked with him.

"Every time he went to a game," Shea continues, "he kept his own notes. He was a doer. He loved life. He was not a cheap man, as some have charged. He was not an exponent of overpaying, but when he worked for someone, he felt he would pay employees what the value of these employees was to the owner. He was not generous to himself. He never held anyone up for any real monies. He used to get checks from Pittsburgh and stuff them into his pocket. . . . Two months later the checks were still there. He may have had three suits but not more than that. He had the same hat, the same bow tie.

"We were fighting to bring another team into New York City to replace the Dodgers and the Giants. We were turned down cold by the National League. They appointed a committee that never met. Mr. Rickey said the only thing to do was to create a third major league."

Many baseball writers, politicians, and major-league executives were intrigued by Rickey's ideas on the need for a third league and its chances for success. He argued that the existing arrangement was too cumbersome, that too many teams were out of pennant contention, and that contention and competition were needed for financial success in baseball.

"Mr. Rickey had all the arguments and all the figures," Shea recalls. "He had the whole thing down to numbers. He said that the average fellow coming up to the majors would have something like three years and three months in the minors. He argued that after three years, if we had the opportunity to get the right players, we would have the cream of the crop and be able to compete with the major leagues."

In 1959, at the age of seventy-eight, Rickey was appointed president of the Continental League. Within an hour after his appointment, he conducted the new major league's first meeting. Eight franchises were formed: New York, Buffalo, Toronto, Minneapolis–St. Paul, Houston, Dallas–Fort Worth, Atlanta, and Denver.

Jack Kent Cooke owned the new Toronto franchise in the Continental League and the old Toronto franchise in the International League. Rickey went to the Canadian city for a victory celebration after Cooke's team won the International League pennant. But in Toronto, Rickey received the news that his son, Branch Jr., who been suffering from diabetes for quite some time, had died.

Rickey was devastated. The father-son relationship between the "Branch" and the "Twig" had always been very close. Branch Jr. had attended prep schools selected by Rickey and went to Ohio Wesleyan at his father's urging. With the Cardinals, with the Dodgers, and in the Continental League, Branch Jr. was always his father's deputy. It was the Twig, not Branch Rickey, who was on the scene that

October day in 1945 in Montreal when Jackie Robinson signed his historic contract with the Royals.

The loss of his only son affected Rickey to the very depths of his being. They had shared so much together through the years—religion, family, baseball. "When his son died," Shea recalls, "Mr. Rickey would not permit anything to be said or done. He stayed until a certain time and then left to go down to his son's funeral. He was back again at work in a couple of days. His grief was private, but very deep."

In 1960 the Pittsburgh Pirates won their first pennant in thirty-five years and defeated the New York Yankees in the World Series. Clemente, Law, Friend, and others whom Rickey had acquired for Pittsburgh had come of age. And the Mahatma's concepts for expansion had also come of age. That same year the American League shifted the Washington Senators to Minnesota, and added franchises in Los Angeles and Washington. Houston and New York were awarded the new National League franchises.

The new home of the Mets in Flushing, New York, was named Shea Stadium in honor of the man who brought back National League baseball. "I didn't know when they were considering naming the stadium that Mr. Rickey went before the Board of Estimate," notes Shea. "He went to the mayor and reporters and argued that there should be no other name but Shea Stadium. He was helpful in all the details and the plans for the building of the stadium.

"I thought he was going to be with the Mets," continued Shea, "but it did not work out. He and Jack Cooke were trying to work out ways to be part owners. M. Donald Grant was a stumbling block. He had other owners in mind . . . and Walter O'Malley figured a lot in the opposition."

Branch Rickey, who created the farm system, who pioneered dozens of baseball innovations, who shattered baseball's color line, never did set up the stakes in his last frontier—the Continental League. Rickey's expansionist vision set off a chain reaction, not only in baseball, but in other sports as well. The American Football League, the American Basketball Association, and the World Hockey Association can all be traced back to the Continental League, the original stalking horse for sports expansion. "The consensus is now that the majors would have been better off accepting the Continental League," observes baseball executive Bill DeWitt, who began his career in 1913 as an office boy for Rickey. "It would be more feasible to have Rickey's concept of three major leagues of eight clubs each, instead of the present four divisions in the two leagues." It is worth noting that of the eight cities chosen by the Continental League in 1959, six (New York, Toronto, Minneapolis–St. Paul, Houston, Dallas–Fort Worth, and Atlanta) have major-league franchises today.

In 1963, with the Continental League behind him, now in his eighties, Rickey still quested for new challenges. He returned to the St. Louis Cardinals as a consultant. Rickey was recommended to St. Louis owner August Busch by Bob Cobb, his old Hollywood Pacific Coast League connection. Critical of manager Johnny Keane, general manager Bing Devine, and other St. Louis executives, Rickey fired off cantankerous tirades and pointed memoranda. He ached to be part of one more winner. In 1964, the Cardinals won the World Series. Their last World Championship had come in 1946, when a Rickey-built team had triumphed.

Jackie Robinson was nearly half Branch Rickey's age as the turbulent decade of the 1960s began. He was still young. He had celebrated his fortieth birthday in 1959. He had spent ten exhausting years in the frenzied give and take of a difficult and consuming baseball life, in the intrusive eye of the media. Combat had been a way of life; now he could elect harmony. But the beat of a more powerful drummer made him march into new battles. His prime concern, the main issue, was now race.

Robinson was active with the Harlem YMCA and the

Freedom National Bank, a project in black capitalism. "There are many of us who attain what we want and forget those who help us along the line," he remarked. "We say, 'Why should I jeopardize my position? Why should I slip back? We've got to remember that there are so many others to pull along. The further they go, the further we all go.'"

"Jackie never forgot the struggle of his mother, and he never forgot what caused that struggle—bigotry in America," says Mal Goode. "And to his dying day, he never stopped fighting. There were reporters who abused him in their columns. 'Why doesn't Jackie keep quiet? Baseball's been good to him.' People said, 'Where did you ever have the chance to make thirty thousand dollars if not for baseball?' I'm sure he was offered bribes to keep quiet, to stop complaining. He couldn't be bribed. He couldn't be bought."

Just as Robinson had placed his stamp on baseball, his historic role in baseball had stamped him. It was baseball across those long seasons that had enabled him to experience firsthand how the hearts and minds of people could be changed, how prejudice could be defused, how gains could be made, and how one man could become an instrument of change and make a difference.

In 1960, impressed by Sen. Hubert Humphrey's civil rights record, Robinson campaigned for Humphrey in the Democratic presidential primaries. After Humphrey lost, Connecticut governor Chester Bowles set up a meeting between Robinson and the Democratic victor, Sen. John F. Kennedy.

"He couldn't or wouldn't look me straight in the eye," Robinson said later of the meeting with Kennedy in a private residence in Washington. The Massachusetts senator asked him, "How much would it take to get Jackie Robinson to work for the election of John F. Kennedy?"

"Look, senator," snapped Robinson, "I don't want any of your money. I came here simply to determine which candidate was the best one for black Americans because the struggle for civil rights and its solution is basic to making America what it's supposed to be."

With Kennedy found wanting, Robinson worked for Richard Nixon. He felt that the Republican had a good civil rights record, and was impressed by a statement made by Nixon's running mate, Henry Cabot Lodge, that if Nixon were elected president there would be an appointment of a black cabinet member. The endorsement evoked much criticism. Robinson's friends could not understand his support of the Republican candidate.

"Jackie saw no grays; he just saw black and white. The issue was right or it was wrong," explains Irving Rudd. "He went for Nixon because Nelson Rockefeller, a master politician who had stroked him, had convinced him that Nixon was a man who could do great things for the Negro."

Events disillusioned Robinson. Nixon never publicly acknowledged the statement made by his running mate, Lodge. When Martin Luther King, Jr., was jailed in Georgia for a minor traffic violation, Robinson urged Nixon to intervene. He refused to get involved. John F. Kennedy did, even using his brother Bobby to work on obtaining King's release.

There was mounting pressure on Robinson to dissociate himself from the GOP. He stayed. He argued that it helped keep the Republican party from going completely "white," and gave blacks a chance of at least being represented in both political parties.

Robinson was a life member of the National Association for the Advancement of Colored People. "It hurt him badly that it was difficult to get black athletes to support the organization," Goode recalls. During a period of internal strife in the NAACP, Robinson quit the national board rather than choose sides in the struggle.

He was a friend and admirer of Martin Luther King, Jr. Paradoxically, the man who wore the badge of martyrdom to break baseball's color line did not accept King's philosophical approach to civil rights. "As much as I loved him," said Robinson, "I would never have made a good soldier in Martin's army. My reflexes aren't conditioned to accept nonviolence in the face of violent provoking attacks." Robinson's development from pacifist to activist was a living embodiment of the direction the civil rights movement was to take. During his first two years as a member of the Brooklyn Dodgers he was, willingly or not, the personification of the nonviolence Martin Luther King would transform into an internationally recognized crusade. One may only wonder just how much of an influence Robinson's behavior during his early years as a pioneer had on King. Vigorous outspokenness and activism characterized Robinson in the latter years of his career. This was again a precursor of the direction the civil rights movement would take.

There was public disagreement between Robinson and black activist Malcolm X. Robinson defended United Nations Undersecretary Ralph Bunche late in 1963 against attacks by Malcolm X that the black diplomat was muzzled because of the job "the white mob" gave him. Malcolm X then turned against Robinson. He charged that Robinson too tried to please the white bosses. Robinson's reply was that he did nothing to please white bosses or black agitators "unless they are things that please me."

In 1962, in his first year of eligibility, he became the first black man admitted to the Baseball Hall of Fame. Even here there was controversy.

"I was really proud that Jack made it into the Hall of Fame and just could not understand Bob Feller saying he did not want to go in with Jackie," Willa Mae recalls. "He wanted to go into the Hall of Fame with Campanella. Jackie told him, 'Go wait on Campanella.' Maybe it was a racial thing, and maybe it was just dislike. In Feller's mind and in a lot of the others', their mind was made up before they started playing as soon as they found out the black was coming."

The Hall of Fame plaque reads:

JACK ROOSEVELT ROBINSON
Brooklyn N.L. 1947–1956

Leading N.L. batter in 1949. Holds fielding mark for
second baseman playing 150 or more games with .992.
Led N.L. in stolen bases in 1947 and 1949. Most
Valuable Player in 1949. Lifetime batting average .311.
Joint record holder for most double plays by second
baseman, 137 in 1951. Led second basemen in double
plays 1949–50–51–52.

During the ceremony at Cooperstown, Robinson called
three people up from the audience to stand beside him,
three people who had special significance in his life and
career: his mother, Mallie; his wife, Rachel; and his friend
and confidant, Branch Rickey. It was to be one of the last
times together for Rickey and Robinson.

On November 13, 1965, against the advice of his doctors,
the eighty-three-year-old Rickey insisted on being released
from a St. Louis hospital where he had been confined after
suffering another heart attack. He said he wanted to watch
the Missouri-Oklahoma football game that day, and he had
to make an acceptance speech that night for his induction
into the Missouri State Hall of Fame. He promised his doctors that he would return to the hospital after the speech.

The pale Rickey watched Missouri's football team defeat
Oklahoma on that cold November day, and went almost
immediately afterward to the early dinner in Columbia,
Missouri.

"He got to his feet as the final inductee," Bob Broeg,
sports editor of the *St. Louis Post-Dispatch*, recalls. "He was
inducted along with George Sisler and the late publisher of
the *Sporting News*, J. G. Taylor Spink. He wove a tale of
three types of courage: physical, mental, and spiritual. And
he had just launched into a parable about a biblical tailor

when he suddenly put his hand over his heart and said, 'I don't believe I can continue.' "

The audience was stunned. Rickey had suffered another heart attack.

"He sat slumped down at the head table in the modest-sized dining room of the old Daniel Boone Hotel," Broeg remembers. "He would have died at once if it had not been for the presence of a Kansas City doctor, Dr. D. M. Nigro, the last man to see his old friend Knute Rockne alive when he put the famed coach on the fatal plane in 1931."

An ambulance sped Rickey to Boone County Memorial Hospital. Placed in the intensive care unit, supplied continuously with oxygen, the dying Rickey lay, his wife keeping a constant vigil at his bedside.

Branch Rickey died at 10:00 P.M. on December 9. It was just eleven days before his eighty-fourth birthday. His father, of whom he often spoke, lived to the age of eighty-six and "until the very end was still planting peach and apple trees on our farm near Portsmouth, Ohio," Rickey was fond of saying. "And when I asked him who would take care of the fruit, he said, 'That's not important. I want to live every day as if I'm going to live forever.' " The Deacon left behind his wife, five daughters, many grandchildren, and several great-grandchildren. Strangely, few blacks attended the funeral of the man who had given Jackie Robinson the chance to break baseball's color line. Rickey had always refused to accept any public honors for signing Robinson. "I have declined them all," he said. "To accept honors and public applause for signing a superlative ballplayer, I would be ashamed."

Jackie Robinson was ashamed and angered at the skimpy black representation at the funeral. He criticized black athletes. "Not even flowers or telegrams, and they're earning all that money," he raged.

Monte Irvin felt "the warm feeling for Branch Rickey had worn thin. Seemingly since Jack had acted the way he did and become arrogant and alienated a lot of people, they might have associated Jack's arrogance with his association with Branch. They were still grateful for what Branch had done, but the warm feeling wasn't there the way it was at the beginning."

Roy Campanella still had that warm feeling, but he was physically unable to attend the funeral. "Mr. Rickey went out of his way to do so much to put blacks in the major leagues. He could tell you so many things, Mr. Rickey, just like my mother or father reading a book to me as a youngster. He made me a better catcher, a better person on and off the field. He made me a completely changed individual."

Among the mourners was Rickey's good friend Bill Shea. He remembers his thoughts that day: "My friend, Mr. Rickey, there's nobody in baseball like him. There never will be again. There's nobody in any way like him."

On that December day in St. Louis in 1965, there were moments when Jackie Robinson's mind traveled back twenty years to an August day in Brooklyn when he and Branch Rickey first met. The passing years had seen them go their separate ways. But their relationship had always been more than a business one.

"The passing of Mr. Rickey is like losing a father," said Jackie Robinson, who never knew his own father. "My wife and I feel we've lost someone very dear to us. Mr. Rickey's death is a great loss not only to baseball but to America. His life was full, and I'm sure there are no regrets as far as fulfillment in life. I think he did it all."

In 1967, the teller of more than a thousand homespun tales, many of which he heard from his mother, was admitted to the Hall of Fame. His plaque reads:

WESLEY BRANCH RICKEY

St. Louis A.L. 1905–1906–1914
New York A.L. 1907

Founder of farm system which he developed for St. Louis
Cardinals and Brooklyn Dodgers. Copied by all other
major league teams. Served as executive for Browns,
Cardinals, Dodgers and Pirates. Brought Jackie Robinson
to Brooklyn in 1947.

The Branch Rickey Physical Education Center on the
grounds of Ohio Wesleyan was the first building to bear his
name. "It is impossible for me to give back to the University
what it gave me," Rickey once wrote. "If it were not for my
family, all I have or all I should leave at my death would go
to the University. . . . Without the experience I had at Delaware, I would have been at best a trustee of Rush Township in Scioto County, and, hopefully, a good country
schoolteacher."

Three years after the death of Branch Rickey, another
symbolic and much-loved figure in the life of Jackie Robinson passed away. His mother, Mallie, died in Pasadena.
Jackie received a phone call about her illness and flew out to
California to be with her. When he arrived, she was dead.

Robinson pressed on without Mallie and without Rickey.
His job and social concerns kept him moving, and wherever
he went, he met with the respect won by his achievements.
At the first Martin Luther King game in Dodger Stadium in
Los Angeles, Ben Wade was supervising batting-practice
pitchers. A Brooklyn Dodger from 1952 to 1954, Wade was a
good friend of Robinson's. "I had the locker right next to
him. We talked a lot. He loved to play cards. We played in
hotel rooms, in trains. We played poker. He was a very good
bluffer."

Wade remembers somebody's tapping him on the shoulder that day in Dodger Stadium. It was Jackie Robinson.
"We talked a bit about the old times. He asked me how my
family was. I told him everyone was fine and I mentioned
that the boy catching batting practice was my middle son.
'I'll see you later' were his words that ended our conversa-

tion. The game was about to start. A little while later when my son came up to me in the stands, Robbie made it a point to come over and he said to my son, 'You don't know me. I'm Jackie Robinson. I used to play ball with your dad. He's quite a guy.' My son will never forget that."

"I guess I had more of an effect on other people's kids than I did on my own," Robinson once said. "I thought my family was secure, so I went running around everyplace else."

On June 17, 1971, driving his brother David's 1969 MG Midget on the Merritt Parkway to his Connecticut home, Jackie Jr. lost control of the car. There was a crash, and he died. He was twenty-four years old. Three years earlier, the youngster who looked so much like his father, who had the same pigeon-toed walk, who had batted .500 in Little League baseball, had been arrested for possession of drugs. His addiction had begun when he was wounded in Vietnam. Convicted on a drug charge, Jackie Jr. was ordered to undergo treatment at the Daytop Drug Abuse Facility in Seymour, Connecticut, and recuperated. At the time of his death, he was working to help young drug addicts. "You don't know what it's like to lose a son, find him, and lose him again," Robinson said.

Early in June 1972, at Dodger Stadium in Los Angeles, Jackie Robinson, Roy Campanella, and Sandy Koufax were reunited at a ceremony retiring their uniform numbers. The three Hall of Famers stayed at the Biltmore Hotel in Los Angeles. "I saw Jackie in the hallway," Campy remembers. "His son David was with him, and a fellow was holding him by the hand. I called out to Jackie from my wheelchair, 'Hi, Jackie,' and that's when he told me that he couldn't see too well. That stunned me. Not that I couldn't believe it. I knew all the time he played he had sugar diabetes. I knew our trainer had to sometimes get Jackie to take insulin. Still, I could never believe that we'd come out together to the Biltmore Hotel here in Los Angeles for an old-timers' game, that Jackie would hardly be able to see and that I would be in a wheelchair."

At Dodger Stadium the two brothers Mack and Jackie got together just miles away from the Rose Bowl and Muir Tech, Pasadena Junior College and Pepper Street. "He told me that his legs were killing him," Mack recalls. "His sight was bad—he could no longer drive a car because he was going blind. I was shocked. I didn't know his condition was that far gone. I was on the field with him when some fellow threw a baseball to him out of the stands for him to autograph. The ball bounced off the top of his head because he couldn't even see the ball coming. He got a terrific headache from that, and I guess it bothered him a lot to have the public see how much he had deteriorated."

Mal Goode saw his old friend Jackie Robinson at a banquet luncheon at Mamma Leone's Restaurant in New York City in July. "I was standing there talking, and he said, 'That sounds like Mal.' I was about a foot away from him. 'That you, Mal?' He was looking right at me. I knew then. You talk about something tearing you up." Robinson was bleeding behind the eyes. Efforts to cauterize the ruptured blood vessels with laser beams had not been successful.

At Riverfront Stadium in Cincinnati in October, Jackie Robinson threw out the first ball in the second game of the seventy-fifth World Series. There was halting movement in his legs and his hair was pure gray. A fan brought him a baseball. "I'm sorry," he apologized. "I can't see it. I'd be sure if I wrote only to mess up the other names you have on it."

The fan pushed the ball forward. "There are no other names, Mr. Robinson. The only one I want is yours."

It was almost twenty-seven years to the day since he signed a contract to become the first black player in organized baseball. Robinson was still persisting, still pressing.

"I'd like to live to see a black manager," he said over

national television. "I'd like to live to see the day when there is a black man coaching at third base."

Today Mal Goode winces at the uproar caused by those modest demands. "They asked him why he had to use the World Series to ask for things like that. And he said, 'What better place? What better time?' "

Nine days after his appearance at Riverfront Stadium, on October 24, 1972, Jackie Robinson collapsed in the hallway of his Stamford home. Rachel called the police. External massage and oxygen were administered to the stricken fifty-three-year-old Robinson. A fire department ambulance took him to the Stamford Hospital. He died at 7:10 A.M.

"I spoke to Rae," Campanella recalls. "She said Jackie had gone to Albany to make a speech for Governor Rockefeller, and at the time, Jackie was bleeding from behind the eyes and she suggested to him not to go. But he said he had made a commitment and he had to go. He came back home still bleeding behind the eyes, and he died."

In California, on hearing news of Robinson's death, Los Angeles Mayor Sam Yorty ordered all flags on municipal buildings flown at half mast.

Mack, the brother who taught him to broad jump, notes, "One of the things that probably led to his early death was that he didn't recognize the problems that diabetes could cause. At times he did not keep up with his diet, and there were the pressures of his son's drug problems and death."

While many felt the singular pressures of Robinson's life caused his untimely death, Rachel Robinson, the one person closest to him, maintains, "He didn't die of heartbreak or pressure. He died of a very virulent disease that may have been advanced by the stress."

At the Duncan Brothers Funeral Home at Seventh Avenue and One hundred thirty-fifth Street, the ones who stood on line, the ones who filled the bleachers, the ones who traveled on the subways to the Polo Grounds and Yankee

Stadium and Ebbets Field came to pay their last respects. Mostly middle-aged or elderly, sad-faced and full of stories, they lined up outside the funeral home and passed in single file before the coffin. "The whites and fancy blacks will see him at Riverside Church," one of them said. "First they gotta give the poor people a look. This is all family here."

The funeral was held in Riverside Church at noon on October 27, a Friday. A congregation of more than twenty-five hundred filled the Gothic church, with its thirty-story tower that overlooks the Hudson River and Grant's Tomb. Three daughters and the grandson of Branch Rickey were there, and so were Roy Campanella, in a wheelchair, Willie Mays, Monte Irvin, Hank Aaron, Joe Louis, Governor Nelson Rockefeller, and baseball commissioner Bowie Kuhn. President Nixon sent a forty-man delegation to honor Robinson.

Mal Goode was there and remembers thinking, "Jackie's head was white when he was thirty years old—that came from the anger he was holding in. He didn't run from a fight, but he ran from fights those first two years, and it helped to hasten his death, a psychological kind of death."

The Reverend Jesse Jackson stood near the silver blue coffin draped with red roses and delivered the eulogy. He spoke of how the body corrodes and fades away, but the deed lives on. "When Jackie took the field, something reminded us of our birthright to be free."

Television personality Ed Sullivan; baseball executives Peter O'Malley, Warren Giles, and Bill Veeck; political leader Sargent Shriver; civil rights leader Roy Wilkins, A. Phillip Randolph, and Bayard Rustin; singer Roberta Flack; and others listened as Jackson pointed out that on Jackie Robinson's tombstone would be recorded the years "1919 dash 1972—but on that dash"—Jackson's voice rose—"is where we live. And for everyone there is a dash of possibility, to choose the high road or the low road, to make things better or worse. On that dash, he snapped the barbed wire of prejudice."

The eulogy was couched in poignant baseball metaphors. Near the end of his remarks, Jackson's words made many in the huge congregation break into tears or sobs.

"His feet danced on the base paths," said Jackson.

"Yes, sir," a woman's voice toward the back of the church answered him. "Yes, sir, that's right."

"But it was more than a game," continued Jackson.

"Yes it was," the woman said.

"Jackie began playing a chess game, he was the black knight."

"Yes, sir, go ahead, all right."

"In his last dash," said Jackson, "Jackie stole home and Jackie is safe."

"Yes, sir, you're right."

"His enemies can rest assured of that."

"Yes, they can, hallelujah!"

"Call me nigger, call me black boy, I don't care!"

"Hallelujah!" The woman's voice was joined by hundreds of others, and the Jackson eulogy was ended.

Ralph Branca, Larry Doby, Junior Gilliam, Don Newcombe, Pee Wee Reese, and Bill Russell were the pallbearers. They moved the casket bearing the body of their friend into the waiting hearse. The funeral cortège moved solemnly through the streets of Harlem and Bedford-Stuyvesant. Tens of thousands lined the route. Jackie Robinson was laid to rest in Cypress Hills Cemetery, just a few miles from where he touched millions of people, where there used to be a ballpark named Ebbets Field.

The meaning and the memory of Jack Roosevelt Robinson have remained strong through all the years with Irving Rudd, Jack's brother Mack, his sister Willa Mae, and his wife Rachel.

"While Jack was making world history I was basically a common laborer," says Mack with some bitterness. "None of his fame really rubbed off on me. The city of Pasadena has not recognized Jack's achievements, nor did they recognize my achievements. They chose not to lower themselves, as they would call it, by placing his name in any type of historical place here in Pasadena. We came from Georgia, but we lived in Pasadena. There's no amount of money that Pasadena could ever spend to bring it the fame that Jack and I brought and continue to bring to this city. In the field of athletics our name will never die.

"The one thing that has upset me more than anything else is that so many black players feel no commitment to what he did. We should never forget where we came from. If some of those players can wind up with a lifetime batting average of three eleven under those pressures, then they can say anything they like.

"I was shocked to learn that the Pittsburgh Pirates had a statue of Roberto Clemente in their park and the Dodger organization didn't think to place any importance in that type of recognition for Jack.

"From time to time," Mack muses, "I'm watching sporting events and I look at the TV screen and I see Jackie Robinson. I look at the whole spectrum of black America's life from 1947 on, against that from 1900 to 1947. We're no longer the butlers, the servants, the maids; we're senators and congressmen. We're baseball managers. I trace it back to his breaking the color line and creating a social revolution in a white man's world. Blacks have excelled in all areas because Jackie Robinson showed the world we could."

Willa Mae's memories are more tender. "I can still see him in the house with the family or out with a bunch of kids playing ball in the field. I believe that your days are numbered, and when you get to a certain point you have to step aside. He had been ill, and he told me and he told others that he knew he was going. I can just picture him all the way through to his passing. I have people who stop me and say their brother, their son, should have been the one. I say involve me out. I tell them if your brother or son was going to be the one, he would have been, because Jack sure wasn't looking for it."

Rachel continues the work begun by her husband. Five years after his death, thirty years after he broke baseball's color line, the Jackie Robinson Foundation was formed "to perpetuate some of Jackie's goals, including educational, cultural, and recreational opportunities." Rachel was its inspiration and functions as chairperson of the board of directors. The foundation is located just around the corner from the old Brooklyn Dodger office on Montague Street where Rickey and Robinson first met.

"In remembering Jack," Rachel says, "I tend to de-emphasize him as a ballplayer and emphasize him as an informal civil rights leader. That's the part that drops out, that people forget. My memories of him are very good, very satisfying to me."

Perhaps the ultimate commentary on Jackie Robinson, however, comes not from an intimate but from one who has been intimately associated with the world of sports for many years:

"I'm sure that being the pioneer in baseball killed him," says sports publicist Irving Rudd. "Black bastard, nigger, spade, coon—those were the words they called him, and there was all that time he could do nothing about it, and he had a short fuse. I always used to think of who I would like going down a dark alley with me. I can think of a lot of great fighters—Ali, Marciano, gangsters I was raised with in Brownsville, strong men like Gil Hodges—but for sheer courage, I would pick Jackie. He didn't back up."

AFTERWORD

This story appears in *It Happened in Brooklyn,*[1] the oral history I wrote with my wife Myrna Katz Frommer:

MAX WECHSLER: When school was out, I sometimes went with my father in his taxi. One summer morning, we were driving in East Flatbush down Snyder Avenue when he pointed out a dark red brick house with a high porch.

"I think Jackie Robinson lives there," he said. He parked across the street, and we got out of the cab, stood on the sidewalk, and looked at it.

Suddenly the front door opened. A black man in a short-sleeved shirt stepped out. I didn't believe it. Here we were on a quiet street on a summer morning. No one else was around. This man was not wearing the baggy, ice-cream-white uniform of the Brooklyn Dodgers that accentuated his blackness. He was dressed in regular clothes, coming out of a regular house in a regular Brooklyn neighborhood, a guy like anyone else, going for a newspaper and a bottle of milk.

Then, incredibly, he crossed the street and came right towards me. Seeing that unmistakable pigeon-toed walk, the rock of the shoulders and hips I had seen so many times on the baseball field, I had no doubt who it was.

"Hi Jackie, I'm one of your biggest fans," I said self-consciously. "Do you think the Dodgers are gonna win the pennant this year?"

---

1. Harvey Frommer, and Myrna Katz Frommer. 1993. *It Happened in Brooklyn: An Oral History of Growing Up in the Borough in the 1940s, 1950s, and 1960s.* New York: Harcourt Brace.

His handsome face looked sternly down at me. "We'll try our best," he said.

"Good luck," I said.

"Thanks." He put his big hand out, and I took it. We shook hands, and I felt the strength and firmness of his grip.

I was a nervy kid, but I didn't ask for an autograph or think to prolong the conversation. I just watched as he walked away down the street.

At last the truth can be told. I am blowing my cover. That kid, MAX WECHSLER, was me, Harvey Frommer, and it now seems to me that morning moment on a street in East Flatbush was when the seeds for *Rickey and Robinson* were first planted.

It is gratifying to see this book, written more than twenty years ago, back in print. I have written many other books since then, but *Rickey and Robinson* remains one of my favorites. Perhaps it is because I was fortunate enough to interview such special people for this work: Rachel Robinson, Roy Campanella, Mack Robinson, Irving Rudd, Monte Irvin. Perhaps it is because this story is such a significant piece of American sports history and culture. Perhaps it is because it traces the lives of two very different people who came together on common ground to shatter baseball's age-old color line.

APPENDIX

Box Score of Jackie Robinson's First Game, April 15, 1947

BOSTON (N.)

	ab	r.	h.	po	a.	e.
Culler, ss	3	0	0	0	2	0
bHolmes	1	0	0	0	0	0
Sisti, ss	0	0	0	0	0	0
Hopp, cf	5	0	1	2	0	0
McCormick, rf	4	0	3	2	0	0
R. Elliott, 3b .	2	0	1	0	2	0
Litwhiler, lf ..	3	1	0	1	0	0
Rowell, lf	1	0	0	0	0	0
Torgeson, 1b .	4	1	0	10	1	1
Masi, c	3	0	0	4	0	0
Ryan, 2b......	4	1	3	4	7	0
Sain, p	1	0	0	0	1	0
Cooper, p	0	0	0	1	0	0
aNeill	0	0	0	0	0	0
Lanfranconi, p	0	0	0	0	0	0
Total	31	3	8	24	13	1

BROOKLYN (N.)

	ab	r.	h.	po	a.	e.
Stanky, 2b ...	3	1	0	0	3	0
Robinson, 1b .	3	1	0	11	0	0
Schultz, 1b ...	0	0	0	1	0	0
Reiser, cf	2	3	2	3	0	0
Walker, rf	3	0	1	0	0	0
Tatum, rf	0	0	0	0	0	0
eVaughn	1	0	0	0	0	0
Furillo, rf	0	0	0	0	0	0
Hermanski, lf .	4	0	1	3	0	0
Edwards, c ...	2	0	0	2	0	1
dRackley	0	0	0	0	0	0
Bragan, c	1	0	0	3	0	0
Jorgensen, 3b .	3	0	0	0	4	0
Reese, ss	3	0	1	3	2	0
Hatten, p	2	0	1	1	1	0
cStevens	1	0	0	0	0	0
Gregg, p	1	0	0	1	0	0
Casey, p	0	0	0	0	0	0
Total	29	5	6	27	10	1

aHit by pitcher batting for Cooper in eighth.

bFlied out for Culler in eighth.

cStruck out for Hatten in sixth.

dRan for Edwards in sixth.

eGrounded out for Tatum in seventh.

Boston .... 0 0 0   0 1 2   0 0 0—3
Brooklyn .... 0 0 0   1 0 1   3 0   —5

Runs batted in — Edwards, Hopp, Ryan 2, Jorgenson, Reiser 2, Hermanski.

Two-base hits — Reese, Reiser. Sacrifices — Sain 2, Culler, Masi, Robinson. Double plays — Stanky, Reese and Robinson; Culler, Ryan and Torgeson. Left on bases — Boston 12, Brooklyn 7. Bases on balls — Off Hatten 3, Sain 5, Gregg 2. Strike outs — Hatten 2, Sain 1, Gregg 2. Lanfranconi 2, Casey 1. Hits — Off Sain 6 in 6 innings; Cooper 0 in 1; Lanfranconi 0 in 1; Hatten 6 in 6; Gregg 2 in 2 1/3; Casey 0 in 2/3. Hit by pitcher — By Hatten (Litwhiler); Sain (Edwards); Gregg (Neill). Wild pitch — Hatten. Winning pitcher — Gregg. Losing pitcher — Sain. Umpires — Pinelli, Barlick and Gore. Attendance — 26,623. Time of game — 2:26.

Jackie Robinson's Playing Record

Jackie Robinson

ROBINSON, JACK ROOSEVELT　　　　　　　　　　　　　　　　BR　TR　5'11½" 195 lbs.
B. Jan. 31, 1919, Cairo, Ga.　　D. Oct. 24, 1972, Stamford, Conn.
Hall of Fame 1962.

1947 **BKN N**	151	590	175	31	5	12	2.0	125	48	74	36	29	.297	.427	0	0	1B-151
1948	147	574	170	38	8	12	2.1	108	85	57	37	22	.296	.453	2	1	2B-116, 1B-30, 3B-6
1949	156	593	203	38	12	16	2.7	122	124	86	27	37	.342	.528	0	0	2B-156
1950	144	518	170	39	4	14	2.7	99	81	80	24	12	.328	.500	2	1	2B-144
1951	153	548	185	33	7	19	3.5	106	88	79	27	25	.338	.527	3	1	2B-153
1952	149	510	157	17	3	19	3.7	104	75	106	40	24	.308	.465	2	0	2B-146
1953	136	484	159	34	7	12	2.5	109	95	74	30	17	.329	.502	5	1	OF-76, 3B-44, 2B-9, 1B-6, SS-1
1954	124	386	120	22	4	15	3.9	62	59	63	20	7	.311	.505	7	1	OF-64, 3B-50, 2B-4
1955	105	317	81	6	2	8	2.5	51	36	61	18	12	.256	.363	9	1	3B-84, OF-10, 2B-1, 1B-1
1956	117	357	98	15	2	10	2.8	61	43	60	32	12	.275	.412	10	1	3B-72, 2B-22, 1B-9, OF-2
10 yrs.	1382	4877	1518	273	54	137	2.8	947	734	740	291	197	.311	.474	40	7	2B-751, 3B-256, 1B-197, OF-152, SS-1

WORLD SERIES

6 yrs.	38	137	32	7	1	2	1.5	22	12	21	14	6	.234	.343	0	0	3B-13, 2B-12, 1B-7, OF-6
					8th			9th		8th	10th						

Branch Rickey's Playing Record

Branch Rickey

RICKEY, WESLEY BRANCH (The Mahatma)　　　　　　　　　　　　BL　TR　5'9"　175 lbs.
B. Dec. 20, 1881, Stockdale, Ohio　　D. Dec. 9, 1965, Columbia, Mo.
Manager 1913-15, 1919-25.
Hall of Fame 1967.

1905 **STL A**	1	3	0	0	0	0	0.0	0	0	0		0	.000	.000	0	0	C-1
1906	64	201	57	7	3	3	1.5	22	24	16		4	.284	.393	7	2	C-54, OF-1
1907 **NY A**	52	137	25	2	3	0	0.0	16	15	11		4	.182	.241	12	1	OF-22, C-11, 1B-9
1914 **STL A**	2	2	0	0	0	0	0.0	0	0	0	1	0	.000	.000	2	0	
4 yrs.	119	343	82	9	6	3	0.9	38	39	27	1	8	.239	.327	21	3	C-66, OF-23, 1B-9

Branch Rickey's Managing Record

Branch Rickey

RICKEY, WESLEY BRANCH (The Mahatma)
B. Dec. 20, 1881, Stockdale, Ohio
D. Dec. 9, 1965, Columbia, Mo.
Hall of Fame 1967.

1913 **STL A**	12	5	6	.455	8	8
1914	159	71	82	.464	5	
1915	159	63	91	.409	6	
1919 **STL N**	138	54	83	.394	7	
1920	155	75	79	.487	5	
1921	154	87	66	.569	3	
1922	154	85	69	.552	3	
1923	154	79	74	.516	5	
1924	154	65	89	.422	6	
1925	38	13	25	.342	8	4
10 yrs.	1277	597	664	.473		

INDEX